Mexican Travel Writing

Hispanic Studies: Culture and Ideas

Volume 9

Edited by
Claudio Canaparo

PETER LANG
Oxford · Bern · Berlin · Bruxelles · Frankfurt am Main · New York · Wien

Thea Pitman

Mexican Travel Writing

PETER LANG

Oxford · Bern · Berlin · Bruxelles · Frankfurt am Main · New York · Wien

Bibliographic information published by Die Deutsche Bibliothek
Die Deutsche Bibliothek lists this publication in the Deutsche National-
bibliografie; detailed bibliographic data is available on the Internet at
‹http://dnb.ddb.de›.

A catalogue record for this book is available from The British Library.

The graphic design of this book was made by Florian Ziche.
Cover photo taken by Kerry Shields and Gaspar Ortega.

ISSN 1661-4720
ISBN 978-3-03911-020-9

© Peter Lang AG, International Academic Publishers, Bern 2008
Hochfeldstrasse 32, Postfach 746, CH-3000 Bern 9, Switzerland
info@peterlang.com, www.peterlang.com, www.peterlang.net

All rights reserved.
All parts of this publication are protected by copyright.
Any utilisation outside the strict limits of the copyright law, without the
permission of the publisher, is forbidden and liable to prosecution.
This applies in particular to reproductions, translations, microfilming,
and storage and processing in electronic retrieval systems.

Printed in Germany

Contents

	Acknowledgements	7
INTRODUCTION	'Mexicans Don't Write Travel Books'	11
CHAPTER 1	Tropes and Chronotopes	31
CHAPTER 2	The Tradition of Mexican Travel Writing	49
CHAPTER 3	The Postmodern and the Postcolonial in Contemporary Mexican Travel Writing	85
CHAPTER 4	Postmodernist or Postcolonialist? Juan Villoro's *Palmeras de la brisa rápida*	105
CHAPTER 5	Virtual Journeys: Héctor Perea's *México: crónica en espiral*	131
CHAPTER 6	Archival Travel Writing: Fernando Solana Olivares's *Oaxaca: crónicas sonámbulas*	155
CONCLUSION	'Mexicans Aren't Great Travellers'	177
	Bibliography	181
	Index	199

For a list of abbreviations used in this volume, refer to p. 181.

Acknowledgements

> One says Mexico: one means, after all, one little town away South in the Republic; and in this little town, one rather crumbly adobe house built round two sides of a garden *patio*: and of this house, one spot on the deep, shady veranda facing inwards to the trees, where there are an onyx table and three rocking-chairs and one little wooden chair, a pot with carnations, and a person with a pen. We talk so grandly, in capital letters, about Morning in Mexico. All it amounts to is one little individual looking at a bit of sky and trees, then looking down at the page of his exercise book.[1]

D.H. Lawrence was very candid about the limitations of his work in the opening paragraph of *Mornings in Mexico* (1927) and I would like to make a similar disclaimer for the shortcomings of the work presented here. As I sit at my desk in Otley, looking up at a bit of Yorkshire sky and trees, then looking down at the screen of my laptop, trying to remember Mexico and the years I spent researching this topic, I should acknowledge that the selection of primary material included in this study is deliberately limited to salient examples rather than exhaustive coverage of a vast and fast-growing field of scholarly enquiry. The reader who dips in expecting to find a detailed study of all Mexican travel writers from the last two centuries will inevitably be disappointed.

In the first place, works studied are restricted to those that focus on travels in Mexico rather than abroad – this is because the main focus of the development of Mexican travel writing in the nineteenth century was the desire to wrest the description of their country from the pens of foreign writers and this 'nationalist' urge continues even today. Mexican travel writing, then, should be understood as the rather more awkward Mexican 'national' travel writing, or Mexican travel writing in/about Mexico.

Furthermore, notable writers whose work sadly does not figure here to any great degree include Salvador Novo, Jorge Ibargüengoitia

---

1 D.H. Lawrence, *Mornings in Mexico* (Harmondsworth: Penguin, 1986), p. 7.

and Fernando Benítez. Their work has been missed out not because of any oversight, but rather, in order to advance my argument about the most significant changes that have taken place in the field of Mexican travel writing, I have preferred to concentrate my attentions on the early group of writers who established a tradition of Mexican travel writing in the mid-nineteeth century, and the most recent wave of postmodernist travel writers whose work has the ability to consciously challenge the imperialist underpinnings of the genre. Hence those writers such as Novo, Ibargüengoitia and Benítez who fall between these two poles have unfortunately slipped the net.

Similarly, the amount of critical writing on the subject of travel literature that has been published both in Mexico and particularly in the Anglophone academy since I started work on this topic in the early 1990s has been substantial and this study cannot claim to incorporate it all. Simply, it hopes that its findings will harmonise with those of other critics working in the field. Where false notes are detected, all mistakes are, needless to say, entirely my own.

An earlier draft of part of Chapter 1 appeared as 'The Construction of National Identity in the Mexican Travel Chronicle, 1843–1893', *Journeys: The International Journal of Travel and Travel Writing*, 2:1, 1–23 (2001). An earlier draft of Chapter 4 appeared as 'Postmodernity, Post-Tourism and Postmodern Irony: Juan Villoro's *Palmeras de la brisa rápida* and the Possibility of a Postmodern Travel-Chronicle', *Bulletin of Spanish Studies*, 81:1, 77–97 (2004). And an earlier draft of Chapter 5 appeared as 'An Impossible Task?: Héctor Perea's *México: crónica en espiral* and the Problems of Writing a Travel-Chronicle of Contemporary Mexico City', *Studies in Travel Writing*, 7:1, 47–62 (2003). I would like to thank the editors of *Journeys*, the *Bulletin of Spanish Studies*, and the *White Horse Press* respectively, for their kind permission to reproduce those materials in revised form here.

I would like to thank Professor Jason Wilson for his support and counsel during the research for this book, and the British Academy for providing funding without which it would never have been completed; the staff at Peter Lang, especially Alexis Kirschbaum, Hannah Godfrey and Florian Ziche, for their patience and understanding in the long and tortuous route that this project has followed from initial proposal to final manuscript; the School of Modern Languages and Cultures at the

University of Leeds for financial aid in the publication of this book; Kim Stringer for her meticulous preparation of the index; the staff of Quench Café in Otley who tolerated my slow coffee-drinking habit while the book was in the final stages of preparation; and colleagues and friends who have provided succour, sound advice and fresh perspectives over the years, in particular Claire Taylor, Steph Dennison and Claire Lindsay. Thanks are also due to the following Mexican writers, critics, and editors for giving so generously of their time, books and advice: Sealtiel Alatriste, Christopher Domínguez Michael, Alfonso de María y Campos and Aurelia Álvarez Urbajtel at the Dirección General de Publicaciones of the Consejo Nacional para la Cultura y las Artes, Carlos Monsiváis, Héctor Perea, Guillermo Sheridan, René Solís, Fernando Solana Olivares, and Juan Villoro. For all their emotional and financial support while I wrote this book, I would like to thank my parents, Maureen and Leonard Pitman, my brother, Tim, and my husband, Haynes. And finally, thank you to Noah and Louis for both helping and hindering the final stages of preparing the book for publication.

Thea Pitman, Otley, West Yorkshire, July 2007.

Introduction
'Mexicans Don't Write Travel Books'

Mexican Travel Writing

What might the 'Mexican' in the term 'Mexican travel writing' actually mean? In the field of English studies in the United Kingdom, its meaning is assumed to be quite straightforward. Thus a critic such as Nigel Leask can publish an article entitled 'The Ghost in Chapultepec: Fanny Calderón de la Barca, William Prescott and 19th Century Mexican Travel Accounts' safe in the knowledge that 'Mexican travel accounts' are those works written about travels in Mexico by foreign writers.[1] But in Mexico the two-volume publication *Viajes en México* (Mexican Journeys) is explicitly divided into 'Crónicas mexicanas' (Mexican chronicles or accounts) and 'Crónicas extranjeras' (foreign accounts).[2] So here, by dint of comparison, the 'Mexican' in 'Mexican accounts' refers quite clearly to those accounts that are written by writers of Mexican nationality. It seems perfectly acceptable that both meanings should co-exist – and indeed, to avoid confusion many publications concerning travel writing and a certain nation or nationality find ways to make questions of destination and the origin of the author(s) of the work more explicit. Nevertheless, the fact that almost no publications exist in the English language that understand the 'Mexican' in 'Mexican

---

[1] Nigel Leask, 'The Ghost of Chapultepec: Fanny Calderón de la Barca, William Prescott and 19th Century Mexican Travel Accounts', in *Voyages and Visions: Towards a Cultural History of Travel*, ed. by Jás Elsner and Joan-Pau Rubiés (London: Reaktion Books, 1999), pp. 184–209.

[2] *Viajes en México: crónicas mexicanas*, ed. by Xavier Tavera Alfaro, ill. by Alberto Beltrán, 2nd edn (Secretaría de Obras Públicas, 1972); and *Viajes en México: crónicas extranjeras (1821–1855)*, ed. and trans. by Margo Glantz, ill. by Alberto Beltrán, 2nd edn (Secretaría de Obras Públicas, 1972).
See Chapter 1 of this study for a detailed analysis of the term '*crónica de viaje*'.

travel writing' to refer to citizens of Mexican nationality reveals a rather colonialist mentality at work: travellers are presumed to be citizens of the imperial powers of the Western World and places like Mexico are the passive receptors of their gazes. In other words, Mexicans are presumed not to write travel books so there is no need to distinguish quite what is meant by the adjective 'Mexican'.

It is my contention that, while evidently there exist travel books written by Mexican authors – the subheadings of Tavera Alfaro's *Viajes en México* are sufficient proof –, the prevailing metropolitan assumptions about travel writing and the motivations that underpin the genre's development mean that Mexican writers frequently display an ambivalent position in this regard, claiming that they do not write travel books, even as they do just that. Ambivalence towards the genre is hardly suprising. However, since Mexicans do write travel books, the most important question to address is how a genre that has been so closely linked with the construction of great empires can be practised by citizens of a former colony, and this will merit a detailed study of both the genre's politics and its rhetorical strategies.

The first section of this introduction addresses the first interpretation of the term 'Mexican travel writing', analysing the varying different types of travel writing written by foreigners such as Alexander von Humboldt and Fanny Calderón de la Barca on the subject of Mexico, and the impact of such works on Mexican writers. The second section then goes on to examine in detail two key statements by Mexican writers concerning their relationship to travel writing and imperialism/colonialism, the first made by Manuel Altamirano in the late nineteenth century and the second by José Emilio Pacheco in the late twentieth century. This analysis of the different types of 'Mexican' travel writing is designed to succinctly expose the politics of the genre. The remainder of the study will then go on to probe more closely the rhetorical features of the genre and how these work in tandem with its political underpinnings.

Mexican Travel Writing, I: The Legacy of Foreign Travel Writers in Mexico

The most significant demographic movement between Europe and Latin America has tended to flow from the metropolis to the colonies and this has generated an awful lot of travel writing penned by Europeans (and later citizens of the United States) on the subject of Latin America. Of this fact Latin Americans are painfully aware. In the case of Mexico, the names of the most significant foreign travel writers to have published their observations and impressions of Mexico are repeated *ad infinitum* in Mexican cultural production, both creative and critical.

The reasons why certain foreign travel writers have more impact than others in the country about which they are writing differ. Availability and translation into the native tongue might be one *a priori* factor. Broadly speaking, in the case of nineteenth-century Mexico it would appear that a lack of translations was not a factor that significantly hindered the capacity of a book written in English or French to reach Mexican readers and that the Mexican intelligentsia of the day avidly imported anything written on the subject of their new-born nation.[3] In the twentieth century, the translation into Spanish of foreign travel books has greatly widened the influence of such writers in the Mexican psyche. It started slowly in the early years of the century with a backlog of translations of nineteenth-century works: the Marquise Frances Calderón de la Barca's *Life in Mexico during a Residence of Two Years in that Country* (1843) was first published in translation in 1920 and Jean Frederic de Waldeck's *Voyage pittoresque et archéologique dans la Province d'Yucatan (Amérique Centrale) pendant les années 1834 et 1836* in 1930.[4] Brantz Mayer's *Mexico: As It Was and As It Is* (1844) appeared in 1953 in the Fondo de Cultura Económica's

---

3   Juan A. Ortega y Medina, *Humboldt desde México* (UNAM, 1960), pp. 24–25.
4   Fanny Calderón de la Barca, *La vida en México*, 2 vols, trans. by Enrique Martínez Sobral, prol. by Manuel Romero de Terreros (Librería de la Viuda de Bouret, 1920); Federico de Waldeck, *Viaje pintoresco y arqueológico a la Provincia de Yucatán, 1834 y 1836*, trans. by Manuel Mestre Ghigliazza (Mérida: Carlos R. Menéndez, 1930).

'Biblioteca Americana, Serie de Viajeros' – the first initiative by a Mexican publisher to edit a series of foreign travel writing. And from the 1970s onwards the printing and reprinting of foreign travel writing has become a major enterprise for Mexican publishers. Indeed, a sizeable percentage of the two thousand six hundred authors listed in Iturriaga de la Fuente's extensive bibliography of foreign travel writing concerning travels in Mexico has now been published in the country.[5] The publishers most closely involved in the enterprise to translate and/or reprint works of foreign travel writing on the subject of journeys in Mexico have been the Secretaría de Educación Pública (SEP) with the series 'SepSententas' and 'Sep/80' in the 1970s and 80s; the Fondo de Cultura Económica (FCE), working in conjunction with the SEP, in its first 'Cien de México' series in the 1980s; and, since the 1990s, the Consejo Nacional para la Cultura y las Artes (CNCA) has continued the efforts of both the SEP and the FCE with its 'Lecturas Mexicanas' and 'Mirada Viajera' series. The fact that so many of these publishers are government-sponsored institutions gives an idea of quite how important and/or inescapable many Mexicans deem foreign travel writing on the subject of their country to be.[6]

Sheer availability, however, is not enough to explain the impact of such books, merely their potential for impact. In fact the influence of a foreign travel book is dependent upon either how strategically helpful the foreign writer might be to the local intelligentsia or how controversial or offensive the writer's observations are, with the more appreciative texts falling somewhere in between these two poles. Over time the reasons for impact have changed. The stategically helpful account had more influence in the early Independence period – the first half of the nineteenth century – when Mexicans most urgently needed to define themselves as a nation and when 'homegrown' material was in short supply. The interest in more offensive texts has existed all along, but current Mexican writers' fascination with the whole back catalogue

---

5   José Iturriaga de la Fuente, *Anecdotario de viajeros extranjeros en México, siglos XVI-XX*, 1st edn, reprinted, 4 vols (FCE, 1993–94), I, 251–314; IV, 327–59.
6   A foreign travel writer's personal contacts in Mexico would constitute another *a priori* reason which might have an impact on their circulation in Mexico.

of such texts is perhaps the ultimate proof of the irony inherent in one contemporary travel writer's comment that 'Nuestra relación con el extranjero no da para resentimientos de largo alcance'.[7]

The obvious example of the strategically helpful account is the work of Baron Alexander von Humboldt. Humboldt was one of the very few foreign travellers that Spain allowed to visit her American colonies in the years before they variously gained independence, making his trip to Mexico in 1803–04.[8] His most immediately influential publication in Mexico concerning his time there was the *Essai politique sur le royaume de la Nouvelle-Espagne* (1811) although his *Vues des cordillères et monumens* (sic) *des peuples indigènes de l'Amérique* (1810) would grow in terms of its importance to Mexicans by the late nineteenth century.[9]

The effect of these publications on the Mexican intelligentsia of the day was far reaching. Although relying on substantial amounts of information provided by various local institutions and individuals, Humboldt's *Essai politique* provided a comprehensive analytical overview of the country, particularly its material wealth. For this synthesis of available information, many Mexicans were genuinely grateful.[10] Furthermore, the terms in which Humboldt couched such an analysis 'granted [Mexicans] parity' with Europe – they were an 'antique' culture.[11] And, following on from this, Humboldt's work was thus 'partly aimed at vindicating the American continent and its inhabitants from criticisms made by enlightenment savants' such as the

---

7   Juan Villoro, 'Todos somos gondoleros', *LJS*, 17 May 1998, p. 15.
8   Insurrection against the Spanish crown dates from 1810 although Mexicans did not officially gain independence until 1821.
9   The 'primer bosquejo' of Humboldt's *Essai*, the 'Tablas Geográficas Políticas del Reyno de Nueva España', was actually distributed in Mexico in December 1803 (Ulrike Leitner, 'Humboldt's Works on Mexico', in *Alexander von Humboldt im Netz*, 1:1 [2000], http://www.uni-potsdam.de/u/romanistik/humboldt/hin/leitner3.htm, accessed 22 June 2006).
10 Ortega y Medina, *Humboldt desde México*, p. 23.
11 Nigel Leask, *Curiosity and the Aesthetics of Travel Writing, 1770–1840: 'From an Antique Land'* (Oxford: Oxford UP), p 258. Leask notes that, despite this, Humboldt simultaneously tried to 'insist upon [Latin America's] cultural *difference* from, and hierarchical subordination to, Europe' (author's italics).

Comte de Buffon, the Abbé Raynal and William Robertson,[12] arguing that there was nothing inherently inferior about the Mexican 'race', simply that they were the product of many centuries of colonial misrule.[13] As a result, Humboldt's works can be seen to have helped Mexicans free themselves from the shackles of the Spanish Empire by proving their suitability for independence, even though he never 'publicly fomented revolution'.[14] Mexican historians of the era repeatedly cite Humboldt as 'el incitador de la Independencia' both for what he wrote about the country as well as for what he brought with him in terms of ideological baggage from the French Revolution.[15]

Furthermore, some Mexicans writing later in the century, after independence was well established, felt that, as an independent nation, Mexicans really needed to cultivate all branches of the arts and the sciences themselves. Where they perceived a certain scarcity in the field of travel writing, Humboldt's works also proposed a pertinent aesthetic model to follow. Ortega y Medina notes that there was a revival of interest in Humboldt's work in the late 1860s and early 1870. Whereas in earlier decades appreciation of his work had been more focused on the political message and the strategic information that it contained, after 1869 appreciation turned to the literary qualities of his work – he even became the object of 'romanticisation' in some Mexican writers' imaginations.[16] And in terms of the proposal of an aesthetic model for travel writing, nineteenth-century Mexican travel writing tends to correspond to the 'integrated' model of travel writing that Wilson credits Humboldt with having popularised in Europe, a

---

12   Leask, *Curiosity*, p. 257.
13   Rayfred Lionel Stevens-Middleton, *La obra de Alexander von Humboldt en México: fundamento de la geografía moderna* (Instituto Panamericano de Geografía e Historia / Sociedad Mexicana de Geografía y Estadística, 1956), p. 219.
14   Jason Wilson, introduction to Alexander von Humboldt, *Personal Narrative of a Journey to the Equinoctial Regions of the New Continent*, abridged and translated by Jason Wilson, with an historical introduction by Malcolm Nicholson (Harmondsworth: Penguin, 1995), p. xlvi.
15   See, for example, Ortega y Medina, *Humboldt desde México*, pp. 1–30.
16   Ortega y Medina, *Humboldt desde México*, p. 84.

model that combines the strictly scientific with the literary and/or the popular, observation and enquiry with the personal impressions and experiences of the traveller.[17] Furthermore, particularly in his *Vues des cordillères*, Humboldt helped trigger the development of a new aesthetic awareness in Mexico. Although it cannot be claimed that he was the first to describe Mexican flora, fauna or climate – Francisco Xavier Clavijero and other Mexican 'encyclopaedists' had already laid strong foundations for this in the eighteenth century – Humboldt was the first to describe Mexican 'landscapes'.[18] He also revived interest in the pre-Columbian civilisations of Mexico and gave an aesthetic appreciation of their architecture and artefacts.

To sum up, Humboldt's works significantly enhanced Mexicans' political and aesthetic self-awareness. His writings, in particular the *Essai politique*, are referred to and quoted from endlessly in nineteenth-century Mexican writing, both for the factual data they contain and for their descriptions of the country. Nevertheless, his most enduring legacy is perhaps not to be found in his own works, but in the hordes of other works by foreign travellers that his accounts inspired. While some of these were, at least in part, in the spirit of Humboldt's own enterprise – see for example John Lloyd Stephens and Frederick Catherwood's *Incidents of Travel in Yucatan* (1843) – they also tended to correspond to the interests of a group that Mary Louise Pratt terms 'the capitalist vanguard'; travellers who functioned as 'advance scouts

---

17   Wilson, introduction to Alexander von Humboldt, *Personal Narrative* p. lxii. It should nevertheless be noted that it was Jean-Jacques Rousseau who initiated this model and Humboldt who popularised it (see section on *Paisajismo* in Chapter 1), and that Humboldt was not the only conduit through which Rousseau's influence would have reached Mexico.

Wilson's claims for Humboldt's popularisation of the integrated model stand in contrast to Leask's argument that Humboldt is the '*terminus*' for such accounts (Leask, *Curiosity*, p. 282 [author's italics]). As an endorsement of Wilson's argument, it should be noted that the disintegration of the Humboldtian model only occurs in Mexican travel writing at the very beginning of the twentieth century.

18   Humboldt did not invent the Romantic topos of the description of landscape, but he was the first to describe specifically Mexican landscapes in this way (see Ortega y Medina, *Humboldt desde México*, p. 182). See section on *Paisajismo* in Chapter 1.

for [predominantly] European capital' and who made inroads on Mexico in the years after Spain had reliquished her hold on the ex-colony.[19] Despite Humboldt's best efforts, it is these sorts of works that have led Mexicans to view foreign travel writing as the genre *par excellence* that accompanies imperialist exploitation. And it is on account of these exploitative accounts that Humboldt himself has been condemned as an out-and-out 'colonialist' by some.[20]

In the case of the more controversial and/or offensive accounts, there are countless examples to be taken, from the Marquise Frances Calderón de la Barca's *Life in Mexico* of 1843 to the writings of expatriate British novelists, the French Surrealists or members of the North American Beat Generation in the course of the twentieth century. Calderón de la Barca, for example, was a gifted social satirist, with access to all the most important figures of the day – she was the wife of the first Spanish ambassador in Mexico after Independence. Her acerbic criticisms of Mexican society and its mores were the subject of much irritation in Mexico at the time of her book's publication and her impact in the Republic clearly has a lot to do with Mexican writers' usually defensive reactions to her depiction of their culture.[21] In particular, the Mexican intelligentsia of her time objected not just to what she got

---

19   Mary Louise Pratt, *Imperial Eyes: Travel Writing and Transculturation* (London: Routledge, 1992), p. 146. For an interesting study of the balance of imperialism and Humboldtian scientific observation in the work of John Lloyd Stephens, see Daniel Cooper Alarcón, 'The Ruins of Manifest Destiny: John L. Stephens's *Incidents of Travel in Central America, Chiapas, and Yucatan*', in *A través del espejo: viajes, viajeros y la construcción de la alteridad en América Latina*, ed. by Lourdes de Ita Rubio and Gerardo Sánchez Díaz, (Morelia: Instituto de Investigaciones Históricas, Universidad Michoacana de San Nicolás Hidalgo, 2005), pp. 333–42.

20   Daniel Cosío Villegas, cited in Ortega y Medina, *Humboldt desde México*, p. 36.

21   See *Women through Women's Eyes: Latin American Women in Nineteenth-Century Travel Accounts*, ed. by June E. Hahner (Wilmington, DE: Scholarly Resources, 1998), p. xx. María Bono López also comments on the number of Mexican intellectuals, as well as foreign travel writers, who expressed criticism of Calderón de la Barca's work (María Bono López, 'Frances Erskine Inglis Calderón de la Barca y el mundo indígena mexicano', http://www.bibliojuridica.org/libros/1/252/8.pdf, p. 4, accessed 5 September 2005).

wrong or misinterpreted based on partial knowledge or prejudiced views, but more to the flippant and willfully mordant way in which she described members of the social élite. She contravened the strict rules of respect, courtesy and hospitality that govern Mexican social relations.[22]

Other writers who have since acquired equal infamy in the Republic to Calderón de la Barca have achieved this in similar ways: through their partial knowledge and their misinterpretations, through their prejudices – particularly with respect to race –, but also through their often witty prose style which at once seduces on a literary level and repulses when one happens to identify with the object of such writers' attentions. For writers such as Graham Greene, Evelyn Waugh, D.H. Lawrence, and later William Burroughs, despite the perhaps exaggerated appeal of the country which prompted them to travel there in the first place – the Revolution, the 'magical' aspects, the indigenous lifeways and handicrafts, and of course the availability of drugs – Mexico largely produced a feeling of disillusionment, or at least of radical ambivalence. Their texts do not seek to fully describe or explain the country and its cultures, but to capture a deliberately fragmentary perspective, highly coloured by the author's personality and experience. Graham Greene in *The Lawless Roads* (1939) claimed that the food was awful, said that he hated all Mexicans because they were over-demonstrative, and dismissed the ruins at Palenque as uninteresting simply because he had dysentery at the time.[23] In *Queer* (written 1951–53; published 1985), William Burroughs was equally as offensive with respect to Mexicans and Mexican culture for similarly petty reasons.[24] D.H. Lawrence acknowledged that *Mornings in Mexico* (1927) was made up of the limited number of mornings he spent sitting at a desk in a courtyard in a small town in Mexico, although he still extrapolated

---

22   Michael P. Costeloe, 'Prescott's *History of the Conquest* and Calderón de la Barca's *Life in Mexico*: Mexican Reaction, 1843–44', *The Americas*, 47:3 (1991), 337–48. I would like to thank Claire Lindsay for alerting me to Costeloe's work.
23   Graham Greene, *The Lawless Roads* (Harmondsworth: Penguin, 1982), pp. 35, 48, 139–42.
24   William S. Burroughs, *Queer* (New York: Viking, 1985).

wildly to encompass the whole country in his fatalistic vision.[25] And Evelyn Waugh famously refused to re-edit his *Robbery Under Law: The Mexican Object Lesson* (1939) because even he acknowledged its libellous nature. Of course, all of these texts, even Waugh's, are currently available in translation in Mexico.[26] And while these texts do not focus on the direct exploitation of Mexico as those of the 'capitalist vanguard' did, they quite clearly all partake of the discourse of imperial relations where independent Mexico is still all too often posited as undeveloped, uncultured, unstable, unhealty and/or unsuited to self-governance. This discourse is prevalent in the genre of travel writing as practiced in the West.[27]

Mexican Travel Writing, II: Why Mexicans Say They Don't Write Travel Books

In a succinct overview of the importance of foreign travel writers in Mexico from the time of the Conquest to the 1990s, Mexican journalist and critic Hermann Bellinghausen has noted,

> En general, los extranjeros no han entendido a México, pero lo han mirado con una atención que se agradece: Madame Calderón de la Barca, D.H. Lawrence, Graham Greene, Malcolm Lowry, Max Frish (*sic*), Humboldt, Lumholtz, Artaud, Kerouac, Huxley, Calvino. Pero sólo aquellos suficientemente locos como para parecer mexicanos dieron en el clavo: Bernal Díaz, John Reed, y algún otro (como los cineastas Eisenstein y Buñuel). Los demás cronistas que importan, sin excepción, son mexicanos.[28]

---

25   D.H. Lawrence, *Mornings in Mexico* (Harmondsworth: Penguin, 1986), p. 7.
26   Greene, Lawrence and Waugh were all published in the Consejo Nacional para la Cultura y las Artes's 'Mirada Viajera' series in the mid-1990s. Burroughs was published by Anagrama in 2002.
27   See for example Pratt, *Imperial Eyes*; David Spurr, *The Rhetoric of Empire: Colonial Discourse in Journalism, Travel Writing, and Imperial Administration* (Durham, NC: Duke UP, 1993), and Steve Clark, ed., *Travel Writing and Empire: Postcolonial Theory in Transit* (London: Zed Books, 1999).
28   Hermann Bellinghausen, 'Testigos del caso: la crónica en México', *Nexos*, 162 (June 1991), 17. In a similar line-up Carlos Fuentes has deemed Antonin

Although Bellinghausen does his best in the last sentence to promote the value of Mexican contributions to the genre of chronicles written about the country, some of which fall within the parameters of travel writing, many other Mexican writers have expressed concern about Mexicans' ability to write travel books. Furthermore, this concern has most often been expressed in the course of works of travel writing themselves, or in introductions or critical responses to such works. The fact is that Mexicans say that they do not write travel books while simultaneously writing them, and it is the function of such a rhetorical strategy that interests me in this study.

The reasons that Mexican writers most often put forth for the dearth of Mexican travel writing are the following: Mexicans do not have either the means or the desire to travel; they are put off by, or simply choose to rely on, the sheer volume of foreign accounts concerning the country; and/or, perhaps most importantly, they have reservations about their relationship to the genre of travel writing as such. The focus on the latter reason has grown in importance over time as a postcolonialist sensibility has taken root in the country.

By way of example, the Liberal statesman, pedagogue and novelist Ignacio Manuel Altamirano made the following, deliberately provocative, remarks in his introduction to the Mexican writer Luis Malanco's *Viaje a Oriente* published in 1882:

> Los mexicanos viajan poco, y los que viajan no escriben, ni publican sus impresiones o sus recuerdos. Esta es una verdad tan notoria en México, que no necesita demostrarse. [...]
>
> Sólo los mexicanos hemos escrito poco a cerca de nuestro país. Figúrasenos que hablar de nuestras poblaciones, de nuestras montañas, de nuestros ríos, de nuestros desiertos, de nuestros mares, de nuestras costumbres y de nuestro carácter, es asunto baladí, y que al ver escrito en una página de viaje un nombre indio, todo el mundo ha de hacer un gesto de desdén. [...]
>
> Hay cierta repugnancia para conocer el país nativo, y ésta es la causa de que no puedan desarrollarse vigorosamente todas las ramas de nuestra literatura

---

Artaud to be the writer who comes closest to understanding Mexico (prologue to Fernando Benítez's *Los indios de México: antología*, edited by Héctor Manjarrez [Era, 1989], pp. 13–14).

> nacional. Sólo el tiempo y la civilización harán desaparecer estos hábitos de la vida colonial.
>
> Por eso nuestra literatura de viajes, en el interior del país, es singularmente escasa. No tenemos una sola colección pintoresca o descriptiva; artículos sueltos, narraciones aisladas, algún pequeño estudio publicado hace años en el *Museo Mexicano*, en el *Liceo*, en el *Álbum*; algunas estampas litográficas: eso es todo. Muchas veces tenemos que acudir a los libros extranjeros para tomar algunos datos.[29]

Altamirano corroborates the first two reasons listed above to justify why Mexicans do not write travel books: they do not travel in the first place and they rely on the texts of foreign travellers for strategically helpful information – he is clearly referring to Humboldt and his followers here. But this reliance on foreigners' accounts is a *faute-de-mieux* rather than a choice in Altamirano's argument – what he really wanted was to stimulate Mexicans to travel in their own newly-formed nation-state and to write about it in order to describe and prescribe what the recipe for independent Mexican national identity might be. When he observes that Mexicans feel awkward about writing travel books about their own country because of its indigenous cultures he clearly has his own axe to grind since he was himself from an indigenous Nahua community in the state of Guerrero and wanted to contest the racism of the *criollo* and *mestizo* sectors of contemporary Mexican society by locating the essence of independent Mexican national identity in the indigenous communities. In Altamirano's words, this racism, this constant privileging of the European over the indigenous, is a 'colonial habit' and an impediment to the creation of a sense of national identity.

Altamirano wanted Mexicans to get over this impediment, but rather than identifying foreign travel writing on the subject of Mexico as another colonial/imperial problem because of the nature of its discourse, Altamirano simply advocated that Mexicans should get out more in their own country and write about it following the generic mould formed by foreign writers such as Humboldt. This would be a 'creolisation' of the genre – one which worked well for his nation-building purposes – but

---

29 Ignacio Manuel Altamirano, *Obras completas*, ed. by Nicole Girón (SEP, 1986-), 13 vols, *Escritos de literatura y arte, II* (1988), pp. 215, 229–30.

it would not really take into account the all too frequent imperialist associations of the genre *per se*.³⁰ It should be noted that this creolising manoeuvre was quite typical of Mexican culture at this historical juncture rather than an oversight or failing on the part of Altamirano and friends – as Jorge Klor de Alva notes, Latin American society in the post-Independence era was founded on its desire to emulate Europe (particularly Spain and France) and was thus not postcolonial in any critical sense, and although there are the seeds of a postcolonialist sensibility in Altamirano's comments regarding colonial habits, he was perhaps the exception to the rule by dint of his indigenous ancestry.³¹

In his role as one of the key figures in the development of the modern nation-state of Mexico and of the attempt to create a corresponding sense of national identity, particularly in the field of literature, Altamirano was determined that there should be a national brand of travel writing to compete with the works of Europeans and United States citizens regarding travels in Mexico, particularly those with imperialist designs on the country. From at least 1870 he was making statements to this effect, and indeed, by the early 1880s his words were beginning to produce results. A significant number of travel books were published

30   See Susan Castillo, *Performing America: Colonial Encounters in New World Writing, 1500–1786* (London: Routledge, 2006), pp. 189–90 for a good discussion of 'creolisation'.

   Altamirano's comments on the lack of Mexican travel literature have since been quoted and annotated on a number of occasions: by Felipe Teixidor in the prologue to the first edition of his anthology of Mexican travel writing at home and abroad, *Viajeros mexicanos: siglos XIX y XX* [1939], 2nd edition (Porrúa, 1982), pp. 3–4; by Francisco López Cámara in his book *Los viajes de Guillermo Prieto: estudio introductorio* (Cuernavaca: Centro Regional de Investigaciones Multidisciplinarias, UNAM, 1994), pp. 13–14; and again by Emmanuel Carballo in the introduction to his anthology of Mexican travel writing concerning travel in the United States, *¿Qué país es éste?: los Estados Unidos y los gringos vistos por escritores mexicanos de los siglos XIX y XX* (CNCA, 1996), pp. 11–12. Ironically, given the context, all three critics uphold (with nuances) Altamirano's declarations on the lack of Mexican travel writing.

31   Jorge Klor de Alva, 'The Postcolonization of the (Latin) American Experience: A Reconsideration of "Colonialism," "Postcolonialism," and "Mestizaje"', in *After Colonialism: Imperial Histories and Postcolonial Displacements*, ed. by Gyan Prakash (Princeton, NJ: Princeton UP, 1995).

in the 1870s, and from the 1880s onwards many more came into print – even ones concerning travel well before that date were finally written up and published.³² By the time that Altamirano made the statements quoted above Mexicans were already busy making up for lost time. His comments that only three writers – Antonio García Cubas, Guillermo Prieto and Ignacio Ramírez – had bothered to publish travel books or articles on the subject of Mexico and that there was even less material by Mexicans concerning travel abroad are, of course, a deliberately exaggerated view, designed to provoke even more Mexicans to publish travel books.³³ As proof of the success of the efforts of Altamirano and his friends and colleagues at *El Renacimiento*, the literary journal he founded in 1869, the contemporary cultural critic Carlos Monsiváis has since identified travel writing as the 'género decimonónico predilecto' in Mexico.³⁴

Writing over a hundred years after Altamirano's 'manifesto for Mexican travel writing', Mexican novelist, journalist and poet José Emilio Pacheco, returns once again to the question of why Mexicans do not write travel books. The sheer volume of foreign accounts – particularly the offensive sort – are mentioned as an impediment, but Pacheco is more precise:

> El libro de viajes es sobre todo un género del Norte: la mirada sobre las tierras conquistadas o por conquistar. [...]
> Si los toros pudieran escribir una historia de la tauromaquia seguramente no contendría el elogio de los grandes diestros. Los mexicanos estamos en una situación parecida respecto de los libros de viajes. No debe de haber muchos otros países que hayan inspirado tantos relatos donde se juzgue a sus habitantes con tal vehemencia para condenar y con tan poca generosidad para entender.³⁵

Jorge Klor de Alva has argued that a tacit and retrospective/ anachronistic postcolonialist sensibility reached Latin America in the

---

32 See the bibliography to Teixidor's *Viajeros mexicanos*, pp. 221–25.
33 Carballo corroborates the bias and selectiveness of Altamirano's vision in *¿Qué país es éste?*, p. 12.
34 Carlos Monsiváis, *A ustedes les consta: antología de la crónica en México* (Era, 1980), p. 347.
35 José Emilio Pacheco, 'Bitácoras', *Hoja por hoja*, 13 December 1997, p. 13.

late 1970s.[36] Thus in Pacheco's analysis of Mexicans' relationship with travel writing, the problem is not the 'colonial habit' of being embarrassed about one's own non-European country, but that travel writing itself is cited as an imperialist genre and hence as something with which a technically postcolonial people will necessarily have a problem. Pacheco subsequently overlooks Altamirano's success in stimulating a tradition of Mexican travel writing and implies that Mexicans simply do not write travel books. Nevertheless, towards the end of his article Pacheco inadvertently reveals that the genre of travel writing is practised in contemporary Mexico and, indeed, is booming:

> En los tiempos del turismo masivo, la internet, el correo electrónico, los discos que ponen en nuestra pantalla el Museo del Prado o los tesoros del Nilo sin riesgo de ser aniquilados por los integristas, el libro de viajes se diría un género tan anacrónico como la novela epistolar o la tragedia en cinco actos y en verso. A pesar de todo, en las grandes librerías se alza un estante dedicado a estas obras y en los grandes periódicos dominicales este tipo de narración se ejerce cada semana. Hay, por lo visto, algo que sólo pueden transmitir las palabras sobre la página.[37]

Pacheco's statement is ambivalent. Since he has so far omitted to acknowledge the existence of Mexican travel writing, one might presume that the bookshelves dedicated to travel literature and the articles in the Sunday papers are those that Pacheco has seen in the United States or in Europe. Nevertheless, one cannot help suspecting that this statement does acknowledge the existence of Mexican travel writing: Pacheco's article was published in Mexico for a Mexican reading public, and the contents of these bookshelves and newspapers must surely be accessible to the Mexicans for whom he is writing. Thus, although for different reasons, Altamirano and Pacheco concur in their denial of a practice that they inadvertently reveal to exist.

Indeed, travel writing in contemporary Mexico is booming. 1989 saw the launch of a short-lived but influential series of travel writing by Alianza Editorial Mexicana designed to revive the nineteenth-century

---

36 Klor de Alva, 'The Postcolonization of the (Latin) American Experience', p. 263.
37 Pacheco, 'Bitácoras', p. 13.

Mexican tradition of travel writing, as well as to wrest the description of the country, once again, from the hands of foreign travel writers.[38] As the editors of the series noted on the back cover of the first of the texts published in that series, Juan Villoro's *Palmeras de la brisa rápida: un viaje a Yucatán* (1989):

> En un país como el nuestro, pródigo en paisajes naturales y humanos retratados con abundancia durante el siglo XIX, extraña no encontrar hoy en día una literatura igualmente copiosa que lo describa, acote y reflexione sobre él. [...]
> Con este volumen, Alianza Editorial Mexicana inicia una colección de relatos de viajes que pretende cubrir las notorias ausencias en este género.[39]

And with respect to the work of foreign travel writers in Mexico, René Solís, vice-president of Alianza at the time of the commissioning of the series, also noted pointedly that the field of travel writing about Mexico, 'había sido monopolizado por viajeros extranjeros que escribieron sus observaciones y experiencias de viaje, de Thomas Gage hasta Lawrence, Greene, Waugh, Paul Theroux *et al.*',[40] and that the series aimed to redress the balance in that regard.

The success of Villoro's chronicle subsequently inspired a further series – Cuadernos de Viaje – which was published during the 1990s by the Consejo Nacional para la Cultura y las Artes.[41] Although a travel

---

38 Information concerning the series stems from personal interviews with René Solís, 24 May 1996, and with Sealtiel Alatriste, series editor at Alianza Editorial Mexicana at the time, 19 July 1996. The chronicles published in the series are Juan Villoro's *Palmeras de la brisa rápida: un viaje a Yucatán* (1989), Rafael Ramírez Heredia's *Por los caminos del sur: vámonos para Guerrero* (1990), a translation of Tom Miller's *On the Border, En la frontera: imágenes desconocidas de nuestra frontera norte* (1991) and Dante Medina's *Sólo los viajeros saben que al sur está el verano: un viaje por Francia, Italia, Yugoslavia, Bulgaria y Grecia* (1993).
39 Villoro, *Palmeras de la brisa rápida*, back cover.
40 René Solís, personal letter, 8 November 1995.
41 Information concerning the 'Cuaderno de viaje' series stems from personal interviews with Alfonso de María y Campos, director of publications at the CNCA at the time of the commissioning of the series, 21 May 1996, and Aurelia Álvarez Urbajtel, series editor at the CNCA at the time, 20 January 1997. The travel chronicles published in the series up until 1998 are Fernando Solana Olivares's

writing competition dreamt up by Alianza Editorial Mexicana in the early 1990s to coincide with their reinvention of Mexican travel writing was never organised, another international travel writing competition promoted by the Catalan publisher Ediciones B in conjunction with Iberia airlines has helped to raise the profile of Hispanic travel writing as a whole since the late 1990s.[42] Finally, two large international conferences on the subject of the conjunction of Latin America and travel writing have been organised in the country since 2003 and academic interest in travel writing by Mexican authors is growing.[43]

But if travel writing is booming in Mexico, we must ask whether contemporary travel narratives can offer any advance on Altamirano's appropriation of the genre; whether they can effectively challenge its imperialist associations? It is my contention that where contemporary Mexican travel writing takes on board certain aesthetic innovations associated with postmodernist literature, in so far as they can be applied to this stubbornly Realist narrative form, it can offer a variety of travel writing that challenges the genre's imperialist legacy. This, I will argue, takes place at the level of the chronotope, whereby the imperialist 'chronotope of the road' is exchanged in more contemporary,

---

Oaxaca: crónicas sonámbulas (1994), Hugo Diego Blanco's *Ángelus* (1995), Francisco Hinojosa's *Un taxi en L.A.* (1995), María Luisa Puga's *Crónicas de una oriunda del kilómetro X en Michoacán* (1995), Luis Zapata's *Paisaje con amigos: un viaje al occidente de México* (1995), Orlando Ortiz's *Crónica de las Huastecas: en las tierras del caimán y la sirena* (1995), Héctor Perea's *México: crónica en espiral* (1996), Silvia Molina's *Campeche: imagen de eternidad* (1996), Alvaro Ruiz Abreu's *Los ojos del paisaje* (1996), Ana García Bergua's *Postales desde el puerto* (1997), Hernán Lara Zavala's *Viaje al corazón de la península* (1988), José Martínez Torres's *Chiapas: crónica de dos tiempos* (1998) and Adolfo Castañón's *Lugares que pasan* (1998).

42 Carlos García-Tort, 'Escriba (una crónica de viajes) ahora, viaje (con un premio) después', *LJS*, 23 May 1999, p. 11. The only Latin American to win the prize to date is the Argentine writer Mempo Giardinelli for his *Final de novela en Patagonia* (2000).

43 The conferences were the II Congreso Internacional Alexander von Humboldt, Morelia, Michoacán, 2003 and the III Congreso Internacional Alexander von Humboldt, Veracruz, 2005. The most recent Mexican publication on the subject travel writing by Mexicans and others is *Espacio, viajes y viajeros*, ed. by Luz Elena Zamudio (Aldus and UAM – Unidad Iztapalapa, 2004).

postmodernist work for the 'chronotope of the net'.[44] While such a form of travel writing may not be the exclusive preserve of 'postcolonial' authors, it does suggest a way in which writers from former colonies might reconcile themselves with such a pervasive and persuasive vehicle for imperialist discourse.

Although much contemporary travel writing overlooks the challenge that the absorption of modernist and postmodernist narrative innovations might present, casting itself in a traditional, popular, Realist mould, notable examples of Mexican travel writing from the late 1980s and 1990s question the founding principles of the travel narrative as practised in Mexico, its aesthetics and politics. Such texts include Villoro's *Palmeras de la brisa rápida: un viaje a Yucatán* of 1989; Héctor Perea's *México: crónica en espiral* (CNCA,1996) and Fernando Solana Olivares's *Oaxaca: crónicas sonámbulas* (CNCA, 1994). Villoro's text is particularly interesting for its postmodernist deconstruction of the traditional generic mould of travel writing in conjunction with what I define as a 'postimperialist' critique of the genre of travel writing, as well as of the tourist industry in late twentieth-century Mexico.[45] Perea's and Solana Olivares's works are both important for the ways in which they establish an intense dialogue with a wide variety of other (travel) narratives, thus revealing their disinclination to produce 'totalising', coherent, authoritive forms of travel narrative themselves.[46] Perea's is also notable for its exploration of the complexities of Spanish–Mexican postcolonial relations through such dialogue. Solana Olivares's text constitutes what I will define as a postmodernist 'archival' form of travel chronicle that blends the 'postimperialist' critique found in Villoro's work with the exploration

---

44   For more on chronotopes see Chapter 1 and 3 in this study.
45   I use the term 'postimperialism' in this study to refer to a contestatory attitude expressed by Mexicans vis-à-vis nineteenth- and twentieth-century Northern European and United States imperialism as distinguished from a contestatory attitude vis-à-vis Spanish colonialism which the term postcolonialism might imply. The 'post'-prefix clearly refers to the contestatory stance adopted rather than to any sense of having moved beyond imperialism.
46   For postmodernism's assault on 'totalising' narratives see Linda Hutcheon, *The Politics of Postmodernism* (London: Routledge, 1989), especially pp. 62–92.

of Mexican postcolonialism found in Perea's.[47] In particular Solana Olivares offers a *mestizo,* Mexican, anti-totalising reading of Western modes of historiography and an implicit critique of the validity of the traditional imperialist travel narrative in Mexico. Despite their different approaches, however, all three authors can be seen to use postmodernist narrative strategies to postcolonialist effect.

Synopsis of the Book

In order to answer fully the questions raised in this introduction, the remainder of this study is divided into six chapters. Chapter 1 introduces the reader to key critical concepts and terminology relevant to the study of specifically Mexican travel writing as well as considers the imperialist propensity of the genre to be found in its basic 'chronotope' – Mikhail Bakhtin's 'chronotope of the road'. Chapter 2 evaluates the development of a tradition of Mexican travel writing during the nineteenth- and early twentieth-century with regard to its major achievements in the creation of a discourse of Mexican national identity, as well as in the light of critical work on imperialist discourse in travel writing. Chapter 3 then makes a case for the, albeit problematic, development of postmodernism and postcolonialism in contemporary Mexican culture. Specifically, it examines the development of forms of postmodernist and/or postcolonialist writing travel writing in said context, thus mapping out the theoretical terrain for the following chapters. Chapters 4, 5 and 6 focus in detail on the works mentioned above by Juan Villoro, Héctor Perea and Fernando Solana Olivares which can all be viewed as offering a variety of postmodernist-informed responses to the conundrum of how one might write a travel narrative in and of contemporary Mexico, and which also unpick the imperialist legacy of the genre.

---

47 For an analysis of Latin American 'archival fictions' see Roberto González Echevarría, *Myth and Archive: A Theory of Latin American Narrative* (Cambridge: Cambridge UP, 1990), especially pp. 142–86. See also Chapter 6 in this study.

CHAPTER 1
Tropes and Chronotopes

Introduction

The central argument of this study is that the poetics of travel writing – tropes and chronotopes – reveal its politics, and that a genre that is so closely associated with imperialist desires and colonialist expansion must surely present some problems when practised by citizens of a postcolonial nation and that these should be visible in the poetics of such texts by, in this case, Mexican authors. In the introductory chapter to this study, I argued that foreign – particularly Northern European and United States – travel writing on the subject of Mexico had been perceived as the major hindrance to the writing of travel books in Mexico, both because of its volume and authority, and because it accompanied imperialist exploitation of the country. However, it is not only this kind of travel writing on the subject of Mexico that is a potential problem for Mexicans who want to travel in and write about their own country. Travel writing *per se* is potentially problematic, and Mexican writers' practice of the genre must thus negotiate with a much wider, predominantly European, tradition of travel writing. Their relationship with this tradition is highly complex, ranging from emulation and adulation, to ironic appropriation, to pointed politically-motivated critique.

In what follows, I want to plot out the generic features of travel writing as it has evolved in post-Independence Mexico, with a predominant focus on the nineteenth- and early twentieth-century form in which the genre was practised. I will thus examine the defining characteristics of what I will refer to as the *crónica de viaje* such as its close relationship to Mikhail Bakhtin's 'chronotope of the road' model, as well as its use of the topoi of *costumbrismo* and *paisajismo*, and I will also emphasise the complex genealogies of these imported literary forms and themes, looking in particular at how the importations were passed off in Mexico itself. The presentation of such features here is deliberately neutral, with a more critical evaluation being reserved for the closing pages of Chapter 2.

The *crónica (de viaje)* as a Literary Genre

Although there are a great many terms in Spanish that can be used to designate a work of travel writing, within Mexico itself, and gaining in popularity from at least the 1860s onwards, *crónica de viaje* or travel chronicle is the most commonly used term to describe a work of specifically literary travel writing.[1] The term *crónica*, of course, immediately suggests its very clearly colonialist ancestry – the *crónicas de Indias* or chronicles of the Conquest were those texts written by the conquistadors as they made inroads into Latin America in order to report their achievements to the Spanish crown and the Spanish people. The texts themselves perform that act of taking possession at a rhetorical level through, for example, the enumeration of the features and attributes of the conquered territory, and the construction of a centred, unified narrative voice that makes sense of the new environment and imposes its ordering, hierarchising vision on the land and its people.[2] However, rather than interrogating the genre for the rhetoric of colonialism, most Mexican writers and critics choose to consider the genre as the foundation-stone of Mexican literature – they simply appropriate it.

---

1   For the sake of accuracy, this study translates *'crónica de viaje'* throughout as 'travel chronicle'. The term is a relatively obscure denomination in English, although it does exist. In fact, 'travelogue' would be the closest English translation for *'crónica de viaje'* in terms of its semantic relationship to other less exclusive terms such as 'travel literature' and 'travel books'. This study prefers not use it because it does not preserve the etymological link to the practice of chronicling.

2   There is a huge amount of criticism available concerning imperialist rhetoric in the chronicles of the Conquest. One of the most useful is Stephen Greenblatt's *Marvelous Possessions: The Wonder of the New World* (Chicago: U of Chicago P, 1991). See also Mary Louise Pratt's seminal *Imperial Eyes: Travel Writing and Transculturation* (London: Routledge, 1992).

Thus, in the words of Alfonso Reyes, 'Nuestra literatura es hecha en casa. Sus géneros nacientes son la Crónica y el Teatro Misionero o de evangelización. [...] La crónica primitiva no corresponde por sus fines a las bellas letras, pero las inaugura y hasta cierto instante las acompaña'.³ The *crónica* is thus deemed Mexican, if not entirely literary, even at the time of the Conquest.

Nevertheless, the popularity of the term *crónica (de viaje)* in Mexico is not only due to the chronicles of the Conquest. Indeed, as Estuardo Núñez, one of the very few scholars of travel writing in and of Latin America, argues, the term *crónica* fell into disuse in the seventeenth and eighteenth centuries.⁴ It was then revived in the mid-nineteenth century to designate a particular kind of journalistic practice and the catalyst for its revival is usually traced back to the light-hearted *chroniques* of social mores and character types (i.e. *costumbrista* sketches) published in Parisian newspapers from the 1850s onwards which were read and emulated by Mexican authors, aware of their readership's desire for French fashions, in literature as well as in other fields.⁵

With regard to the importation of these foreign genres, it should be noted that Mexican writers were, in general, quite happy to cherry-pick their way through foreign products, using those that appeared most

---

3   Alfonso Reyes, *Obras completas*, 26 vols (FCE, 1955–92), XII: *Letras de la Nueva España* (1960), 313.
4   Núñez finds the most appropriate term for Latin American travel writing to be *viaje* rather than *crónica*. He posits that chronicles are merely temporal narratives of more historical than literary value, and that *viajes* display a more spatial consciousness in their desire to describe Latin American reality. *Viajes* are hence more literary. He then substantiates his argument by looking at the fall-off in usage of the term *crónica* in the Colonial period, and the increase in the publication of *viajes*. He is, in part, correct – there is a change in usage of terminology over this period that continues into the nineteenth century – but the use of the term chronicle has since mutated and made a come-back. In Núñez's own bibliography the use of the terms *crónica* and *crónica de viaje* in the titles of travel books is evident from 1928 onwards (Estuardo Nuñez, ed., *Viajeros hispanoamericanos: temas continentales* [Caracas: Biblioteca Ayacucho, 1989], pp. ix-xx).
5   Aníbal González, *La crónica modernista hispanoamericana* (Madrid: Porrúa Turanzas, 1983), pp. 64–65; and *Journalism and the Development of Spanish American Narrative* (Cambridge: Cambridge UP, 1993), pp. 84–87.

useful to them by simply transplanting them and changing their content. The form and function of these imports may mutate somewhat over time to fit the new context, but it is not necessarily a conscious decision on the part of those writers who import the new product. This will to appropriate such foreign genres as the Spanish *crónica* and the French *chronique* without too much consideration for any underlying political baggage is indicative of the fact that Mexico, even after Independence, continued to conceive of itself in the image of Spanish (and French) culture rather than rebelling against such influences.[6] Mexicans would only become alerted to the problematic nature of the genre of travel writing when faced with examples of travel books written about their own country by Northern European and United States travellers that began to appear in increasing numbers from the mid-nineteenth century onwards. This is why their reactions to the genre are more specifically postimperialist than they are postcolonialist.

The *crónica* is thus a common genre in Hispanic letters and one that has become increasingly popular throughout Latin America since the Independence movements of the early nineteenth century. But what of its development in Mexico and its contemporary form? How has it evolved to become something which many Mexicans would identify as particularly Mexican? There have been two main booms in the production of *crónicas* in Mexico: the first in the late nineteenth century and the second in the late twentieth century. In his *Antología de la narrativa mexicana del siglo XX* Christopher Domínguez Michael notes that: 'Desde el siglo XIX la crónica fue una de las manifestaciones más libres y creativas de la literatura mexicana'.[7] The chronicle as a vehicle for committed journalism was given a major boost by Carlos Monsiváis in the wake of the Tlatelolco massacre of 1968, and, according to Domínguez Michael, 'Desde los años setenta, en México, *todo lo que*

---

6   Jorge Klor de Alva, 'The Postcolonization of the (Latin) American Experience: A Reconsideration of "Colonialism," "Postcolonialism," and "Mestizaje"', in *After Colonialism: Imperial Histories and Postcolonial Displacements*, ed. by Gyan Prakash (Princeton, NJ: Princeton UP, 1995).
7   Christopher Domínguez Michael, ed., *Antología de la narrativa mexicana del siglo XX*, 2nd edn, 2 vols (FCE, 1996), II, 73.

no es ficción, es crónica' (author's italics).[8] Hermann Bellinghausen has also commented on the contemporary proliferation of the chronicle: 'Van por el mundo, decenas, cientos de textos, que se suponen crónicas. Suposición que comparten lectores, autores y editores, de manera que la crónica existe a pesar de su aparente confusión polimórfica.'[9]

Analysts of the contemporary chronicle as a journalistic practice such as Bellinghausen, Raymundo Riva Palacio and Federico Campbell tend to define it as 'a subjective vision of the news'; the Mexican equivalent of American New Journalism.[10] It needs to be about something of interest to the general public, but it must be a personalised rewriting of events mixing narrative, description and critical discourse with 'intensidad, humor, fantasía, el desmadre que ordena el universo postapocalíptico'.[11] It needs to pay particular attention to the recording of pertinent details, to providing a 'nota de color', in order to make the reader relive events for him/herself. The personalisation of the rewriting may be on the narrator's own behalf if he/she was an eyewitness, or from the imaginary perspective of any other real witness of the events. In either case 'being there' must be demonstrated through the inclusion of pertinent details that only an eyewitness could record, and this exercise of personalising the style of writing, insists upon the literary value of the chronicle.

This definition is not so very far from that which might be given for the chronicles of the Conquest, although current advice on the writing of chronicles also deems chronological order to be optional; a choice that was not on offer in the genesis of the genre. It also reveals some of the literary considerations, however involuntary, that underpinned the original chronicles. The best chronicles of all time hold literature and

---

8   Christopher Domínguez Michael, personal letter, 12 February 1996.
9   Hermann Bellinghausen, 'Testigos del caso: la crónica en México', *Nexos*, 162 (June 1991), 15.
10 Federico Campbell, *Periodismo escrito* (Ariel, 1994), pp. 42–53; and Raymundo Riva Palacio, *Más allá de los límites: ensayos para un nuevo periodismo* (Gobierno del Estado de Colima / Fundación Manuel Buendía, 1995), pp. 187–205.
11 Carlos Monsiváis, prologue to *El fin de la nostalgia: nueva crónica de la ciudad de México*, ed. by Jaime Valverde Arciniega and Juan Domingo Argüelles (Nueva Imagen, 1992), p. 25.

history (or journalism) in the balance. The sixteenth-century chronicle might have focused more on its news value than its literary style, thus meriting the definition as a 'texto histórico en el que se van recogiendo los hechos según sucedieron cronológicamente', but increasingly literature prevails over news in the Mexican chronicle: it has become an 'artículo literario, generalmente de no mucha extensión, que versa acerca de algún comentario o juicio de sucedidos'.[12] Monsiváis's definition in the introductory notes to his *A ustedes les consta* is the most extreme in its evaluation of the literary value of the chronicle:

> Reconstrucción *literaria* de sucesos o figuras, género donde el empeño formal domina sobre las urgencias informativas. [...] En la crónica, el juego literario usa a discreción la primera persona o narra libremente los acontecimientos como vistos y vividos desde la interioridad ajena. Tradicionalmente – sin que eso signifique ley alguna –, en la crónica ha privado la recreación de atmósferas y personajes sobre la transmisión de noticias y denuncias.[13] (author's italics)

This fully ratifies the chronicle as a literary practice, giving it the autonomy to exist independent of its role in the press.

One point that merits no particular comment in these definitions is that travel is almost always involved in the production of a Latin American chronicle, from the time of the *crónicas de Indias* onwards: 'being there' as an eye-witness usually requires 'getting there'. However, where some chronicles omit the narration of the journey to concentrate on the investigative goal of the journey, others narrate the personal journey as well. In general, contemporary chronicles that have a more journalistic focus are those that omit the journey – unless it constitutes part of the news in question (the chronicle of a pilgrimage, for example). The remainder are travel chronicles and they are usually even more of a literary practice, both in their intentions and in their results.

---

12 First acceptation of the word 'crónica' in the *Gran Diccionario de la lengua española*, 2nd edn (Madrid: Sociedad General Española de Librería, 1988), p. 495; and the acceptation currently given by the *Diccionario de Mejicanismos*, ed. by Francisco de Santamaría, 5th edn (Porrúa, 1992), p. 312, respectively.

13 Carlos Monsiváis, *A ustedes les consta: antología de la crónica en México* (Era, 1980), p. 13.

The narration of one's own travels – the *a priori* defining characteristic of the travel chronicle – forces the narrator to take an active part in his/her own narrative. It is this recording of the details of private life as well as of matters of potential public interest that distinguishes the tone of the travel chronicle from that of the chronicle (although this is arguably a matter of degree). The travel chronicle thus tends to foreground questions of identity in the traveller's confrontation between self and other on the road. Yet as a complement to its focus on personal identity, the travel chronicle also inevitably focuses on group identity. In the case of Mexicans travelling in Mexico since Independence, this group identity tends to be of a national order and it is this potential to provide a vehicle for debates on national identity that Mexican writers have typically found to be the most useful characteristic of the travel chronicle. This is precisely the reason why writers such as Altamirano argue that the genre should be promoted in Mexico.

The preference in the travel chronicle for chronological order, linear, goal-orientated journeys and the presentation of an authoritative, unified narrative voice that interprets his surroundings for the reader back home (at least until the publication of a number of postmodernist-inspired travel chronicles studied in Chapters 4, 5 and 6 of this study) is also indicative of the fact that travel chronicles are generally more traditional in their approach, whereas the practice of writing chronicles has become more experimental, more amorphous. Realism is the dominant style of writing and intertextuality within the field of travel writing is continually used in these texts to acknowledge respect for and (slight) deviance from the tradition. Both the development of the narrator as a protagonist, and the use of intertextuality to signal an awareness of tradition, are key factors in the increased literary construction of the travel chronicle.[14]

---

14   For an interesting recent analysis of the chronicle genre as a whole in Mexican letters, see Ignacio Corona and Beth E. Jörgensen, eds., *The Contemporary Mexican Chronicle: Theoretical Perspectives on the Liminal Genre* (Albany: State U of New York P, 2002).

Costumbrismo and Paisajismo

Inextricably entwined in the history of the importation(s) of the *crónica* are the equally imported topoi of *costumbrismo* – the description of the idiosyncratic characters and customs of different regions – and *paisajismo* – the aesthetic appreciation of landscapes.[15] In their regional specificity, both have a clear application in the creation and propagation of a sense of national identity, hence their popularity with nineteeth-century Mexican writers intent on creating their own brand of Mexican national identity in literature.

Costumbrismo and *paisajismo* are parallel topoi in nineteenth-century Mexican literature; however *paisajismo* is technically the first to be used and is clearly related to the influence of Romanticism in Mexico, spread by travelling European artists and writers.[16] Many critics also associate *costumbrismo* with the Romantic movement; nevertheless, it is essentially a Realist, and even, Naturalist subject. While the movements of Romanticism, Realism, and Naturalism may be seen to follow on from one another in clear succession in a country such as France, where at least the two latter movements originated,

---

15   This is described as 'the special attention given to the portrayal of manners and customs characteristic of a region or country' in *The Oxford Companion to Spanish Literature*, ed. by Philip Ward (Oxford: Clarendon Press, 1978), p. 137. Neither *costumbrismo* nor *paisajismo* has been thoroughly studied with respect to its practice in Mexico. There is no individual publication dedicated to the study of Mexican *costumbrismo* as there are for other Latin American nations. The works available on *paisajismo* are dated: Manuel Maples Arce, *El paisaje en la literatura mexicana* (Porrúa, 1944), and María de los Ángeles Mendieta, *El paisaje en la novela de América*, prol. by Alberto Delgado Pastor, Tercera Época, 203 (SEP, 1949). Neither book deals with the specific case of the chronicle, concentrating on poetry and novels respectively. *El paisaje mexicano en la pintura del siglo XIX y principios del XX*, by Consuelo Fernández Ruiz, Leticia Gámez Ludgar & María de los Ángeles Sobrino Figueroa (exhibition catalogue: June–October 1991, Mexico City [Fomento Cultural Banamex, 1991]), is better and more up-to-date, but strictly limited to *paisajismo* in painting.
16   See María Esther Pérez Salas, 'El costumbrismo del siglo XIX, origen del nacionalismo en la plástica mexicana' in *Identidades y nacionalismos: una perspectiva interdisciplinaria*, ed. by Lilia Granillo Vázquez (UAM / Gernika, 1993), pp. 149–70.

in Mexico the influence of these movements tended to be either simultaneous or alternating. Realism reached Mexico within only a few years of Romanticism, and Romantic novels were still being written at the time that the first influences of Naturalism were being felt. In fact, it is possible to view Mexico as being under the sway of Romanticism throughout the *modernista* period, right up until the 1930s and 40s. Realism, then, blends with Romanticism and it is perhaps this blend of 'realismo romántico' which allows for the enduring popularity of *costumbrismo* throughout the nineteenth century.[17]

Paisajismo: The experience of the lone traveller reflecting on the correspondence of nature to his moods and looking to experience new emotions through contact with the 'exotic' and the 'wild' is a leitmotif in Romantic literature. Jean Jacques Rousseau's *Rêveries du promeneur solitaire* (written c.1776; published posthumously in 1782) signified the beginning of Romanticism: with its Liberal, back-to-nature rêveries in the Swiss countryside, his descriptions of the 'picturesque' Swiss landscape infused with introspective sentiment, plus his recommendation of travel for educational, consciousness-raising purposes, he created the paradigm for the nineteenth-century travel writer.[18] The integration of personal narrative, description (in particular of landscape) and thought, in a step-by-step guide in his *Rêveries* was also a new development in the travel writing of that period; one which has arguably endured as the model for literary travel writing ever since. Much modern travel writing, with its integration of the narrator-protagonist's personal experience of travel and sense of self in counterpoint to changing surroundings, might even now be considered a specifically Romantic genre.

---

17 See John S. Brushwood, *La barbarie elegante: ensayos y experiencias en torno a algunas novelas hispanoamericanas del siglo XIX*, trans. by Lucía Garavito (FCE, 1988), pp. 13–34; and Emmanuel Carballo, ed., *Historia de las letras mexicanas en el siglo XIX* (Guadalajara: Universidad de Guadalajara / Xalli, 1991), pp. 64–65. Brushwood's analysis of the practice of Romanticism and Realism in Latin America has informed much of the following discussion of *costumbrismo*.

18 The paradigm is valid for the individualistic journeys of the Romantics and also the more scientifically-orientated journeys of naturalists such as Humboldt who used the Romantic aesthetic to give their descriptions of nature more impact (see Pratt, *Imperial Eyes*, p. 56).

During the course of the nineteenth century almost every Romantic writer was known for some travel literature, most of which dealt with external journeys in search of new 'exotic' landscapes. In a French context, Mme de Staël's *De l'Allemagne* (1810) and René de Chateaubriand's *Voyage au Mont Blanc* (1806), *Itinéraire de Paris a Jérusalem* (1811), *Voyage en Italie* (1826), and most importantly his *Voyage en Amérique* (1827) should be viewed as the immediate precursors of fully-developed Romantic travel writing. These are followed by works by Lamartine, Gautier, Stendhal, Hugo, Vigny, Musset, Senancour, Constant, Dumas (père), Nerval, Michelet, Georges Sand, Verlaine, Taine, Flaubert, Maupassant and others.[19] None of this travel writing deals with travel in Mexico; however, nineteenth-century Mexican writers were almost obsessed with French representations of the exotic 'other' whether it referred directly to themselves or not, and much of their writing is directed to the negotiation, through illustration and example, of Mexico's difficult relationship between exoticism and culture.

Whether directly from Rousseau's texts, via Humboldt, or via any of the French Romantics, *paisajismo* and one of its preferred vehicles (travel writing) had a profound and lasting effect on the development of Mexican travel writing. Nineteenth-century Mexican travel chroniclers refer ceaselessly to the descriptions of nature in the travel writing of the great Romantics: Chateaubriand in North America, Lamartine in the Holy Land, Gautier in Spain and many others, alongside their more direct appreciations of the work of Humboldt. While seemingly acknowledging the mastery of these great writers in the frequent suggestion that Mexican writers do not have adjectives enough to capture the beauty and subtlety of their natural surroundings, they simultaneously laud Mexican landscapes as equal or better than those of Europe: they require more of the average writer.

Costumbrismo: Romanticism was also responsible for the development of interest in natural and/or undeveloped ways of life and

---

19   Goethe should also figure on this list of Romantic travel writers, were it not deliberately limited to French writers. Tocqueville's historical analysis of North American democracy which stemmed from a journey there to study the penal system was extremely influential in its own right.

the cult of the Noble Savage, yet it was the Realist movement which more thoroughly espoused the ethnological slice-of-life approach to the middle, lower middle and working classes of society who are the most frequent subjects of *costumbrismo*: the water carrier, the working-class girl ('la China Poblana'), the night watchman and others. If *costumbrismo* is only seen to be part of Romanticism, it must, then, be considered an ironic part on account of its focus on the lower classes rather than the Romantic individual.[20] Nevertheless, the moralising aspect of much *costumbrismo* stems more clearly from Romanticism than from Realism. In the long run, the best *costumbrismo* balances Romantic retouched 'local colour' with Realist photographic documentation.[21]

The proto-anthropological/sociological study of people and customs was not a Realist invention. In Spain Cervantes and other Golden Age writers had occasionally made *costumbrista*-style descriptions in their work.[22] In the early eighteenth-century in England, Joseph Addison and Sir Richard Steele, influenced by the Spanish Picaresque, both wrote articles on the subject of customs and characters which they published in their journals, *The Tatler* and *The Spectator*. Influenced in turn by Addison and Steele, the Frenchmen Louis-Sébastien Mercier and Joseph Étienne de Jouy wrote extensively on *costumbrista* topics. Mercier's twelve-volume *Tableau de Paris* (1779–89) contains many sketches of typical events and characters; Jouy's satirical descriptions of both metropolitan and provincial French society are collected as *L'Hermite de la Chaussée d'Antin* (1812–14) and *L'Hermite en province* (1824).[23]

---

20   This is how José Luis Martínez accounts for it (quoted in Carballo's *Historia de las letras mexicanas*, p. 129).
21   The development of photography in the nineteenth century was central to the perceived need for a Realist approach in literature.
22   See Ward, *The Oxford Companion to Spanish Literature*, p. 137.
23   Data paraphrased from Margarita Ucelay da Cal, Los españoles pintados por sí mismos, 1843–1844: estudio de un género costumbrista (El Colegio de México, 1951), pp. 13–65.

　　Honoré de Balzac's *Comédie humaine* (1830–), with its studies on human behaviour – the 'études des moeurs' –, divided into sections of 'scènes de la vie privée', '...de la vie de province', '...de la vie parisienne' etc., was no doubt influential in the development of early *costumbrismo*. Taine's deterministic

The encroachment of French culture on that of Spain in the early years of the nineteenth century was seen as an imposition by the Spanish intelligentsia of the day.[24] Romanticism, in particular, was seen as an import that was threatening to destroy the Spanish sense of identity in a wave of francophilia: Spain for the French Romantics was just another exotic destination. In the Spaniards' struggle to assert their own national identity through the celebration of autochthonous culture and the derision of imported behaviour patterns, they adopted *costumbrismo* as a literary genre and movement in itself, despite its most immediate French origin. Newly independent Latin American nations trying to create national literatures of their own felt a similar need to that of Spain to find and develop their own local repertoire of topoi: they thus looked to the Spanish (and French) practices of *costumbrismo* for inspiration.

In his article 'The *Costumbrista* Movement in Mexico',[25] Jefferson Rea Spill traces the development of the movement in Spain and its adoption in Mexico. Although, as Rea Spill notes, Fernández de Lizardi had independently produced some articles satirising the customs of Mexican society in 1812 – a fact that has prompted some critics to claim that Mexican *costumbrismo* was more of a spontaneous, homegrown product than 'una importación servil' from Spain[26] – the movement

---

    theory of 'la race, le milieu et le moment' as a means of explaining human nature and society in general, conveyed through his plentiful travel writing, was also of importance for the practice of naturalist-inspired *costumbrismo* in the latter decades of the century.

24   Indeed, France had quite clearly imperialist designs with respect to her Southern neighbour at that point in time (see Nancy Vogeley, 'The Discourse of Colonial Loyalty: Mexico, 1808', *in Macropolitics of Nineteenth-Century Literature: Nationalism, Exoticism, Imperialism*, ed. by Jonathan Arac and Harriet Ritvo (Philadelphia: U of Pennsylvania P, 1991), pp. 37–55).

25   In Jefferson Rea Spill, *Bridging the Gap: Articles on Mexican Literature* (Libros de México, 1971), pp. 295–315 (repr. from *PMLA*, 50 [March 1935], 290–315).

26   Carballo, *Historia de las letras mexicanas*, p. 129. Carballo notes: 'El influjo de Larra, Mesonero Romanos, Estébanez Calderón si bien se advierte entre los costumbristas, en ningún momento es decisivo. La posición ante el mundo y el hombre de nuestros escritores costumbristas coincide con la del Pensador Mexicano más que con la de estos prosistas españoles. Simplemente adaptan el costumbrismo dinámico del autor del Periquillo al estatismo propio de sus cuadros de costumbres'.

did not really get started in Mexican journalism until about 1840, and when it did, it acknowledged mainly Spanish sources: Mariano José de Larra's satirical articles and 'cuadros', and also those of Ramón de Mesonero Romanos, Serafín Estébanez Calderón, and Manuel Bretón de los Herreros.[27] Many of the articles by these Spanish writers were reproduced in Mexican magazines and journals of the day, although other writers whose *costumbrista* sketches were published in Mexico in the early nineteenth century were Jouy and the North American/ Englishman, Washington Irving. Both Manuel Payno and Guillermo Prieto, two of the key writers of travel accounts in nineteenth-century Mexico, recognised the positive influence of Larra and Mesonero Romanos in their early *costumbrista* articles.

In Mexico, as in Spain, *costumbrismo* was in part a tool of political resistance and in part a complacent, or at best neutral recreation of 'the good old days'. Depending on who was in power, Mexican writers used *costumbrista* sketches either to fête their own social achievements and revel in their own idiosyncratically Mexican *savoir-vivre*, or to deride the other party's social image through ridiculous sketches of its adherents' manners and lifestyle. In the long run it was a tool most used by Liberal writers, since it was they who were least frequently in power, and most conscientious about the creation of a new, independent Mexican society. Their *cuadros* were generally written 'not with the intention of furnishing entertainment but [...] with the hope of effecting reforms', as they tried to goad a sense of national identity into existence.[28]

---

27 The Spanish *costumbrista* movement lasted from approximately 1830–1860.
28 Rea Spill, 'The *Costumbrista* Movement in Mexico', p. 295. Two periods of *costumbrismo* may be discerned in nineteenth-century Mexico: a more critical one which lasted until Porfirio Díaz came to power in 1876, and a more complacent one thereafter. This complacent form of *costumbrismo* was probably what got the movement a bad name, and although *costumbrismo* will never disappear from literature, the movement was well over by the beginning of the Mexican Revolution. (Rea Spill actually dates it 1840–1890.)

Costumbrista Travel Chronicles in Nineteenth-Century Mexico

Spanish *costumbrismo* started with the description of *madrileño* society, but in order to describe the full range of inhabitants of Spain, and to document the customs which were rapidly falling into disuse in the capital on account of their exposure to foreign influences and modernisation, it became necessary to travel to the provinces. The Spanish *costumbristas* wrote travel articles and even whole series of *cuadros de costumbres* concerning their travels: Larra wrote the articles *Las antigüedades de Mérida* and *Impresiones de viaje* in 1835; Mesonero Romanos wrote his *Recuerdos de viaje por Francia y Bélgica* in 1840–41, and fragments of his *Viaje de los dos donceles* (1943), covering a trip to Andalucia, were published posthumously in 1883.[29] Such travel chronicles were much appreciated by the Mexican *costumbristas* and, spurred on by their desire to create a nation, they also travelled extensively within Mexico.

In Carlos Monsiváis's concise overview of the work of the *costumbrista* writers in his introduction to the anthology *A ustedes les consta*, he notes that they,

> Seleccionan las estampas que respiran en lo literario calor hogareño; en lo político efusión patriótica; en lo nacional la riqueza de lo pintoresco, y en el recuento de viajes comprensión y alabanza del mundo. (Las crónicas viajeras son los prenoticieros de la época.)[30]

And he goes on to sum up their aims and procedures:

> De acuerdo al plan de afirmar la nacionalidad glosándola, la crónica oscila entre el turismo interno (de lances de charrería y paseos por Ixtacalco al descubrimiento de paisajes y caracteres a las figuras de veladores de barriada y policías hostiles) y una suerte de 'filosofía nacional', el interrogatorio a lo desconocido o inexpresado: debemos indagar en la psicología colectiva que

---

29 Data paraphrased from Don Carlos Seco Serrano's prologue to the *Obras de Ramón de Mesonero Romanos*, 5 vols (Madrid: Biblioteca de Autores Españoles, 1967), I, pp. il-liii.
30 Monsiváis, ed., *A ustedes les consta*, p. 25.

norma fatalmente nuestra conducta. [...] Se necesita – además de la burla como escuela de continencia – fortalecer a la Nación infundiéndole y aclarándole sus orgullos locales y regionales, recreando literariamente las formas de vida más ostensiblemente 'mexicanas' y subrayando el desdén por la imitación de lo francés y la nostalgia servil de lo hispánico.[31]

The task of the Mexican *costumbristas* was not easy. As the writer and politician Guillermo Prieto noted very early on, 'Los cuadros de costumbres eran difíciles, porque no había costumbres verdaderamente nacionales, porque el escritor no tenía pueblo, porque sólo podía bosquejar retratos que no interesan sino a reducido número de personas.'[32] But Prieto also took heart: 'No por esto debe desmayar el escritor de costumbres; sus cuadros algún día serán [...] como el tesoro guardado bajo la primera piedra de una columna.'[33] The endeavours of these writers are the subject of Chapter 2 of this study.

The Chronotope of the Road

The above analysis of the genealogy of the *costumbrista* (travel) chronicle has focused on the genre as part of a broadly Hispanic tradition (dating from the time of the Conquest) and has placed emphasis on its increasing acceptance as a specifically Mexican genre, yet it has also argued that this was achieved largely at the level of rhetorical claims of ownership, and, at the level of content, through a repackaging with local material, rather than in terms of any substantial change in the form of the genre. But the fundamental form of the genre, I shall argue, is the key to understanding what may lead it to have such pervasive imperialist tendencies, particularly when practised by Northern European and

---

31 Monsiváis, ed., *A ustedes les consta*, p. 27. In Monsiváis' analysis *paisajismo* is a branch of *costumbrismo*: the *costumbristas* seek 'el descubrimiento de *paisajes y caracteres*' (my italics).
32 First published in the *Revista Científica y Literaria de México*, 1845; quoted in Monsiváis, ed., *A ustedes les consta*, p. 24.
33 First published in *El Siglo XIX*, 6 June 1842; quoted in Monsiváis, ed., *A ustedes les consta*, p. 26.

United States writers, and how the genre might thus be adapted to make it work for 'postcolonial' writers.

Although many critics have had their say on quite how difficult it is to define a genre such as travel writing, or put in a rather more circumspect manner, to define travel writing as a genre,[34] what I want to do here is consider what most readers would unproblematically identify as travel writing in the light of Mikhail Bakhtin's study of chronotopes associated with different prose genres, as presented in *The Dialogic Imagination* (1975), in order to shed light on the genre's politics.[35] Bakhtin's theory of chronotopes classifies works of literature – usually novels – according to their particular combination of time (real versus fantasy, historical versus ahistorical/fictional, and so on) and space (public versus private, familiar versus unfamiliar, specific types of places, and so on). These chronotopes can be very broad (the 'adventure chronotope' or the 'chronotope of the road') or specific to an individual writer (for example, Dostoyevsky's 'staircase', 'street' and 'carnival chronotopes'). While any reader can classify works in this manner,[36] the value of Bakhtin's work lies in what he then goes to deduce about the implications of a selection of the most common time-space combinations: what certain chronotopes can tell us about a given society and its politics. In essence, the chronotope works as a kind of literary DNA.

Traditional (European) travel writing – linear, chronological, goal-orientated, broadly Realist work with a unified and authoritative narrative voice – most closely corresponds to Bakhtin's 'chronotope of

---

34 See, for example, the introduction to Helen Gilbert and Anna Johnston's *In Transit: Travel, Text, Empire* (New York: Lang, 2002), especially pp. 8–13.

35 Mikhail Bakhtin, 'Forms of Time and of the Chronotope in the Novel: Notes toward a Historical Poetics', *in The Dialogic Imagination: Four Essays by M.M. Bakhtin*, ed. Michael Holquist, trans. Caryl Emerson and Michael Holquist (Austin: University of Texas Press, 1981), 84–258 (especially pp. 243–45).

36 Since Bakhtin's ground-breaking research, significant numbers of researchers have worked with his original set of chronotopes, refining them and adding new specifications to the more generic chronotopes. See, for example, Michael Larsen, 'The Bakhtinian Chronotope: Origins, Modifications and Additions', unpublished doctoral dissertation, U. of Kent at Canterbury, 1997.

the road' model whereby the historical time of the narrative advances apace with spatial displacement through real terrain. According to Bakhtin, this chronotope has the advantage of introducing the widest possible cross-section of the community travelled through, without the contrivance of plot, and is hence ideal for the articulation of group identities, as mentioned above with regard to the function of nineteeth-century Mexican *crónicas de viaje*. As Bakhtin notes,

> The road is a particularly good place for random encounters. On the road ('the high road'), the spatial and temporal paths of the most varied people – representatives of all social classes, estates, religions, nationalities, ages – intersect at one spatial and temporal point. People who are normally kept separate by social and spatial distance can accidentally meet; any contrast may crop up, the most various fates may collide and interweave with one another.[37]

In this discussion of specifically fictional travel narratives, Bakhtin further refines the 'chronotope of the road' to specify that 'the road is always one that passes through *familiar territory*, and not through some exotic *alien world*'.[38] That is to say, in such fictional accounts the depition of unfamiliar worlds is always a fairly transparent vehicle for the analysis of one's own society and hence the territory remains familiar, even if the place names marking the way are supposedly foreign to the narrator.

Bakhtin did not write about how this might be different in non-fictional European travel writing where, in the vast majority of cases, the narrator does experience an unfamiliar territory. It is evident, however, from the now copious body of critical literature on the subject, that the discourse of 'exoticism' figures highly in such non-fictional travel accounts, working in close counterpoint with that other very common process in travel writing of translation of the unfamiliar into the familiar of home.[39] Thus, while such accounts can be useful for

---

37 Bakhtin, 'Forms of Time', p. 243.
38 Bakhtin, 'Forms of Time', p. 245 (italics in original).
39 Although there are far too many works to mention them all here, of particular relevance are Pratt's *Imperial Eyes,* Spurr's *The Rhetoric of Empire*, and Patrick Holland and Graham Huggan's *Tourists with Typewriters: Critical Reflections on Contemporary Travel Writing* (Ann Arbor: U of Michigan P, 2000).

helping to elucidate the functionings and even the centrality of home, in so far as they have the ability to articulate group identities related to the host society, this chronotope is particularly prone to being harnessed to imperialist projects because the group identities to be articulated are always those of 'others' who live in unfamiliar, *exotic* terrain and who are thus differentiated (negatively) from the narrator of the account. Articulating the identity of such groups frequently runs hand-in-hand with an attempt to contain and to dominate them, or at the very least to harness their potential for the production of capital. Thus this chronotope in which the historical time of the narrative advances apace with spatial displacement through real and *unfamiliar, exotic* terrain has clear imperialist tendencies in its fundamental conception, and these are then echoed in many of the tropes and other rhetorical features of such works.

It is this basic chronotope that nineteeth-century Mexican travel writers imported when they decided to kick-start a Mexican travel writing tradition. However, given that they were travelling in their own country and writing for a domestic reading public, these non-fictional Mexican travel accounts stand half way between the imperialist 'chronotope of the road' outlined above for non-fictional European travel writing and the more domestic, nationalist 'chronotope of the road' that Bakhtin discussed with reference to European fictional travel accounts. To a large extent, as we shall see in Chapter 2, the nationalist drive in their work will dominate. Nevertheless, some features of the imperialist chronotope such as the question of the authority of the voice/gaze persist to a greater or lesser extent depending on the author and his politics, and these will be explored at the end of Chapter 2. The study will then go on to propose that a new chronotope has emerged in recent Mexican travel writing – the 'chronotope of the net' – and that this chronotope has the advantage of helping to avoid the pitfalls of the original imperialist chronotope, thus facilitating a more 'postcolonialist', Latin American approach to travel writing.

CHAPTER 2
The Tradition of Mexican Travel Writing

Introduction

Nineteenth-century Mexican travel writing was a European import that was conveniently used by Mexican writers as a 'vehicle' for the development of Mexican national identity in literature. The outstanding characteristics of Mexican travel chronicles in this period are their sense of purpose (the creation of national identity), coupled with the detailed attention paid to the description of all things Mexican, in particular local natural phenomena and the idiosyncrasies of the Mexican people (*paisajismo* and *costumbrismo*, respectively), and the consistency of their formal features (a clear, chronologically-ordered and goal-orientated journey structure, and an active first-person narrator who presents himself as a unified, centred subject with the authority to comment on a wide range of subjects).

This characteristic format is reinforced by intertextual references to other travel narratives – those written by foreign travellers in Mexico, those by Mexicans travelling in Mexico, and those by foreign travel writers describing other parts of the world entirely. The use of intertextuality is often a way of corroborating the truth value of the text – someone else has done or seen or said the same thing, even in nigh-on virgin territory.[1] Furthermore, in the case of references to specifically Mexican writers, it also expediently creates a canon of Mexican travel writing: the content, the form, the continuity of purpose are seen to be handed down from one writer to another; literally, a tradition is in

---

1 See Lily Litvak's *El ajedrez de estrellas: crónicas de viajeros españoles del siglo XIX por países exóticos, 1800–1913* ([Barcelona: Laia, 1987], p. 220) for an analysis of the relationship between verisimilitude and intertextuality in nineteenth-century Spanish travel chronicles.

the process of being invented.² It is in part through this intertextual invention of a tradition, of an 'imagined community' of increasingly Mexican writers, and in part through the overlap between the subject matter and target audience of the travel chronicles, an 'imagined community' of Mexican readers, that Mexican national identity is created in literature.³

This chapter, then, will consider the work of some of the key nineteenth- and early twentieth-century travel writers in Mexico, giving them full credit for their achievements in the field, and exploring in particular the nuances of their changing relationship with European travel writing and the discourse of exoticism. It will also consider how the tradition was developed in the mid-nineteenth century by the friends Manuel Payno and Guillermo Prieto and follow it through to its demise in the early twentieth century, paying particular attention to different writers' attitudes to the question of tradition, in line with Carlos Monsiváis's apt observation that Mexico is 'un país experimental donde las tradiciones por excelencia son la improvisación continua y el rechazo de la tradición'.⁴ It will then go on to consider evidence of imperialist discourse and the balance of creolisation and transculturation in nineteenth- and early twentieth-century Mexican writers' appropriation of the genre.

---

2   Mexican travel chronicling is an 'invented' tradition in itself, in the sense discussed by Eric Hobsbawm and Terence Ranger in the introduction to their *The Invention of Tradition* [Cambridge: Cambridge UP, 1983], pp. 1–14), and it also invents other traditions such as the Day of the Dead through its subject matter.
3   See Benedict Anderson's introduction to his *Imagined Communites: Reflections on the Origin and Spread of Nationalism*, revd edn (London: Verso, 1991), pp. 1–7.
4   Carlos Monsiváis, 'Notas sobre la cultura mexicana en el siglo XX', *Historia general de México*, ed. by Daniel Cosío Villegas, 2nd edn, 4 vols (Colegio de México, 1977), IV, 309.

Manuel Payno and Guillermo Prieto: Creating the Nation, Creating the Tradition

In the years following Independence in all the different Latin American nations, political thinkers and activists, usually Liberals, perceived a need to travel around their newly-won countries to establish for themselves what they actually 'owned'.⁵ At the same time, sometimes by choice and sometimes by obligation, these writers also travelled abroad, thus observing how other, more advanced nations were developing, with a view to returning to their own nations to have another attempt at establishing national identity. Indeed, Walter D. Mignolo summarises on the subject of the difference between nineteeth-century (North and Latin) American and European travel writing that, rather than seek otherness and the exotic as European travel writers did, Americans, and I would add, particularly Latin Americans, sought 'the complicitous identification of the self-same with national territories'; that is to say, they sought to compare and to emulate.⁶ The biggest name associated with this project in Latin America as a whole is undoubtedly that of the Argentinian Domingo Faustino Sarmiento whose *Viajes por Europa, África i América* (1849–51) illustrates one of the fullest itineraries

---

5   In Mexico the Liberals were generally committed to a federal approach to government and thus more interested than the Conservative centralists in letting the provinces know that they were part of the Mexican Republic while allowing them to retain a large degree of autonomy; hence their interest in travel writing. Conservatives who produced works concerning travel tended to write guidebooks, often of major cities, for the use of foreign visitors to Mexico, opting for a more sedentary and/or utilitarian approach – see for example, Marcos Arróniz's *Manual del viajero en México* (Paris: Librería de Rosa y Bouret, 1858; repr. Instituto Mora, 1991). (The suggestion concerning the sedentary nature of nineteenth-century Conservative politics was made by Carlos Monsiváis, personal interview, 30 January 1997.)

6   Walter D. Mignolo, 'Human Understanding and (Latin) American Interests: The Politics and Sensibilities of Geohistorical Locations', in *A Companion to Postcolonial Studies*, ed. by Henry Schwarz and Sangeeta Ray (Oxford: Blackwell, 2000), p. 181.

of any Latin American of his day.⁷ Alongside Sarmiento, one should also mention the life and works of the Venezuelan Simón Bolívar, the Peruvian Manuel Lorenzo de Vidaurre and the Colombian Juan Montalvo.

The major Mexican writers and politicians caught up in this polarised programme of nationalist travel chronicling are Manuel Payno (1810–94) (*Un viaje a Veracruz en el invierno de 1843*; *Memorias e impresiones de un viaje a Inglaterra y Escocia, por Manuel Payno, ciudadano mexicano* (1853); *Barcelona y México en 1888 y 1889, por don Manuel Payno, Cónsul General de México en España*); and Guillermo Prieto (1818–97) (*Viajes de orden suprema, 1853–1855*; *Viaje a los Estados Unidos por Fidel* (1877–78)).⁸ Payno and Prieto dominated the Mexican travel chronicling scene from the 1840s to the 1870s. In fact, this nationalist travel chronicling impetus continued on through to the 1930s and 40s, culminating with José Vasconcelos's memoirs, although nowhere is the polarised pattern for establishing the Mexican nation with respect to other nations so clear as in the works of Payno and Prieto.⁹

Payno's didactic obsession with creating a concept of nation and nationhood through travel is unmistakable. The sole purpose of his

7   According to Estuardo Núñez, Latin American travellers hardly ever go to Africa, Central Asia or Australasia (*La imagen del mundo en la literatura peruana* [FCE, 1971], p. 227).
8   Fidel was one of Prieto's pseudonyms.
    Another example of this type of travel chronicler is Melchor Ocampo (*Viaje a Veracruz, Puebla y Sur de México* [1839]; *Viaje de un mexicano a Europa* [c. 1840/1]); however, his internal travel chronicle was not published at all until very recently and hence cannot be considered as part of the nationalist programme.
9   Neither author actually refers to his travel chronicles as 'chronicles' *per se*, although both authors' works are now classified as chronicles (Payno's *Viaje a Veracruz* and Prieto's *Viajes de orden suprema* now appear in their respective collected works under the heading '*crónica de viaje*'). This thus corroborates Estuardo Nuñez's argument concerning the preference for the term '*viaje*' over '*crónica*' in Latin American travel writing as a whole (cf. Nuñez, ed., *Viajeros hispanoamericanos: temas continentales* [Caracas: Biblioteca Ayacucho, 1989], pp. ix–xx). However, the recent reclassification of these works by Payno and Prieto also corroborates my argument that the term has made a come-back since the late nineteenth century, the reasons for which will be explored in more detail later in this chapter.

narration of travel in Mexico is to illustrate the customs and character of the nation's inhabitants; to describe the beauty and fertility of the land; and to map it out with the landmarks of national history and the stories of national heroes, thereby conveniently backdating Mexican nationality at least to the beginning of the Colonial era. In order to back up his arguments he quotes liberally from the writings of previous travellers in Mexico, in particular Humboldt and Fanny Calderón de la Barca, producing what is virtually a collage of 'lo mexicano' as seen by foreign commentators. Furthermore, he manages to squeeze in the opinions of foreigners whom he meets on his travels, who reassure him that Mexico is at least as good as France: 'Un francés que venía en la Diligencia, me dijo que esos campos estaban labrados lo mismo que se usa actualmente en Francia', he notes happily.[10]

Foreign influence is also discernible in his references to, and adaptations of, the works – in particular, the travel writing – of the French Romantics (Chateaubriand, Lamartine, Dumas, Hugo *et al.*), and of that idiosyncratic English traveller in France, Laurence Sterne. Payno flaunts false humility in his repeated bows before the master Lamartine: doubting his own capacity as a writer, he tells Prieto (to whom all the letters which compose the *Viaje* are addressed), 'Así, si yo fuera Lamartine, te describiría un cuadro brillante y espléndido...', and yet this is precisely what he goes on to do in the following paragraphs, describing the 'éter azul' of a sky dotted with clouds 'volando como los ángeles del sol' (p. 20).

With respect to Sterne, one assumes that Payno hopes to be at least as amusing and as risqué as the author of *A Sentimental Journey through France and Italy*, although one also senses that the satirical drive in Payno's text is not as all-encompassing as Sterne's. Payno's work does have a critical edge to it, though. There is some indication of a tension in his work between rose-coloured Romanticism and abrupt Realism, between fabulous accounts and documentary evidence. It is as much

---

10   Manuel Payno, *Un viaje a Veracruz en el invierno de 1843*, prol. by Esther Hernández Palacios (Xalapa: Universidad Veracruzana, 1984), p. 27. All further quotations from Payno's work are from this edition and will be given parenthetically in the text.

prescriptive as it is descriptive of 'lo mexicano'. It aspires to teach its readers about all things inherently Mexican (the country's history and its physical attributes), to cultivate a taste for things which could come to be Mexican with time (French culture and North American democracy), and to point out those lapses in etiquette which let the Mexicans down so. Written during the time of General Antonio López de Santa Anna's increasingly authoritarian second period in office (1841–45), the *Viaje a Veracruz* is also highly critical of contemporary Mexican administration: the state of the roads, the indigents and highwaymen who roam along them, and the amount of foreign investment in the country.

Prieto's acute criticism of Santa Anna's administration is what motivated his *Viajes de orden suprema*: he was sent into internal exile 'on high command' on two separate occasions, once to Cadereyta, in the state of Querétaro, and once to Oaxaca. Although evidently disgruntled by the indignities of being exiled, particularly on the first occasion, Prieto took advantage of the situation. 'Nosotros con pocas diferencias, por impericia, por desdén o corrupción, continuamos siendo extranjeros en nuestra patria', he had commented sometime earlier.[11] Internal exile was a good opportunity to let other Mexicans know who they were – Prieto does not seem to have suffered any self-doubt in this matter, but the humility of the 'nosotros' creates a sense of bonhomie and community spirit.

Acclaimed as the 'national' poet of the nineteenth century, Prieto seems to have had a lot less talent for narrative than Payno, producing a text which is truly Humboldtian in its attempt to be all-inclusive:

> Es un libro periodístico en el que se mezcla la crónica con el artículo de fondo y con las estadísticas; la narración, con la canción y la descripción; la denuncia, con la autobiografía y la profecía [...]. Es [Prieto] al mismo tiempo político, guerrero, poeta, economista, historiador y profeta improvisado y sobre la marcha.[12]

---

11   Guillermo Prieto, first published in the *Revista Científica y Literaria de México*, 1845; quoted in Carlos Monsiváis, ed., *A ustedes les consta: antología de la crónica en México* (Era, 1980), p. 24.
12   José Joaquín Blanco, *Crónica literaria: un siglo de escritores mexicanos* (Cal y Arena, 1996), p. 22.

The narrative might be top-heavy, the style verbose, but the social satire is far more rigorous than Payno's attempts. The chronicle is full of in-jokes about the 'partido santannista' and 'la romería política', and grotesque vignettes of fellow travellers ('[El españolazo] roncaba con despecho, roncaba con inspiración lírica, roncaba terminando en punta, porque silbaba, soplaba o se quejaba; roncaba un ronquido salpicado con palabras mal articuladas; su ronquido era un ronquido que crispaba, que alarmaba, que acalambraba'[13]). It also includes a fair bit of posturing and self-irony (he deems his exile to be 'una invitación de viajar entre soldados' [p. 103]), and a beautiful Sternian send-up of the overly Romantic travel chronicle ('¡Qué tipos tan pintorescos, tan uniformes, tan pedantes...!' [p. 112]). As a result, Prieto's *Viajes* appear to display a certain largesse with respect to the professed aim to create a nation – they certainly have a lot less overbearing didacticism than Payno's travel chronicles. However, as pointed out by the editors of *La Ilustración Mexicana* in 1851, 'Para corregir los vicios y los defectos de que por desgracia adolecen las sociedades, no bastan a veces los consejos, ni son suficientes los preceptos; hay sí una arma terrible: el ridículo'.[14] This is a classic *costumbrista* technique.

Prieto is sometimes less satirical in his approach. For example, in his journey along the 'Ruta de Cortés', on his way from Mexico City to Oaxaca via Puebla, for the second leg of his internal exile, he follows the *topoi* set out by Humboldt, Lamartine and Payno, paying less direct attention to political issues, and more to the description of the landscape and references to Mexican history. However, he is generally a much more self-reliant ('independent') travel chronicler than Payno – the extensive quotation from Humboldt's *Political Essay* (p. 550) is quite exceptional in his work –; and the overall impression is that, at least in

---

13   Guillermo Prieto, *Obras completas*, ed. by Boris Rosen Jélomer (CNCA, 1992-), IV: *Crónicas de viaje 1*, ed. by Francisco López Cámara (1994), 114. All further quotations from Prieto's work are from this edition and will be given parenthetically in the text.
14   Editors, *La Ilustración Mexicana*, quoted by Jefferson Rea Spill, 'The *Costumbrista* Movement in Mexico', in Jefferson Rea Spill, *Bridging the Gap: Articles on Mexican Literature* (Libros de México, 1971), p. 305.

Prieto's self-confident view, a Mexican national identity has already been 'assumed' into existence.

Payno and Prieto's travels abroad illustrate the two main trends in external Mexican travel chronicling of the period. Destinations were either the United States of America or Europe. A place of exile or of diplomatic service, the United States was viewed with some ambivalence by commentators. Certainly, in the early years of Independence the United States was seen as a model democracy, as analysed by Tocqueville and romanced by Chateaubriand.[15] However, after the secession of the northern Mexican states to the United States in 1848, all subsequent travellers by land had at least five hundred miles of 'border' territory to cross. The experience of this dilated border zone, and the sense of loss, frustration and anger it provoked in Mexican travel chroniclers, tempered their experience of the United States. Despite all North America's modernity and prosperity – railways, industries, penitentiaries – this first flexing of US Imperial muscles left Mexican travel chroniclers with a strong feeling that Mexicans were inherently different, in character and in culture, from their nearest neighbours.

Travels in Europe were more positive than in North America, perhaps because they were less politically orientated – European nations were generally perceived as less of a threat to independent sovereignty in Mexico than the United States, particularly after 1848, and despite the continued European invasions of Mexican territory. Whether sent as

---

15   The two most important Mexican travellers to the United States in the early nineteenth century are the diplomat Lorenzo de Zavala (*Viaje a los Estados Unidos* [Paris, 1834; Mérida, 1846], with an introduction by Justo Sierra O'Reilly) and Justo Sierra O'Reilly himself, whose four volumes of *Impresiones y recuerdos de un viaje a los Estados Unidos y Canadá* (1851) describe a political mission made in 1847–48 to make a plea for help to the North American government during the Guerra de Castas. Although Liberals, both writers were antifederalists (Zavala supported the independence of Texas; Sierra O'Reilly that of Yucatan) and their portrayal of the United States is coloured by this distancing from Mexican federal policies. Nevertheless, Zavala and O'Reilly are also critical of the United States. (More detailed discussion of these writers and others who have written on the United States may be found in Emmanuel Carballo, ed., *¿Qué país es éste?: los Estados Unidos y los gringos vistos por escritores mexicanos de los siglos XIX y XX*, [CNCA, 1996], pp. 9–48.)

a diplomat, as an exile, or as a journalist (or any combination thereof), travel chroniclers to Europe tended to seize the opportunity to complete the nineteenth-century Mexican version of the *Grand Tour* – after all, foreign travel for Mexico-born subjects of the Viceroyalty was extremely difficult during the eighteenth century. This being so, the preferred educational destinations were France and Italy, although there were also numerous religious and cultural pilgrimages to the Holy Land during this period. Travels in Spain were largely occasioned by diplomatic tasks but later in the century, probably responding to the interest shown in Spain as an exotic destination by key French Romantic travel writers, it, too, became the subject of leisured, erudite travel, helping Mexicans complete their sense of national identity with reference to a bit of what is really their own ancient history.

Ignacio Manuel Altamirano and Manuel Gutiérrez Nájera: Literary Travels and Early Tourism

In 1870, on the occasion of the first anniversary of the creation of the Mexican Academia Nacional de Ciencias y Literatura, Ignacio Manuel Altamirano (1834–93) gave the keynote speech. After firmly establishing the cultural goals of the institution – the creation and diffusion through state education of a nationally-orientated corpus of cultural material –, he went on to say that,

> *Los viajes de exploración en el interior del país y de nuestras costas*, el establecimiento de jardines de aclimatación, las clasificaciones zoológicas, las observaciones físicas, las indagaciones históricas y el cultivo de las bellas letras, cuyo desarrollo es necesario impulsar hoy que por un movimiento espontáneo la juventud se consagra a tan apacible estudio, son objetos que por descuidados se propone considerar la Academia preferentemente, sin por eso dejar de atender a otros ramos interesantísimos de la ciencia.[16] (My italics)

---

16   Manuel Ignacio Altamirano, *Discursos y brindis*, *Obras completas*, I (1986), 240. See also Altamirano's further comments on the need for Mexicans to write

That is to say, the need for internal travel in Mexico was still acknowledged as an imperative in the late nineteenth century, despite the efforts of Payno and Prieto, and travel chronicling would not entirely lose out with the gradual shift in emphasis from early Liberal to *científico* schools of thought,[17] although it would start to move on from the *costumbrista/paisajista* mode to encompass works of more formal scientific impetus. The focus, according to Altamirano, must also be directed at travel at home rather than abroad – statistics for Mexican travel chronicling in the nineteenth century do show a marked preference for external travel.[18]

Only six years later, in 1876, the Spanish Institución Libre de Enseñanza was founded by Francisco Giner de los Ríos and friends, along very similar lines to those espoused by Altamirano: empirical education for all with an emphasis on scientific method and directed by an overarching nationalist ideology. One of the mainstays of this approach were the hands-on group excursions into the Spanish countryside in search of an essential, intrahistorical Spanish national identity, to be defined through the methodical interrogation of what was really out there, rather than the nitpicking rejection of all that was foreign practised by earlier generations of Spanish *costumbristas*. Much of the travel

---

      both external and internal travel chronicles made in 1882 and quoted in the introduction to this study.

17   The Mexican *científicos* were moderate Liberals inspired by Auguste Comte's positivism.

18   Information culled from the bibliography to Felipe Teixidor's *Viajeros mexicanos: siglos XIX y XX* (Sepan Cuantos…, 350, 2nd edn [Porrúa, 1982]) reveals a total of 47 travel chronicles published by Mexican authors during the nineteenth century (or shortly thereafter and concerning travels which took place in the nineteenth century). Of these 47, only 6 or 7 cover travel in Mexico as their main objective. (Collating bibliographic material from other sources, I estimate the total number of nineteenth-century Mexican travel chronicles to be in the region of 60 volumes, of which around 20 deal exclusively with travel in Mexico, and a further 10 to 20 include travel in Mexico on the way to somewhere else. Many more texts by Mexicans on Mexico were published as individual articles rather than as whole books and have not been subsequently anthologised – for example, Ignacio Ramírez's journey to Baja California in 1864, published in *El Semanario Ilustrado* on 20 November 1868.)

writing of the Generation of 98 stems from this educational background. Although Mexican influence over Spanish cultural institutions cannot be proven at this point, by the 1870s Mexico and Spain were culturally neck and neck: Mexicans were contemporaries of Spaniards, if not yet of all men.[19] Yet from that date on, Mexicans and other Latin Americans would gradually start to exert their cultural influence in the Peninsula, culminating with the spread of the *modernista* movement to Spain in the 1890s.

Altamirano, in line with his proposals for internal, nationalist travel chronicling, restricted his own travel writing to the Mexican Republic (for example, the serialised letter describing a journey to Mazatlán and Acapulco published in *El Semanario Ilustrado* in November 1868, and his series of articles collected under the heading *Paisajes y leyendas: tradiciones y costumbres de México*, first published in periodicals in the early 1880s).[20] The literary journal that he founded in 1869 with Gonzalo Esteva, *El Renacimiento*, was also a major organ for the publication of internal travel chronicles, although it did strike a balance with translations of foreign travel writing on Mexico and the publication of Mexican external travel chronicles. The other main writer of this period to concentrate exclusively on internal travel chronicling is Manuel Gutiérrez Nájera (1859–95) who, despite his obsessive interest in French culture, never travelled abroad. He left only a handful of travel chronicles on trips in Mexico between 1880 and 1893: these he planned to have published in book form as his *Viajes extraordinarios*.[21]

---

19 Both Altamirano and Giner de los Ríos were the progeny of the Romantic tradition: their interest in travel and travel writing stems from this shared heritage rather than from the influence of one over the other. For Spanish travel writing in the late nineteenth century see Josefina Gómez Méndez, Nicolás Ortega Cantero, Dolores Brandis & others, *Viajeros y paisajes* (Madrid: Alianza Editorial, 1988).

20 Altamirano did not travel abroad until only a few years before his death, visiting Europe in the early 1890s.

21 The entirety of Gutiérrez Nájera's travel chronicles may be found partly in his *Cuentos, crónicas y ensayos*, ed. by Alfredo Maillefert, Biblioteca del Estudiante Universitario, 20, 3rd edn (UNAM, 1992); and partly in the recent collection of his *Viajes extraordinarios*, ed. by Rafael Pérez Gay (Breve Fondo Editorial, 1996).

Despite these two authors' slight production in terms of actual travel chronicles, their importance as cultural commentators and as literary innovators cannot be underestimated. Altamirano is credited with having finally inaugurated Mexican national literature; a literature inherently distinct from that of other nation-states, rather than a literature which produces a running commentary on what Mexican national identity should be, as Payno and Prieto had tended to do. Gutiérrez Nájera's place in history is that of one of the main founders of Latin American *modernismo*. This movement is frequently charged with the undiscriminating importation of European – mainly French – literary styles and subject matter: Romanticism, Parnassism and Symbolism. A brief look at Gutiérrez Nájera's travel chronicles does, however, provide material for a refreshing revision of this accusation, and the literary innovations of Altamirano are perhaps the best place to start this revision.

Altamirano was a lot less heavy-handed in his travel chronicles than might have been expected given his didactic profession. Avoiding the style of Payno's and Prieto's overt political catechisms, he was careful to take a more personal, readable approach: 'Todo llevará el sello de la impresión personal, todo tendrá el airecito de la confidencia'.[22] Wooed by modernity – its speed, its accessibility, its aesthetic – and soothed by the first years of the 'paz porfiriana' – the prosperity and the stability – Altamirano appears happy to be almost a tourist in Mexico. Certainly he displays his erudition in terms of Mexican history, with references to a most up-to-date list of commentators, including Joaquín Arróniz and Ernest de Vigneaux, as well as all the old favourites from Bernal Díaz del Castillo to Humboldt, and he also reveals himself to be a connoisseur of Mexican customs and character traits. But all this is presented more as a spectacle than as lessons in the history of the nation and the fundamental characteristics of the Mexican people. Even religious rites are partially depoliticised as picturesque scenes and in

---

22   Manuel Ignacio Altamirano, *Paisajes y leyendas: tradiciones y costumbres de México, primera y segunda series*, prol. by Jacqueline Covo, 4th edn, Sepan Cuantos…, 275 (Porrúa, 1989), p. 137. All further quotations from Altamirano's work are from this edition and will be given parenthetically in the text.

aesthetic appreciation of Santa Anna and Sebastián Lerdo de Tejada's respective birth places in Xalapa, he simply exclaims, '¡Qué dos motivos para una disertación filosófica, histórica o política!' (p. 165).[23]

Not weighed down quite as much as Payno by didacticism and demonstration from first principles, nor as much as Prieto by the sheer bulk of information documented, Altamirano has more space to create himself as a character in his texts. Although, in certain aspects, Prieto is a forerunner in this field, Altamirano casts himself as the self-conscious, hypersensitive individual, eccentric and temperamental, but generous and lovable, with access to a self-irony that simply reinforces his projection of self-importance – he is every bit the Romantic individual. A self-styled father figure for the Mexican nation, demonstrating through personal experience that improvements in infrastructure can put first-hand knowledge of the nation's boundless natural and cultural resources within easy reach of the man in the street, Altamirano heralds the dawn of the Republic's leisure industry. Paradise is a place in Mexico.

In Altamirano's writing Mexico is still, of course, being compared to other places, but no longer as the local *faute-de-mieux* for something European and civilised (Xochimilco as the Venice of Mexico etc.). There is increasing subtlety in the terms of comparison. While in passages of realism Altamirano admits to some disappointment with Mexico as it is – its lack of culture and its natural paradise infected with yellow fever and other hazards –, in his more dreamy moments Mexico is tacitly transformed into a civilised, but still exotic, European nation. He writes: 'Para mí lo que distingue a Jalapa de las ciudades montañosas del África Septentrional y de sus hermanas las ciudades de la costa de Andalucía [... es] la extremada limpieza que se contempla en ella por todas partes' (p. 164). This is a rhetorical device in which Spain is implicitly wild and exotic (twinned with Africa), and Mexico must therefore stand parallel to a northern European nation such as France. Xalapa still has all the positive attributes of a tropical paradise (the luxuriant vegetation, the

---

23 For a good study of Altamirano's take on religion in his travel chronicles, see Edward N. Wright-Rios, 'Indian Saints and Nation-States: Ignacio Manuel Altamirano's Landscapes and Legends', *Mexican Studies/Estudios Mexicanos*, 20:1 (2004), 47–68.

agreeable climate), but the source of its uniqueness is its 'extreme cleanliness', indicative of its purity ('blancura deslumbradora') and civilisation. It is as good, if not better, than France.

Although Altamirano's access to fantasy, frivolity and leisure is still indicative of a nation desperately trying to compare favourably with Europe by casting itself in Europe's traditional role, it also signifies a very different approach to the writing of travel chronicles: they become 'lighter', briefer and more self-conscious. As Francisco Monterde notes of Altamirano,

> Con ella [la crónica], el maestro [Altamirano] prepara el advenimiento de Gutiérrez Nájera, que sabrá ser más ágil y exquisito, como correspondía al cronista de una sociedad que mostraba preocupaciones por la elegancia, en la vida y en las letras.[24]

Altamirano's writing was changing to keep up with modernity, and perhaps ironically, in his attempts to keep up with the times, it was Altamirano who was largely responsible for repopularising the historical term *crónica* to describe his non-fictional literary texts. As Carballo notes, the reviews *El Siglo XIX* and *El Correo de México* started to publish self-styled chronicles by Luis G. Ortiz and José Tomás de Cuéllar respectively in 1867, and Altamirano followed suit in 1868. However, it was Altamirano's journal, *El Renacimiento*, which brought about the real renaissance of the chronicle from 1869 onwards.[25] For Carballo, the chronicles of the Conquest and the work of early nineteenth-century Mexican historians such as Carlos María de Bustamante, Lorenzo de Zavala and José María Luis Mora are the immediate precursors of the revived chronicle, and Altamirano does quote extensively from these three Mexican historians in his *Paisajes y leyendas*. Nevertheless, his work also corroborates Aníbal González's theory of French influence in the revival of the chronicle form: in 1869 Altamirano described

---

24   Francisco Monterde, *Aspectos literarios de la cultura mexicana*, ed. by Evodio Escalante (UNAM / Universidad de Colima, 1987), p. 82.
25   Emmanuel Carballo, ed., *Historia de las letras mexicanas en el siglo XIX* (Guadalajara: Universidad de Guadalajara / Xalli, 1991), pp. 113–28 (115).

himself as 'un cronista', but bemoaned the fact that it was easier to be a chronicler in Paris, Berlin or London than in Mexico.[26]

The increasing move from the production of an overtly political text to one in which politics is disguised in aesthetic terms (the revamped *crónica*) was at once a response to the market forces of an apparently prosperous capitalist society (an ostensibly depoliticised and 'modern' text, in form and content, made its mass consumption easier), and a way of writing Mexico into literature without having to resort to obvious qualifications ('mexicano/a' etc.).[27] As José Joaquín Blanco notes: 'Es Altamirano el primer autor que se exige la universalidad, y no sólo a sí mismo, sino a la nación'.[28] Altamirano was the first post-Independence Mexican writer to gain an international reputation, and he achieved this by packaging Mexico in a way which made it an attractive export (it compared favourably), and at the same time, through his texts, he imported European culture for a Mexican audience without making them feel deprived or marginalised. This is the corner-stone of a national literature.

Manuel Gutiérrez Nájera was the unwilling chronicler and unenthusiastic traveller who further developed these tendencies. Much more so than Altamirano, he had to contend with the increasing

---

26 Manuel Ignacio Altamirano, *Diario íntimo*, quoted in Carlos Monsiváis's prologue to Altamirano's *Crónicas 1, Obras completas*, VII (SEP, 1987), 15.
Aníbal González claims that, 'It was Nájera who, around 1880, [...] imported the genre of the chronicle from France into Spanish America' (*Journalism and the Development of Spanish American Narrative* [Cambridge: Cambridge UP, 1993], p. 87). Gutiérrez Nájera was no doubt influenced by French sources and maybe used them to add to the Mexican definition of the chronicle, but the practice of writing chronicles in Mexico clearly starts with Altamirano and not Gutiérrez Nájera who, although a child prodigy, was only age ten in 1869 when Mexican chronicles became popular. Rafael Torres Sánchez corroborates Altamirano's seminal role in the development of the journalistic chronicle in his 'Ignacio Manuel Altamirano: la cotidianidad en perspectiva', *LJS*, 2 May 1993, p. 18.

27 For an excellent study of Altamirano's contributions in this field, see Erica Segre, 'An Italicised Ethnicity: Memory and Renascence in the Literary Writings of Ignacio Manuel Altamirano', *Forum for Modern Language Studies*, 36:3 (2000), 266–78, especially pp. 275–76.

28 José Joaquín Blanco, introduction to Altamirano's *Textos costumbristas, Obras completas*, V (1986), 17.

split between journalism and literature created by changing modes of production, and the increasing demands of a consumerist audience avid for imports. His complaint in 1893 that, 'la crónica [...] es, en los días que corren, un anacronismo. [...] Ha muerto a manos del *repórter* quien es tan ágil, diestro, ubicuo, invisible, instantáneo, que guisa la liebre antes que la atrapen' (author's italics),[29] sold himself rather short. Although journalistic writing did inevitably lose in literary quality as the market grew and the pace of reporting speeded up, Gutiérrez Nájera kept the chronicle going as a literary element in modern journalism.

Gutiérrez Nájera's chronicles are entertaining, unassuming, impressionistic accounts; incisive, laconic, and highly readable, with access to some social awareness as well as plenty of aesthetic sensibility.[30] Maybe exhaustive and authoritarian texts of the type that Payno and Prieto wrote were, by the 1880s, things of the past, but this lighter chronicle of 'notas', 'apuntes' and 'impresiones' took its place. In retrospect, there was a boom in the production of this sort of chronicle in the *modernista* period, and to this day the practice of the genre retains these references to brevity and subjectivity. This paring down of the text also made it an experimental zone – as Adolfo Castañón has noted, it is precisely this brief, marginal text which is most open to innovation.[31] In his travel chronicling Gutiérrez Nájera found a solution in which he could infuse a diluted version of his poetic experiments with some of his best jokes and favourite quotes. The concoction is lent stability by a more substantial, accessible subject matter: travel.

In the preservation of his embattled artistic integrity Gutiérrez Nájera's greatest resources are irony and fiction. Despite being a staunch

---

29 Manuel Gutiérrez Nájera, quoted in Carlos Monsiváis's prologue to *A ustedes les consta*, p. 39.
30 There is very little human interest in Gutiérrez Nájera's travel chronicles; that is, little *costumbrismo*. It is replaced by an introspective narrative voice whose aesthetic concerns are mainly directed towards landscape and cultural artefacts.
31 Adolfo Castañón, 'Magnitudes del Jíbaro: literatura hispanoamericana contemporánea', *Vuelta*, 241 (December 1996), 82–85. This essay provides an excellent overview of nineteenth-century Latin American chroniclers such as Prieto, Altamirano and Gutiérrez Nájera, and the innovative role of 'las formas breves' in their work.

supporter of the Porfiriato,[32] he is not enthralled at being a pawn in a market economy. Although cautious, his access to irony and fiction within the texts speaks clearly of his critical distance from the role he is being forced to play. Through self-irony he creates the figure of the eccentric and unreliable literary traveller who is fond of fictionalising his personal experience, and who, suffering from a chronic dose of *mal-de-siècle*, is disinclined to abandon the area of Mexico City currently known as the Centro Histórico. ('Guanajuato es un país lejano que está más allá, mucho más allá del Bosque de Chapultepec.'[33]) Armchair travelling through the poetry, and also the travel writing, of his favourite Romantic authors (Lamartine, Musset, Vigny, Gautier, Chateaubriand, Goethe *et al.*), plus a good range of Mexican authors (travel writers and/ or poets such as Prieto, Payno, Altamirano, Luis Malanco, Francisco Bulnes, Gonzalo Esteva, and José María Roa Bárcena), suits him very well. The travel chronicles of contemporary Mexican authors such as Bulnes[34] merely serve to dissuade him from making any journeys, in Mexico or abroad: 'No vayamos a Guanajuato, esperemos a que Guanajuato venga a nosotros', he protests petulantly (p. 28).[35] (His taste for this kind of humour is in itself a novelty in Mexican literature.) Prone to camp exaggeration, he finally overcomes his disinclination

---

[32] His travel chronicles are almost always occasioned by an official visit, and, particularly in the later texts of the 1890s, Gutiérrez Nájera sees fit to throw in a few lines of praise for various state-initiated projects. However he never sinks to the sycophantic simpering of so many official travel chroniclers.

[33] Manuel Gutiérrez Nájera, *Viajes extraordinarios*, p. 27. All further quotations from Gutiérrez Nájera's work are from this edition and will be given parenthetically in the text.

[34] Francisco Bulnes, a scientific travel chronicler, wrote about his trip to Japan to record the passage of Venus, and also about another trip to Italy, excerpts of which may be found in his *Páginas escogidas*, ed. by Martín Quirarte, Biblioteca del Estudiante Universitario, 89, 2nd edn (UNAM, 1995), pp. 155–59.

[35] See also Gutiérrez Nájera's endorsement of armchair travelling in both 'Los tigres de Chiapas' in his *Cuentos completos, y otras narraciones* (ed. by E.K. Mapes [FCE, 1958], pp. 319–20) and his review of Alberto Lombardo's *Notas y episodios de viaje a los Estados Unidos*, in his *Obras: crítica literaria, I* (ed. by E.K. Mapes [UNAM, 1959], pp. 231–32). His comments on the lack of Mexican travel writing in this latter article, written in 1884, echo Altamirano's statements of two years earlier (quoted in the introduction to this study) almost word for word.

to travel, advising himself, 'No lo hagas por ti: hazlo por Théo[phile Gautier], que viene a México y desea leer tus crónicas' (p. 28).

This is the tone of his first travel chronicles, written in the early 1880s, when Gutiérrez Nájera is still in his early twenties. Once he gets on the road, however, his aesthetic appreciation of Mexico is extremely positive. Its mountains are better than the Alps, its cities at least equal to their European twins, and Xalapa is as white as the dove's feathers in a poem by François Coppée. The comparisons with Europe might be over-exercised, particularly in his later work of the 1890s, but the result is the creation, through literature, of a superlative land of beauty and civilisation in Mexico itself. France has been brought to the mountain, as it were. Altamirano certainly recognised Gutiérrez Nájera's techniques as 'la cumbre de la literatura patria'.[36]

Furthermore, the fact that Gutiérrez Nájera never travelled abroad serves to undermine this arsenal of comparisons between Mexico and Europe, thus partially relieving him of the burden of being the subservient bearer of cultural imperialism. Ostensibly he was feeding the general public with what it wanted, yet through the repetition of this repertoire of images of dubious authenticity, his journalism imports French culture and simultaneously comes very close to turning it into a kitsch aesthetic, in a similar vein to Laurence Sterne's invention and derision of sentimentality in *A Sentimental Journey*.[37]

Gutiérrez Nájera's final contribution to the practice of travel chronicling in Mexico concerns his mode of travel. Altamirano might herald the dawn of leisure travel, but Gutiérrez Nájera practices luxury tourism. Writing in 1880, he claims that,

> En esta época de los caminos de hierro, los viajes son un mito. Sale usted y llega. No hay aventuras, no hay incidentes. La maleta y el viajero deben experimentar las mismas sensaciones. No puede uno ni siquiera quejarse de la dureza del carruaje. Un excelente sillón à la Voltaire convida al sueño. (pp. 60–61)

---

36 Letter from Altamirano to Gutiérrez Nájera, written in Paris, 24 December 1891; quoted in Amado Nervo's article 'Sobre Gutiérrez Nájera', in his *Cuentos y crónicas*, ed. by Manuel Durán, Biblioteca del Estudiante Universitario, 95, 2nd edn (UNAM, 1993), pp.173–74.

37 See, for example, the tearful opening lines of 'De México a Guanajuato', p. 27.

This Romantic show of disappointment in modern technological advances is evidently ironic coming from someone for whom the experience of physical discomfort is '¡Cosa rara para un turista como yo!' (p. 61); who expects to be able to read on the train; and who, on arrival at his destination, requires the best food, wine and accommodation in town – 'Creo que estoy en el mejor hotel de Puebla' (p. 67). Gutiérrez Nájera knowingly accepts those elements of modernity which make this mode of travel possible, happy that these signs of prosperity indicate at last the potential of recreating a better kind of France in Mexico. Yet despite his francophilia he is apparently very contented in Mexico, not a 'desterrado en tierras americanas' as many of the *modernistas* have been described.[38]

Justo Sierra and Amado Nervo: The Stifling Tradition

This sudden possibility of leisured travel, both at home and abroad, is a trademark, in politics, of the Porfiriato and, in literature, of the birth of *modernismo*. If the first years of the Porfiriato are marked by the internal travel writing of Altamirano and Gutiérrez Nájera, making 'el verdadero sueño nacional'[39] of travel towards modernity a reality, at least in literary terms, it falls to a younger generation of writers and politicians to live out that 'sueño nacional' abroad, in the United States or Europe, in the late 1890s and first years of the twentieth century. The two most significant travel chroniclers of this period are Justo Sierra (1848–1912) and Amado Nervo (1870–1919).[40]

---

38 See José Emilio Pacheco's introduction to his *Antología del modernismo: 1884–1921*, Biblioteca del Estudiante Universitario, 90, 2 vols (UNAM, 1970), I, p. xiv.

39 Rafael Pérez Gay, introduction to Gutiérrez Nájera's *Viajes extraordinarios*, p. 9.

40 Sierra dreamt of travel to the United States and to Europe from his childhood onwards (see José Luis Martínez's introduction to Sierra's *Viajes* (in Sierra's *Obras completas*, 1st repr., 14 vols [UNAM, 1977], VI, 7–8); Nervo ironically claimed on arriving in Paris for the first time, 'Por fin puedo hablar francés, estoy

Much research could be done on how the literary works of the *modernistas* (mainly poetry) relate to their extensive practice of journalism, including a vast amount of travel chronicles; and on how, in the 1890s, a growing network of Latin American travel chroniclers spread *modernismo* first within South and Central America, and later in Europe. Of note, are José Martí's travels in Central and North America, including Mexico, between 1875 and 1888, which helped pave the way for the initial development of the movement in Latin America itself.[41] Rubén Darío's lifelong travels in the Americas and in Europe from the mid-1880s through to 1916, the year of his death, significantly increased the dissemination of the movement, particularly in Spain. Darío did not go to Mexico until the unfortunate year of 1910, but by the turn of the century Mexico was able to go to Darío. Nervo and Sierra both met Darío in Europe: Nervo in 1900 in Paris where they were both correspondents for the Universal Exhibition; Sierra in Madrid in 1901 at the Congreso Social y Económico Hispanoamericano.[42] In fact, Nervo met Sierra properly for the first time in France in 1901.[43]

The fact that travel within Latin America in the last decades of the nineteenth century was still incredibly difficult on an international level, plus the increasing ease of transatlantic travel and the attractions of Europe mentioned earlier in this chapter, made France, Spain and Italy the top destinations for *fin-de-siècle* Latin American travel chroniclers.

---

en mi patria: "'¡Hacía treinta años que no la veía!'" (*Cuentos y crónicas*, p. 202). All further quotations from Sierra's and Nervo's work are from these editions and will be given parenthetically in the text.

41 Data glossed from Iván A. Schulman and Manuel Pedro González's *Martí, Darío y el modernismo*, prol. by Cintio Vitier (Madrid: Gredos, 1969), pp. 83–205.

42 See Manuel Durán, *Genio y figura de Amado Nervo* (Buenos Aires: Editorial Universitaria de Buenos Aires, 1968), p. 5; and Wilberto Cantón, *Justo Sierra: héroe blanco de México* (SEP, 1967), p. 20, respectively.

43 See Esther Turner Wellman's *Amado Nervo: Mexico's Religious Poet* (New York: Instituto de las Españas en los Estados Unidos, 1936), p. 62. Other Latin-American travel chroniclers in Europe associated with *modernismo* are the Peruvian José Santos Chocano, the Franco-Argentinian Paul Groussac, and the Guatemalan Enrique Gómez Carillo whose entire literary out-put is comprised of travel chronicles (for Gómez Carillo see Aníbal González, *Journalism*, pp. 96–98).

Ironically, in reaching out for Europe, for personal reasons and/or as representatives of their individual nations' foreign policies, Latin Americans found each other. *Modernismo* is the first literary movement to display the characteristics of Panamerican consciousness.

Modernismo is also the first Latin American movement to exercise its influence over Spanish culture. The development of Spanish *modernismo* and the boom in the production of Spanish travel writing at the turn of the century must be, at least in part, related to Latin Americans' presence in, and texts on, Spain. Miguel de Unamuno, José Ortega y Gasset, Pío Baroja, Emilia Pardo Bazán, Ciro Bayo, Azorín and others were all aware of, and involved in, the growing Latin American literary presence in Spain. Darío's *España contemporánea* is in fact considered part of the writing of the Spanish Generation of 98; a 'manifiesto estético e ideológico del Modernismo español'.[44]

Justo Sierra was not a full-time *modernista* writer but the fact that much of his writing was contemporaneous with *modernismo* (1884–1921)[45] meant that certain similarities were inevitable. More important as a politician and a pedagogue than as a creative writer, he really carried on the work of Ignacio Manuel Altamirano. In his politics he developed Altamirano's nascent positivism into full-blown *ciencia*. In his travel chronicles he updated and extended Altamirano's repertoire: they are mostly external rather than internal, but instead of letting aesthetics blur his politics like some of the *modernistas*, he blended the two in the highly readable series of articles published as *En tierra yankee: notas a todo vapor* (1897–1898), and *En la Europa latina* (1901–1903, posthumously collected for publication in book form).

In his series of chronicles on the United States Sierra displays the sources of his knowledge of the country in his passing references to other Mexican travel chroniclers, such as Lorenzo de Zavala and Justo Sierra O'Reilly, his father; and to the travel writing of other well-known authors such as Chateaubriand, José María Heredia, the Cuban Romantic

---

44   Ramón F. Lloréns García, *Los libros de viajes de Miguel de Unamuno* (Alicante: Caja de Ahorros Provincial de Alicante, 1991), p. 27.
45   Dates given in Pacheco's *Antología del modernismo*, I, p. viii.

poet, and John Tyndall, the popular Irish natural historian.[46] In particular, in his reference to his father's chronicle written in 1848 (pp. 153–54), Justo Sierra at once confirms the existence of a tradition (something which is handed down from one generation to another) and rejects this tradition as being too cumbersome (there is, in fact, a fifty year gap between accounts, enough for three generations' worth of tradition...).[47] In his struggle to see for himself he tries to forget all these previous accounts, yet they inevitably cloud his vision with their increasing pessimism about North American society and politics. On leaving the States Sierra writes: 'Todos estos pesimismos [acerca de la democracia estadounidense] me vienen de los libros que he leído sobre la sociedad americana, son "librescos"; yo no vi bien, entreví un gran pueblo... y adquirí una convicción, que la libertad es un aire respirable' (p.192).

This unspontaneous, stifled vision of the United States is contrasted by Sierra's description of his train journey in Mexico itself before reaching the border with the United States – some of the best pages in the history of the genre. Seemingly unfettered by the well-established tradition of travel chronicling in Mexico – probably because he was not really intending to write about travel in Mexico on this trip, and had not read up on the subject – Sierra makes succinct descriptions of the Mexican landscape and takes verbal snapshots of passing faces, advised by a very economical use of *modernista* literary innovation ('la piel de las montañas [...] se tigrea con frecuencia con las sombras rápidas de las nubes' (p.17)), conscious of the subjectivity of his vision and of

---

46 José Luis Martínez also suspects that Sierra had read Prieto's *Viaje a los Estados Unidos* (in his introduction to Sierra's *Viajes*, p. 5).

47 Sierra O'Reilly also travelled in the footsteps of Zavala, whose work he edited in 1846. Despite Justo Sierra's reservations, the tradition also continues up to the present day: the politician and writer Héctor Pérez Martínez edited Sierra O'Reilly's diary in 1938 (*Diario de nuestro viaje a los Estados Unidos: la pretendida anexión de Yucatán*, Biblioteca Histórica Mexicana de Obras Inéditas, 12 [Antigua Librería Robredo / Porrúa, 1938]); and Silvia Molina, Pérez Martínez's daughter, re-edited Pérez Martínez's own travel chronicle, written in 1939–40, in 1994 ('En los caminos de Campeche', in *Obras completas*, 5 vols [Gobierno del Estado de Campeche/Corunda, 1994], V: *Periodismo*, 233–85). This in turn affects Molina's own travel writing (*Campeche: imagen de eternidad*, Cuaderno de Viaje [CNCA, 1996]).

the literary metamorphosis to which writing subjects reality. Sierra's personal voice and political consciousness come through well in the following reflections on the desert regions of Zacatecas:

> Seguimos a todo escape hacia las regiones inhabitadas, seguimos bajo un cielo color de plata viva, por un suelo que se levanta hacia nosotros, se disuelve en átomos infinitos y nos envuelve y nos engulle en su silencioso huracán de polvo. [...] Las cercas de piedras blancas, colocadas prehistóricamente, parecen más bien denunciar un antiguo 'paraje' chichimeca, que una aldehuela en nuestro siglo. Pero nuestro siglo está ahí presente en forma de telégrafo, cuyas altísimas cruces grises, unidas por las fibras metálicas, parece que huyen a grandes zancadas kilométricas hasta el confín del desierto; nuestro siglo va y viene con el tren de vapor... Alguna vez en esta triste tierra que jamás ha bebido agua, el agua vendrá del pozo, de la presa, del oasis, y con sólo eso podrá una nación acampar cómodamente en estas soledades y abonar con su guano estos páramos... Lo triste y lo encantador en nuestro país, son estos contrastes de civilización refinada y de incultura absoluta, de climas que se atropellan en una escalinata de montañas, de ciudades y soledades, de desiertos muertos de sed que se puedan contemplar paladeando un vaso de limonada fría y deliciosa. (p. 21)

Sierra's style is halfway between the baroque flourishes of Romanticism and the succinct imagery and verbal innovation of *modernismo*. His analysis of Mexico is a realistic blend of history and modernity which puts his aesthetic vision of landscape and lifestyle at the service of his politics. The trip to the United States, by taking Sierra far beyond the borders of Mexico, helps him to further refine this symbolic image of Mexico, through contrast and absence. The distillation of the essence of Mexico is further amplified through the emotional register of Sierra's search for himself – his '"yo" casi perdido' – finally relocated on re-entering Mexico (pp. 191–93).

In Europe Sierra is ostensibly happier, less inhibited by the writings of other Mexican travel chroniclers. Although somewhat disappointed by France and Spain, he appears to feel at home on the ancient roads of cultural pilgrimage through Italy, paying homage to the historical investigations of Ernest Renan and the Italian travel writing of Castelar, Goethe, Taine and others. But even here he frequently protests that he 'cannot see' the monuments he has waited so long to visit. What disturbs his vision in Europe is not so much travel writing, but the ubiquitous presence of the *Baedecker* guidebook and its carrier, the tourist: 'El rojo Baedecker a un tiempo útil y odioso; toda la Italia artística me pareció enferma de escarlatina...' (p. 261). The presence of tourists disturbs Sierra mainly because he does not want to be classed as a tourist himself, albeit as a cultural one. Of course, Sierra twists the issue, pointing out that most of the tourists are North American and the trip which was supposed to place aesthetics above politics becomes entangled in his vision of North American society. His disappointment in Europe is thus largely a transference of his disappointed, or at best ambivalent, reaction to the United States.

Amado Nervo's travel chronicles from Europe (collected in *El éxodo y las flores del camino* [1902], plus the posthumously collected articles covering the period 1900–1913) are a classic example of *modernista* overseas travel writing. Nervo – a full-time journalist and diplomat – is an astute and critical observer of himself and others. In line with Gutiérrez Nájera, he keeps his travel chronicles brief, informative, well-written and witty. Their style is taken from the more accessible range of his poetics, using mainly simple constructions and vocabulary, with rather less whimsy and preciosity than Gutiérrez Nájera. He also provides more dialogue and anecdote in exchange for Gutiérrez Nájera's interior monologue and literary speculation, plus more direct political criticism.

Nervo's stock of intertextual references to his French idols and his Hispanic contemporaries are what further define his texts as pertaining to the *modernista* movement – like most movements it was more of a club or a literary network than a particular style and subject matter, although the poetry was admittedly more homogeneous than the peripheral chronicles.[48] However, what is notable about the intertext to Nervo's chronicles is the absence of references to previous generations of Mexican travel chroniclers in Europe – the texts of Ocampo, Payno and others. Like Sierra, Nervo seems to have preferred to avoid references to the tradition in order to get a fresher view.

Although ostensibly chronicling life in Paris, or elsewhere in Europe, Nervo keeps his eye out for the relevance of his observations to

---

48 These chronicles cannot, however, simply be dismissed as not part of *modernista* literary practice. Recent reappraisals of the value of *modernista* chronicles may be found in González's *Journalism* (pp. 83–100), and in Monsiváis's introduction to *A ustedes les consta* (pp. 34–36).

life in Mexico primarily, and to Latin America in more general terms. Aware that comparisons with home are inevitable in external travel chronicles (*'Saliendo de México todo es Cuautitlán. / Saliendo de París, todo es México.* / Para no hacer comparaciones, mejor quedarse en Cuautitlán' [p. 90; author's italics]), he resolves to use them to introduce a destabilising sense of relativity into his work. He points out the errors of Latin Americans' views on Europe, as well as Europeans' views on Latin America, and also (ironically) signals the developments in Europe which could be of use in Latin America.

Even before setting foot in Europe Nervo dedicated a number of articles to the great Latin American inferiority complex: 'Los franceses valen infinitamente más que nosotros, porque a nosotros, a todos los latinos que no somos franceses, se nos ha ocurrido que valen mucho: porque hablan mucho, porque declaman mucho, porque dogmatizan mucho, pero con elegancia'; and, 'Odio mi idioma y lo revuelco, a semejanza de mis compañeros, con un *caló* delicioso. Odio las costumbres de mi país, y pinto en mis escritos las de pueblos que no he visto'.[49] This might be just sour grapes at not having managed to travel to Europe yet, but even after travelling in Europe, Nervo's attitude is still happily flippant. Paris might be the home of his literary idols, but his view of Latin American idolisation of everything French is still scathing.

The European experience also helps Nervo re-evaluate the question of exoticism. If earlier texts by Altamirano and Gutiérrez Nájera had struggled to create an image of Mexico that was at once civilised and exotic, the equal of France, with a little more besides in terms of nature and climate, Nervo, who has experienced Europe for himself, has the freedom to state: 'Los mexicanos, por nuestra parte, gozamos del privilegio de un alto exotismo. En general, se nos toma por todo menos por latinoamericanos' (p. 224); and again '*Chez nous* es un país fantástico que todo latinoamericano lleva en el bolsillo para uso inmediato' (p. 286). If Europe turns out to be less civilised than it might seem from a distance, the perceived exoticism of Latin America

---

49 Amado Nervo, 'Nuestra insignificancia', 13 February 1896, *Cuentos y crónicas*, pp. 95–96.

is revealed to be the fantastic result of cultural ignorance. Nervo makes fun of transatlantic cultural misconceptions, revelling in his newfound role as the interesting stranger with a *carte blanche* for uncivilised behaviour. It is with this ribald challenge to the Old World that Latin American culture enters the twentieth century.

The 'good things' that Nervo has to point out about Europe are its technological advances and its marketing of itself. It should not come as a surprise that *modernismo* is inherently bound up with travel chronicles when the novelty of new modes of travel, the increasing speed, and the fantasy of flight are all part of the fascination with modernity. Nervo wrote about cars, speculated about planes, and marvelled at the facilities of train stations. These developments in infrastructure which made mass tourism a viable activity for Europeans were one of the things that Nervo singled out for application in Mexico, along with all the marketing and opportunism that goes with them:

> ¿Por qué en México no se explotan nuestros admirables paisajes? Aquí hasta en la cumbre de la más alta montaña hay un suntuoso hotel. Y todo, merced a un hábil plan, rinde cuantiosas utilidades. ¿Que se quiere pasar el Rin? Medio franco. ¿Que se quiere entrar al castillo? Un franco. ¿Que se sube a la cámara obscura? Medio franco. ¿Que se vuelve a pasar el Rin para tomar el tren? Medio franco. Y luego las tarjetas postales ilustradas y el no menos próspero comercio de *recuerdos del Rhein fall*, marfiles, maderas, piedras de los Alpes, fotografías, abanicos…, cuanto hay en el mundo.
>
> Los funiculares (que son aquí de lo más atrevido del orbe) dejan un dineral, un dineral los hoteles, todo un dineral. ¡Cuánto no daría entre nosotros un funicular a las cumbres del Popocatépetl, del Iztaccíhuatl, del Orizaba; cuánto una empresa de vaporcitos de recreo en Chapala y en Pátzcuaro, ahora que es tal la afluencia de excursionistas! ('Las caidas del Rin: nuestros maravillosos paisajes mexicanos', p. 233)

In retrospect, Nervo sounds like an extremely dangerous visionary, although such statements should also be read as ironic send-ups of the kind of exploitative travel accounts written about Mexico by the members of the 'capitalist vanguard' during the late nineteenth century.[50] Nervo's

---

50 See Pratt, *Imperial Eyes*, p. 146. For an example of this kind of passage in a work by a member of the 'capitalist vanguard' see Daniel Cooper Alarcón, 'The Ruins of Manifest Destiny: John L. Stephens's *Incidents of Travel in Central America,*

travel writing thus demonstrates an awareness of the predominant mode of travel narrative penned on the subject of Mexico during his lifetime and his practice of the genre can be seen to have a critical edge to it that signals the beginnings of postimperialist discomfort with such a form of writing.

José Vasconcelos and the Demise of the Tradition

The statesman and philosopher José Vasconcelos (1882–1959) recorded his memoirs in four volumes which were first published in the years 1935 to 1939 by the avid publisher of travel books, both Mexican and foreign, Editorial Botas (*Ulises criollo* [1935]; *La tormenta* [1936]; *El desastre* [1938] and *El proconsulado* [1939]).[51] The scope of these 'memoirs' is undoubtedly greater than that of the average travel chronicle, covering Vasconcelos's life in general from his early childhood to his exile in France and Spain during the Calles regime (1924–28), and again, after his failed presidential campaign, during the Maximato (1928–1934) and Cárdenas's regime (1934–1940). However, the narration of travel remains a constant: Vasconcelos made claims to have spent half his life 'de viaje', starting with the '"leit motiv" (*sic*) familiar' of his childhood migrations – *Ulises criollo* is a telling title for the first book of memoirs.[52] These memoirs constitute travel chronicles of epic proportions.

The narration of travel is also a leitmotif in Vasconcelos's more philosophical works: *La raza cósmica* (1925), purported to be an essay

---

Chiapas, and Yucatan', in *A través del espejo: viajes, viajeros y la construcción de la alteridad en América Latina*, ed. by Lourdes de Ita Rubio and Gerardo Sánchez Díaz (Morelia: Instituto de Investigaciones Históricas, Universidad Michoacana de San Nicolás Hidalgo, 2005), pp. 336.

51 Now published as José Vasconcelos, *Memorias*, 2 vols (FCE, 1993), I (3rd repr.): *Ulises criollo* & *La tormenta*; II (2nd repr.): *El desastre* & *El proconsulado*. All further quotations from Vasconcelos's memoirs are from these editions and will be given parenthetically in the text.

52 Quotes from Vasconcelos's *Memorias*, reproduced in Mario Vasconcelos Aguilar's *José Vasconcelos: maestro de América* (Jus, 1978), p. 26.

on *mestizaje* and after only a brief introduction switched to the narration of 'notas de viaje' of his trip to Argentina and Brazil. Many other texts also include a substantial element of travel narrative: *Divagaciones literarias* (1919), *Indología* (1927), *Pesimismo alegre* (1931), *Sonata mágica* (1933) and *Qué es la revolución* (1937). Towards the end of his life Vasconcelos published one book that was unashamedly a collection of travel impressions: *Temas contemporáneos* (1955).

Vasconcelos's memoirs and other pieces of travel writing should really be considered the, albeit inadvertent, swan song of the tradition of the Mexican travel chronicle. To a large extent his work reads as part of the mid-nineteenth-century tradition, back-tracking on the advances of the *modernistas* to the style and purpose of Payno, Prieto and Altamirano.[53] The sheer volume of his memoirs and the prominence of his desire to narrate his travels (as a politician and as a cultured tourist, or writer at leisure), which spills over even into his philosophical works, is indicative of his assumption of the role of an all-round statesman – politician, philosopher, writer, and 'character' – who makes a package of the narration of his itinerant life and works as part of his contribution to the formation of a nation: it is his duty to narrate his travels in order to educate his people.

The narration of travel also attests to his writerly concerns, particularly his descriptions of landscape. Vasconcelos's style is generally forthright and unhampered by literary preoccupations beyond those of clear communication, although he does betray some rather ironic concern for the style of his travel chronicles and evidence of a certain awareness of insufficiency with regard to the European tradition of travel writing in his first attempt at narrating a journey:

> Lápiz en mano, intenté fijar en mi cuaderno siquiera algunas de las impresiones tumultuosas del día. No me guiaba la vanidad, sino el deseo de guardar de algún modo la emoción venturosa del viaje. Pero me estorbaban los adjectivos. En vez

---

53 It should be noted that Vasconcelos himself would have refuted such a link with the nineteenth-century patriots. Indeed, he hated Ignacio Ramírez and Altamirano so much so that he refused to be buried in the same graveyard as them (Christopher Domínguez Michael's *Tiros en el concierto: literatura mexicana del siglo V* [Era, 1997], p. 56).

> de apuntar las cosas, me empeñaba en calificarlas. Cada montaña tenía que ser alta; las ciudades me merecían el mismo epíteto de bonitas y cada paisaje resultaba encantador. Con plena conciencia de que traicionaba mi sentir, escribía y acusaba al lenguaje de llevarnos por sus caminos trillados, pese a la virginidad de la percepción. [...] Recordaba las narraciones amenas de un libro de viajes alrededor del mundo, que en Piedras Negras leyera, y me sentía apocado. (I: 67)[54]

However, despite this false modesty, in his narration of specific travel episodes he excels in the sketching of brief portraits of people and places (towns and countryside), and in the description of his personal emotional response to the stimuli of travel itself. The influence of Humboldt, Chateaubriand and Antonio García Cubas – three authors whom Vasconcelos admired greatly – is clearly perceptible in his descriptions of nature.[55] In *Ulises criollo* he devotes a number of pages to an intense description of his first railway journey from Mexico City to Veracruz (I: 84–88). His entire attention during the journey is dedicated to what he can see from the train window – not to the state of the train itself, nor the company with whom he is travelling. His description is hyperbolic (and not just a bit repetitious), accentuating the impossibility of capturing in language the beauty of the landscape and the national pride that Mexican civil-engineering inspires in him. Life in Mexico, as seen *en route* (the human landscape), is also of interest to him: he thus balances *paisajismo* and *costumbrismo* very much in the manner of the nineteenth-century travel chronicles. All in all, Vasconcelos is a long-winded nationalist, traditionalist and pedagogue in the best tradition of Payno and Altamirano, illustrating the attributes and potential of the Mexican nation in his descriptions of the country, and in comparisons with other countries. Indeed, Octavio Paz referred to him as 'el gran

---

54   The book referred to is probably Jules Verne's *Le tour du monde en quatre-vingts jours* (1873).
55   More contemporary writers of whose opinions Vasconcelos was generally critical are Azorín, Vicente Blasco Ibáñez, Ramón María del Valle-Inclán and Marc Chadourne, especially where they concern Mexico. By the time of *El proconsulado*, D.H. Lawrence's fatalistic opinions met with a more positive response, however (II: 1074).

creador o recreador de la naturaleza y los hombres de América';[56] a kind of homegrown Humboldt.

Vasconcelos's travel writing as described thus far might well come across as just a bit old-fashioned, but good, traditional, nationalist travel writing, nonetheless. However, his travel chronicles also expose some of the contradictions of his political agenda that run so deep as to affect his approach to travel writing as a whole. Although credited by many as being the main spokesperson for the discourse of *mestizaje* in post-Revolutionary Mexico – a discourse that purportedly saw all Mexicans as being equally mixed in racial and cultural heritage and part of one great, successful 'cosmic race' – Vasconcelos would later in life express quite clearly fascist sympathies and 'white' supremacist ideologies, and the seeds for this can be traced even back as far as *La raza cósmica*.[57] In fact his theory of *mestizaje* is really a guise for a process of *mexicanización* where indigenous people can become *mestizo* Mexicans only if they abandon their cultural roots and espouse more Castilian practices and values. Inevitably his travel writing shows evidence of this, and more broadly responds to his split Mexican/Spanish allegiances – it expresses almost 'colonialist' sentiments in places. (Of this, more later.)

At the date of their publication and for quite a while afterwards Vasconcelos's memoirs were the most read books in the Mexican Republic. As Antonio Castro Leal noted in 1940:

> No hay actualmente escritor mexicano más leído, dentro y fuera de nuestro país, que José Vasconcelos. Después de los éxitos de Francisco Bulnes – importantes para las condiciones de su tiempo – ningún libro ha alcanzado el tiro de *Ulises criollo*, ni siquiera de *La tormenta*. Su autor es tan conocido como lo fue en su época don Ignacio Ramírez y tan leído por todos como lo fue Manuel Gutiérrez Nájera. Es sin duda el único autor mexicano vivo que logra mantener durante quinientas páginas la atención de amigos y enemigos, del hombre culto y del 'hombre de la calle', del escritor y del político, del estudiante y del mercader,

---

56   Octavio Paz, quoted in Christopher Domínguez Michael, 'Diccionario de Octavio Paz', *Vuelta*, 259 (June 1998), 68.

57   See Luis Antonio Marentes, 'Narrativizing the Storm: José Vasconcelos and the Writing of the Mexican Revolution' (unpublished doctoral dissertation, University of Texas at Austin, 1994).

del provinciano y del habitante de la capital. Los suyos son los únicos libros de quinientas páginas que han leído y releído muchos.[58]

This is as popular as travel writing gets. In Castro Leal's view, the reason for this success was not the accessible style of the memoirs, nor the notoriety or theories of their outspoken author, but their display of emotion. Nevertheless, the reasons that Castro Leal discounts are still significant factors in the popular appeal of Vasconcelos's travel writing.

However, the long shadow cast by the popularity of Vasconcelos's work really set the seal on what the travel chronicle could aspire to be in the early to mid twentieth century, despite efforts by slightly younger writers such as Salvador Novo to counter Vasconcelos in his own travel writing.[59] As Carlos Monsiváis notes, by the 1950s the chronicle genre as a whole was deemed both nostalgic and reactionary; the Mexico whose identity it purported to capture was a heap of outdated stereotypes that no longer corresponded to the post-Revolutionary nation of the midcentury. In Monsiváis's terms, no contemporary chroniclers could avoid 'la nostalgia embellecedora y las insistencias comparativas entre el Ayer Diáfano y el Hoy Angustioso' in their work, and 'como género, la crónica se obstina en parecer reaccionaria: suyas son las evocaciones que construyen una realidad alternativa'; an outdated, alternative reality.[60]

Further proof of the nostalgic, reactionary reputation that the (travel) chronicle form had garnered by the mid century can be found in the work of a group that Vasconcelos, in his role director of the Secretaría de Educación Pública in the early 1920s, actively promoted. The *Colonialistas* – Manuel Toussaint, Francisco Monterde, Ermilo

---

58 Antonio Castro Leal, quoted in Christopher Domínguez Michael, 'Lecciones de la tormenta', *Gaceta del Fondo de Cultura Económica*, 285 (September 1994), 53.

59 Salvador Novo, *Return Ticket* (1920), *Jalisco-Michoacán* (1933), *Continente vacío: viaje a Sudamérica* (1935), and *Este y otros viajes* (1951), now all collected as *Viajes y ensayos, I*, ed. by Sergio González Rodríguez, Antonio Saborit, Mary K. Long, et al. (FCE, 1966). See also Mary K. Long's thesis on Novo for his relationship in life and in travel writing with Vasconcelos ('Salvador Novo: 1920–1940, Between the Avant-Garde and the Nation' [unpublished doctoral dissertation, Princeton University, 1995]).

60 Carlos Monsiváis, *A ustedes les consta*, p. 58.

Abreu Gómez, Artemio de Valle-Arizpe, and others – were famed for their admiration for Mexico's colonial heritage in art, architecture and literature and they were also well known for their publication, from the 1920s onwards, of travel chronicles that lovingly describe the art and architecture of Mexico's colonial cities rather than the more contemporary faces of the country.[61] In terms of how the travel chronicle was viewed in Mexico, the politics of Vasconcelos and the *Colonialistas* perhaps started to reveal the genre's more dubious political underpinnings, and thus, where the importation of the genre had previously been justified on account of the pressing need to create Mexican national identity in fact and in literature and an unproblematised mimetic relationship with Spain/France, contemporary writers would start to view the genre in a more circumspect manner.[62]

This incipient 'postcolonialist' attitude to travel writing would be substantially reinforced by ever-increasing anti-imperialist sentiment in the country and the growing association of travel writing with the strategies of imperialism. On average, Mexican attitudes towards travel writing are more specifically postimperialist than they are postcolonialist, and although there is some evidence of the latter – the term colonialism has come to be a 'dirty' word in Mexico – the relationship between Mexico and Spain, Mexicans and Spaniards, continues to be more generally fraternal than antagonistic.

The abandonment of the tradition of the travel chronicle is not only due to the politics of the genre, however. Questions of purpose

---

61 See, for example, Manuel Toussaint, *Oaxaca* (written 1926) and *Tasco: guía de emociones* (written 1928), now published together as *Oaxaca y Tasco*, ill. by Francisco Díaz de León, Lecturas Mexicanas, 80 (SEP / FCE, 1985). Other of Toussaint's publications include *Tasco: su historia, sus monumentos* (1931), *Paseos coloniales* (1939), *Pátzcuaro* (1942), and *La catedral y las iglesias de Puebla* (1954).

62 Jorge Klor de Alva does note a certain shift in attitudes to the legacy of empire ushered in by the Mexican Revolution of 1910–20 – after this point a more contestatory stance does take root, although, in my view, it is far from exclusive (Klor de Alva, 'The Postcolonization of the (Latin) American Experience: A Reconsideration of "Colonialism," "Postcolonialism," and "Mestizaje"', in *After Colonialism: Imperial Histories and Postcolonial Displacements*, ed. by Gyan Prakash [Princeton, NJ: Princeton UP, 1995], pp. 241–75).

and content and of narrative style are also significant. The discourse of Mexican national identity moved its focus away from the rural provinces to the growing megalopolis that is Mexico City from the mid-century onwards, thus depriving the Mexican travel chronicle of its typical subject matter: as Domínguez Michael notes of Agustín Yáñez's *Al filo del agua* (1947),

> Al destruir [...] la provincia como ambiente pintoresco, al penetrar en ella con la modernidad de la novela, acabó por vaciarla como proyecto holístico. Sus sucesores renunciaron de principio a recorrer la nación con la ambición cartográfica de fijarla adánicamente en toda su dimensión humana y natural.[63]

Furthermore, the defining features of the travel chronicle typical of the 'chronotope of the road' model – Realism, in particular *costumbrismo*; linear, chronological narrative development; a unified, psychologically coherent narrative voice; viable cause-effect relationships; the conveyance of a clear message, and so on – proved a major hurdle for its adaptation to the influence of modernism that was overtaking Latin American literature by the 1950s.[64] Only by revising the chronotope that underpinned the genre's practice could it survive as anything more than an anachronism in Mexican letters, and fortuitously such a revision would open up a space for a rethink of the genre's imperialist tendencies.

---

63 Christopher Domínguez Michael, ed., *Antología de la narrativa mexicana del siglo XX*, 2nd edn, 2 vols (FCE, 1996), I, 1016.

64 The terms modernism, and later postmodernism, written in English in this study, are distinct from the Spanish term *modernismo* used to identify the turn-of-the-century Latin American literary movement. Modernism, in Latin America, roughly equates to the Latin American 'Boom' period of the late 1950s and 1960s, and postmodernism to the ensuing 'post-Boom' period. (My typification of these periods corresponds more to the point of view of Roberto González Echevarría put forth in *La ruta de Severo Sarduy* [Hanover, NH: Ediciones del Norte, 1987] than to that of Donald L. Shaw as expressed in *The Post-Boom in Spanish American Fiction* [Albany: State U of New York P, 1998].)

Another reason for the demise of the travel-chronicling tradition is that the commercialisation of the travel chronicle sponsored by the publishing houses Botas and Costa-Amic from the 1930s onwards also damaged its literary reputation considerably and hence writers disassociated themselves from the genre.

Imperialist Discourse, Creolisation and Transculturation

The development of a tradition of Mexican travel writing in the nineteeth century was not a naïve enterprise by any means. Although it coincides with the mimetic relationship that newly independent Latin American nations favoured with the ex-colonial power, Mexican writers do demonstrate their awareness of the foreign models they are employing, and, occasionally, of the potential problems that such borrowings might entail – Nervo is the maximum example of this. It should also be noted that, although Spain and Spanish travel writing, both past and present, do not come in for major criticism because of this mimetic relationship, that of more recent imperialist visitors to Mexico – especially those from the United Kingdom and the USA – does. The imperialist politics of foreign travel writing on the subject of Mexico is acknowledged both in the perceived need to reclaim the textualisation of the Republic for Mexican pens – one of the main purposes of the development of Mexican travel writing – and in the more subtle, and increasingly ironic, renegotiation of the tropes of European travel writing, such as the discourse of the 'exotic' or the 'exploitable'.

The extent to which it can be claimed that these Mexican writers either simply effected a 'creolisation' of the genre – where creolisation may be defined as the importation of a European cultural model or custom, which is then reproduced in the New World with little consideration for the way in which its meaning, purpose or politics might be different or nonsensical in the new context – or produced a more fully transculturated form of travel writing – one that substantially and consciously changes the form of the genre at the level of the chronotope in order to enable it to address fully its new context and to contest the imperialist tendencies of the original genre – depends largely on the individual writer and his politics.[65] By and large, what happens is a process of creolisation with some signs of incipient transculturation; however, this does not map onto a developmental continuum. Ironically, although he simply espoused

---

65   For 'creolisation', see Susan Castillo, *Performing America: Colonial Encounters in New World Writing, 1500–1786* (London: Routledge, 2006), p. 189. For 'transculturation' see, Pratt, *Imperial Eyes*, p. 6.

the creolisation of the genre in Mexico for nation-building purposes,[66] Altamirano's travel writing itself shows more signs of transculturation than that of Vasconcelos, the most recent writer to be considered in this overview of the development of the tradition.

Vasconcelos writes from a split, 'dialogic', Spanish/Mexican point of view. For example, he argues for the creation of a *mestizo* Mexican national identity while simultaneously trying to 'white-wash' over the nation's indigenous components. Specifically in the case of the Maya in Yucatan, in 1938 Vasconcelos described the women as 'pintorescas si se quiere, pero totalmente incultas' (*El desastre*, p. 95), the ruins of Chichén Itzá as 'uniformemente bárbaro, cruel y grotesco. Ningún sentido de belleza [...] Decoración utilitaria que, por lo mismo, no nos causa emoción estética alguna' (pp. 106–07), and summed up: 'Una sensación de fracaso domina al visitante y se piensa con alivio y con orgullo en Mérida y en Valladolid, las ciudades creadas por los españoles' (p. 108). Travelling in South America in the travel narrative section of *La raza cósmica*, Vasconcelos even uses the same tropes as the writers of the 'capitalist vanguard', spying the potential for economic exploitation of the Iguazú Falls, although arguably he was scouting that potential for Latin America rather than imperialist exploitation.[67]

On the other hand, a writer like Altamirano writes from a much more 'Mexico-centred' perspective, embracing the indigenous communities of Mexico as the key to Mexican national identity and describing them as agents of their own landscape's fruitful labour: an edenic, cultivated landscape surrounding Tixtla is specifically ascribed to the 'caudillo azteca' who founded the settlement and to the subsequent generations of indigenous inhabitants who have tilled the earth (*Paisajes y leyendas*, p. 11). Where Vasconcelos still equates civilisation with Spanish practices and values, Altamirano finds rhetorical devices with which to complicate the exotic versus civilised opposition – the valley of Tixtla is simultaneously an exotic, tropical paradise and a civilised

---

66   See the introduction to this study.
67   José Vasconcelos, *La raza cósmica: misión de la raza iberoamericana, Argentina y Brasil*, Austral 802, 16th edn (Espasa-Calpe Mexicana, 1992), pp. 198–99.

agricultural hub. His travel writing thus shows evidence of a certain amount of transculturation.[68]

Where traditional Mexican travel writing is most clearly a creolisation of the European genre, it tends to echo more frequently the imperialist rhetoric of Northern European and United States travel writing, as seen above in the racist and exploitative examples from Vasconcelos's work. Such texts tend to attempt to provide an authoritative account that enumerates and totalises the writer's experiences and that is validated by the discursive construction of the writer as a person of some authority and credibility, usually a well-connected statesman; the gaze of the traveller still masters and appropriates its surroundings, albeit for nationalist rather than imperialist purposes. Inevitably, too, these texts also produce descriptions of groups of people – *jalapeños*, *veracruzanos*, and so on – that, though generally flattering and intended to construct a sense of fraternity between the different regions and the administrative, discursive centre of the nation, Mexico City, also essentialise, even patronise, such groups as they translate the backlands and provinces for their urban reading public, thus transferring the dynamics of imperial power relations to the context of a highly centralised nation; one which is still playing out the legacy of colonialism in its internal dynamics.

Where traditional Mexican travel writing shows signs of transculturation it simultaneously starts to revise the basic 'chronotope of the road' model on which European travel writing was based and which, as I argued in Chapter 1, is in itself closely allied to the production of imperialist discourse. However, although there are some signs of the production of a transculturated model for travel writing in Mexico, at this juncture in history, Mexican writers were not really in a position to substantially reinvent this chronotope. The remainder of this study is dedicated to an examination of the more thorough-going transculturation of the genre effected by writers in the late twentieth century; writers who skilfully reinvent the genre's chronotope, employing postmodernist narrative techniques to achieve postcolonialist ends.

---

68   This is endorsed by Segre's argument in her 'An Italicised Ethnicity', p. 268–69.

Chapter 3
The Postmodern and the Postcolonial in Contemporary Mexican Travel Writing

> La vida ribereña se le ofrece, realista, como un haz de impresiones fijas: más que cinematográfica la miseria es atemporal. Esas chozas taimadas, con esas mujeres que calientan tortillas (al abrigo de la superstición gastronómica que indica como supremamente deleitoso lo más barato), con esas niñas de ojos interminables fugitivas de un cuadro de Diego Rivera, con esos perros de la desesperanza y ese borracho pintoresco que musita sin término la misma frase en inglés: – *Ey, Mister, lend me yur irs, lend mi yur irs, lend mi...* bien pudieran ser consignados por Francisco Rojas González en sus cuentos antropológicos, quizás fueron asimilados por Emilio Fernández en las vivencias escenográficas de *La Perla*. No puede haber gran variedad de cronistas en México. La serpiente se muerde la cola. ¿Qué tanto difiere la mentalidad observada por la marquesa Calderón de la Barca de la comentada por Manuel Gutiérrez Nájera de la elogiada por Salvador Novo? Las constantes del ser humano, dirá alguien. Otro enmendará: las constantes del ser colonial.[1]

Carlos Monsiváis's analysis of the reputation of the (travel) chronicle in the mid-twentieth century is most revealing. As noted at the end of the last chapter, in terms of its literary style and its politics, by this point the genre was inevitably considered anachronistic and reactionary.[2] In the above quotation, taken from a rare example of a travel chronicle penned by Monsiváis himself in 1970, he also reiterates the exhaustion of the subject matter of travel writing in Mexico – the provinces have been emptied of their literary charm, and the discourse of contemporary national identity has moved on.

However, following the revival of the role and function of chronicles in general after the 1968 Tlatelolco massacre as the defiant

---

1   Carlos Monsiváis, '7 de marzo de 1970: Dios nunca muere (crónica de un eclipse)', *Días de guardar*, 13th repr. (Era, 1991), pp. 92–93.
2   Carlos Monsiváis, *A ustedes les consta antología de la crónica en México* (Era, 1980), p. 58.

manifestation of a new public forum for the self-expression of civil society – a forum that could quite clearly encompass the sort of revisionist worldview associated with a more postcolonialist agenda –, the travel chronicle genre was deliberately revived in Mexico in the 1980s. It is the work of this chapter to attempt to account for the ways in which Mexican travel writing of the late twentieth century negotiates the charges against it in terms of style, subject matter, and purpose/ political aspirations; in short, how it negotiates the development of postmodernism, particularly in literature, and postcolonialism, particularly as a political agenda, and how it may seek to combine the two in a productive manner. (As an aside, it should be noted that, unless otherwise stated, the term postcolonialism will be used throughout this chapter to refer to a contestatory attitude towards the legacy and/ or practices of both colonialism and imperialism, as experienced in Mexico. Where that contestatory attitude refers only to imperialism, I will use the term postimperialism.)

Postmodernity and Postmodernism in Mexico

In the late 1980s the postmodern era officially reached Mexico, as evidenced by the June 1987 edition of Octavio Paz's cultural journal *Vuelta*.[3] Much has been written already about the difficult relevance of postmodernity and postmodernism to Mexico and other Latin American countries.[4] While a number of critics and practitioners of high culture associated with Paz have been reasonably positive about the new era and its cultural practices, the majority of critics in Mexico have displayed a more sceptical, although not entirely dismissive, approach

---

3   See *Vuelta*, 127 (June 1987), especially Paz's editorial ('¿Postmodernidad?', p. 1) which claims to have been introducing postmodernity to Mexico since at least 1981.

4   See *Nuevo Texto Crítico*, 3:6 (1990) and 4:7 (1991), issues entitled 'Modernidad y posmodernidad en América Latina (I)' and 'Modernidad y posmodernidad en América Latina (II)', respectively; and *Boundary 2*, 20:3 (1993), an issue entitled 'The Postmodernist Debate in Latin America'.

to the postmodern.⁵ Sergio Zermeño, in an article entitled 'La tentación posmoderna', gives the most succinct overview of the postmodern debate. At his most dismissive he writes that, 'No existen las coincidencias de lo latinoamericano con las tesis del posmodernismo'.⁶ An imperfect modernisation project has left most Latin Americans, particularly in rural areas, in a state of premodernity, and only a very small sector of the population (the upper-middle class residents of the Federal District in Mexico, for example) has full access to the infrastructure of postmodernity and benefits from free-market/neo-liberal policies. This eclectic mix of very different stages of development might look like a postmodern social collage ('América Latina es posmoderna y nunca llegará a ser moderna',⁷ he comments ironically), but, for Zermeño, looking postmodern and being postmodern are two very different issues. Western postmodernity's politically correct cult of popular culture, rescuing traditions, and privileging marginalised voices is a choice; a choice made largely by a sector of society removed from the realities of life in the margins and with full access to the perks of postmodernity: the consumerist life-style, the spectacular option on *Weltanschauung*. Latin Americans, for the most part, are left to pick up the scraps of

5   See for example, a series of interviews conducted by Magali Tercero and published in *Sábado*, the cultural supplement of the newspaper *Unomásuno*, from 10 July to 23 August 1988, subsequently reprinted under the rubric '¿Existe el postmodernismo?' in *Casa del Tiempo*, 81 (January 1989). For a slightly divergent assessment of the advent of postmodernity and postmodernism in Mexico, see Raymond Leslie Williams's *The Postmodern Novel in Latin America: Politics, Culture, and the Crisis of Truth* (London: MacMillan, 1995), pp. 21–24. I personally disagree with Williams's all-encompassing periodisation of postmodernism in Mexico and with his general association of postmodernism with radical literary experimentalism and epistemological self-doubt. My understanding of postmodernism in Mexico is closer to the views expressed by Roberto González Echevarría (*La ruta de Severo Sarduy* (Hanover, NH: Ediciones del Norte, 1987), especially pp. 251–52) and Donald L. Shaw (*The Post-Boom in Spanish American Fiction* [Albany: State U of New York P, 1998]). In particular I am willing to concede that the rather less experimental, although not traditionally Realist, Post-Boom is a significant expression of the postmodern in Latin American literature.
6   Sergio Zermeño, 'La tentación posmoderna', *Nexos*, 124 (April 1988), 7.
7   Zermeño, 'La tentación posmoderna', 7.

postmodern fallout: the narcotics trade offers about the only hope of independent life-style for the man in the street. Globalisation for Latin Americans is simply imperialist exploitation by another name and hence one may expect their attitude to the phenomenon to be at least tacitly postcolonialist. Exceptionally, however, Zermeño does allow that cultural practices such as architecture, or art, or – one might add – literature, may have developed a postmodernist form without reference to a fully pre-existing state of postmodernity in Latin America. But does this development of a postmodernist form in the arts deny the possibility of such media containing a postcolonialist critique or can a postmodernist form work with such a critique? The answer, I believe, is that postmodernism and postcolonialism can work together, but of this, more later.

Carlos Monsiváis has also been extremely cautious in his dealings with the postmodern. While it is indisputable that he is the cultural critic most keen on reflecting on new social trends in Mexico – movements, icons, rituals, displays, many of which would appear to be part of the postmodern mood (Gloria Trevi calendars, *La Onda*, Superbarrio, etc.) –, he has clearly resisted the temptation to use this hold-all term in his *vade mecum* to contemporary Mexican society. For the most part he restricts himself to analysing the facets of Mexican modernity more in line with the thinking of radical social theorists such as Guy Debord in his *La Société du Spectacle* (1967) than with any of the theorists of the postmodern such as Jean-François Lyotard or Jean Baudrillard. From the late 1980s onwards he displays a 'post'-consciousness, but reserves usage of 'post'-terminology for disparaging or parodic critique. Mexico, since the beginning of La Crisis[8] is apparently in an era of 'postnacionalismo';[9] the cult of the Virgin of Guadalupe continues even in 'un mundo postradicional';[10] and Mexico City thrives

---

8   The massive financial crisis which started in 1982 at the beginning of President Miguel de la Madrid Hurtado's six-year term in power and which also prompted 'a crisis of authority, of legitimacy, and of truth' (Williams, *The Postmodern Novel*, p. 24)
9   Carlos Monsiváis, 'Muerte y resurrección del nacionalismo mexicano', *Nexos*, 109 (January 1987), 13.
10 Monsiváis, 'Muerte y resurrección', 19.

on the 'desmadre que ordena el mundo postapocalíptico'.[11] Monsiváis here displays the predominant attitude to the postmodern in Mexico: it is something to play with, to tease, and, if possible, to estrange. Postmodernity is seen as a foreigner in Mexico, a transnational capitalist encroachment on 'real' Mexican culture, a tourist phenomenon. But if postmodernity/postmodernism is a tourist in Mexico, will the discourse of postcolonialism be any less foreign to Mexican writers and critics?

Postcoloniality and Postcolonialism in Mexico

Following a similar pattern to the response to the arrival of postmodernism in Mexico, postcolonialism has been viewed with intense suspicion by some Latin American cultural critics and producers, ignored by most, and endorsed by a select few. While the Argentine critic Walter D. Mignolo welcomes the use of the new critical vocabulary despite its potential problems and abuses,[12] the Mexican-born Chicano critic Jorge Klor de Alva is by far the most convincing in his rejection of the new discourse as it pertains to Latin America as a whole.

In his essay, 'The Postcolonization of the (Latin) American Experience: A Reconsideration of "Colonialism," "Postcolonialism," and "Mestizaje"', Klor de Alva queries whether 'an error is being committed when scholars apply tools and categories of analysis developed in the twentieth century for understanding British colonialism, especially in India and Africa, to make sense of the experiences of sixteenth- to eighteenth-century Latin America'.[13] Without regurgitating the bulk of

---

11   Monsiváis, introduction to *El fin de la nostalgia: nueva crónica de la ciudad de México*, ed. by Jaime Valverde Arciniega & Juan Domingo Argüelles (Mexico City: Nueva Imagen, 1992), p. 25.
12   Walter D. Mignolo, 'Human Understanding and (Latin) American Interests: The Politics and Sensibilities of Geohistorical Locations', in *A Companion to Postcolonial Studies*, ed. by Henry Schwarz and Sangeeta Ray (Oxford: Blackwell, 2000), p. 180.
13   Jorge Klor de Alva, 'The Postcolonization of the (Latin) American Experience: A Reconsideration of "Colonialism," "Postcolonialism," and "Mestizaje"', in *After*

his essay, his main arguments regarding the reasons why Latin America is not postcolonial rest on the following: the only people in the region who were really and truly colonised (in the sense of being exploited) were the indigenous communities and they continue to be colonised even in contemporary times; and Independence movements across Latin America were really battles for power between the different factions within the Spanish-orientated, ie. 'colonising', élite rather than decolonising take-overs by the indigenous communities and thus subsequent nation-states were founded as independent but willingly mimetic entities with respect to Spain.

However, with particular relevance to the case of Mexico, Klor de Alva argues that the popular uprising that was the Mexican Revolution (1910–1920) did herald a more critical attitude to the legacy of Spain in the Republic and that certainly by the late 1960s, even if the application of postcolonialist theory should not be applied wholesale to Latin America, one can still talk of the emergence of a feeling of 'postcoloniality' where this

> can be thought of as a form of contestatory/oppositional consciousness, emerging from either pre-existing imperial, colonial, or ongoing subaltern conditions, which fosters processes aimed at revising the norms and practices of antecedent or still vital forms of domination.[14]

It is worth emphasising the fact that this feeling of 'postcoloniality' responds to both colonial and imperial conditions in Klor de Alva's analysis, and, indeed, in my own view, a 'postimperialist' consciousness is far stronger in contemporary Mexico than a postcolonialist one that focuses soley on the legacy of the Spanish empire.

Colonialism: Imperial Histories and Postcolonial Displacements, ed. by Gyan Prakash (Princeton, NJ: Princeton UP, 1995), p. 264.

14 Klor de Alva, 'The Postcolonization of the (Latin) American Experience', p. 245. It might be noted that Kwame Anthony Appiah is as sceptical as Klor de Alva regarding the application of postcolonialism to Africa – the most compelling similarity he find between postmodernism and postcolonialism is the fact that they are both discourses that stem from the Western academy and are only acknowledged locally by what he 'ungenerously' terms 'a *comprador* intelligentsia' (Appiah, 'Is the Post- in Postmodernism the Post- in Postcolonial?', *Critical Inquiry*, 17:2 [1991], 348).

Thus, Mexican writers might not necessarily use the vocabulary of postcolonial studies as we know it in the Anglophone academcy, but some of their work does coincide with such a critical, revisionist agenda. To return to the quotation of Monsiváis that I cited as an epigraph to this chapter, what is most interesting about it are the terms in which he expresses the exhaustion of the Mexican travel chronicle's subject matter – these are 'las constantes del ser colonial'. In a clever rhetorical manoeuvre that avoids being considered an example of metonymic imperialist superiority by ascribing the cause of Mexican peasants' uninterrupted misery to the on-going experience of colonialism itself, Monsiváis gives voice to the emergence of a postcolonialist sensibility in Mexican travel writing.[15]

The Substance of Contemporary Mexican Travel Writing

Monsiváis justified the need for a new wave of more politically committed chronicles in Mexico with the following comments that he made in 1980: 'Hay un nuevo país que se empieza a cronicar y documentar: el México de masas y desempleo, de frustración y esperanzas bajo la tierra. Todo está por escribirse, grabarse, registrarse'.[16] And if Monsiváis felt that the

---

15 In the field of travel writing, the work published from the 1950s to the 1970s by two important precursors of Carlos Monsiváis's form of writing, that of Fernando Benítez and Jorge Ibargüengoitia, attests to an increasingly critical attitude regarding the relationship between Mexico and Europe that shows signs of a postcolonialist sensibility. Benítez charted extensively the contemporary state of Mexico's indigenous communities and hence focused on the legacy of Spanish colonialism in Mexico itself and on the on-going state of colonisation experienced by such communities; Ibargüengoitia's critical edge is most apparent in his ironic travel chronicles of both Europe and Mexico that often target the legacy of colonialism by deconstructing the cultural self-perception of mainstream Mexican *mestizos* and their relationship with European culture. The French and the Spanish also come in for a certain amount of postcolonialist deconstruction. (See bibliography for full details of Benítez's and Ibargüengoitia's publications.)

16 Carlos Monsiváis, *A ustedes les consta: antología de la crónica en México* (Era, 1980), p. 76.

chronicle genre was an ideal vehicle for this revisionist task, the editors of Porrúa's second edition of Teixidor's *Viajeros mexicanos* in 1981 also perceived a need for Mexicans to continue to write about their travels in the Republic. Concluding their foreword with Altamirano's statements concerning the lack of travel writing by Mexican authors,[17] they added their own plea: 'Quizá la lectura de los juicios de Ignacio Altamirano, estimulen a nuestros autores, y al sencillo viandante, para que nos obsequien y trasmitan sus impresiones como *viajeros mexicanos, en México*' (author's italics).[18] But is there any sense in continuing to write travel chronicles in an era where the nationalist project – the traditional purpose of Mexican travel writing – must surely be being eroded by the effects of globalisation? To get a picture of what contemporary Mexican travel chronicles are about, we must examine both what has become of the discourse of national identity and how the effects of globalisation have also come to be a focus in such work; a focus that can result in a writer's revelling in so much postmodern hybridity, but one that may also have a more clear-cut postcolonialist edge to it.

Most theorists of nationalism do not seriously consider its end to be nigh. Homi K. Bhabha, for example, notes that nationalist discourses have still not been 'definitively superseded by those new realities of internationalism, multinationalism, or even "late capitalism"', and he highlights the continuing existence of the 'grim prose of power that each nation can wield within its own sphere of influence', and which circulates beneath the 'rhetoric of these global terms'.[19] Late 1980s Mexico, might, according to Monsiváis, be in an era of 'postnacionalismo' where a sense of national identity has become fragmented, localised, intermittent, spectacular, ironic; separated from official state discourse and from Catholic doctrine, and possibly even

---

17   Quoted in the introduction to this study.
18   Anonymous editors' introduction to Felipe Teixidor, ed., *Viajeros mexicanos: siglos XIX y XX*, Sepan Cuantos…, 350, 2nd edn (Porrúa, 1982), p. xii.
19   Homi K. Bhabha, 'Introduction: Narrating the Nation', in *Nation and Narration*, ed. by Homi K. Bhabha (London: Routledge, 1990), p. 1. See also Benedict Anderson, *Imagined Communities: Reflections on the Origin and Spread of Nationalism*, 2nd edn, revised & extended (London: Verso, 1991), p. 3.

feminised if not feminist;[20] nevertheless, Monsiváis does not mean that Mexico, despite the homogenising effects of transnational capitalism, has gone beyond nationalism. The United States has always been too overbearing a neighbour for Mexicans to forget who they are, even if their national identity is always blurred in this context by issues of racial identity. And Monsiváis continues to point out that, 'la literatura, la pintura, el teatro, han vuelto a un nacionalismo obsesivo, más libre y más inteligente, desprovisto ya de cualquier pretensión de grandeza o de cualquier tentación de xenofobia, pero nacionalismo al fin.'[21]

In Mexican travel chronicles of the 1980s and 1990s the traditional issue of national identity is typically replaced by the fragmented sub-categories of postnational identity such as local or urban identities which may, at times, synecdochically represent national identity. Alternatively, it is often replaced by a self-conscious and ironic treatment of the question of identity *per se* which compromises any attempt to identify a stable ideological position. However, this more postmodernist approach to the question of identity can also be exploited as a means of undermining the authority of the traditional narrative voice in travel writing and of exploring in a more subtle manner the relationships between self and other that travel writing typically describes, all of which may be seen to have a more postcolonialist application. (Of this, more later.)

Contemporary travel chronicles are also often attentive to the influence of globalisation in the region, particularly in the form of the influence of the United States as seen in material goods, changing customs, signs and graffiti. Nevertheless, not all of these travel chronicles simply record and register the traces of this omnipresent dynamic for the sheer love of documenting new hybrid forms of chilliburgers or evidence of American influence in standard Mexican Spanish. Many writers link this apparent revelling in the postmodern with a tacitly postcolonialist critique of the processes of on-going United States imperialism in the region, particularly through their critique of the tourist industry and, also of the spread and influence of postmodernism itself in Mexico.[22]

---

20 Monsiváis, 'Muerte y resurrección', 21.
21 Monsiváis, 'Muerte y resurrección', 21.
22 Juan Villoro's work is exemplary of this approach.

Others will also turn the tables on the sense that Mexico is the passive recipient of this new and insidious form of imperialism by exploring the ways in which Mexican culture is also overrunning that of the United States.[23]

The Possibility of Postmodernist Travel Writing and The 'Chronotope of the Net'

Contemporary travel chroniclers also tend to want to illustrate 'average' daily life in the areas visited rather than exceptional moments in the regions' present situations: a 'viaje repetible', as Juan Villoro has defined it.[24] However, this ostensibly dull thematic trend is supposed to be mitigated by its counterpoint with the quirky features thrown up by the contingencies of daily life and/or by the way in which the journey is narrated. But what might be the poetics of the contemporary Mexican travel chronicle? In particular, how much of postmodernist literary practice will the genre be able to take on board without becoming indistinguishable from other forms of narrative?

On the level of the text, there is much debate about whether postmodernism constitutes a continuation and intensification of the practices of modernism, or a break with the project of modernism altogether. If postmodernism is an intensification of modernism, then the conditions for the survival of the travel chronicle as a literary genre become extremely adverse: the characteristics of modernist literature (the fragmented structure and formal experimentation; the frequent lack of verisimilitude, objectivity, cause-effect relationships, stable truth or message, or coherent characterisation; the creation of independent fictional worlds and totalising narratives; plus plenty of metatextual irony and epistemological doubt[25]) simply intensify, rendering the genre

---

23   For a good example, see Francisco Hinojosa, *Un taxi en L.A.* (CNCA, 1995).
24   Juan Villoro, personal interview, 19 February 1996.
25   Characteristics glossed from Gerald Graff's analysis of modernism, quoted by John Barth in 'La literatura postmoderna', *Quimera*, 46–47 (1985), 16; and from

of the travel chronicle either obsolete or unrecognisable. Such an attack on the tenets of Realism is also intrinsically linked to modernism's attack on the bourgeois rationality that Realism seeks to represent and this too suggests a major problem for a genre that is increasingly associated with middle-class attitudes and values.[26]

If, however, postmodernism is a rupture with, or implosion of, modernism, and an ever-so partial return to the projects of Realism and Romanticism, then the travel chronicle will be revived also. Roberto González Echevarría notes that for him the main characteristics of postmodernism in Latin American literature are the 'regreso de las historias' for the sake of telling stories; the general lack of totalising, authoritarian projects and values; a renewed interest in 'relatos locales', stories from the margins of society, and from the provinces in a country as centralised as Mexico; and a concern with superficiality, 'literatura lite': 'Ni el lenguaje en sus giros y juegos, ni los personajes, ni la figura del autor, prometen un conocimiento profundo. Todo es color, narratividad, acción'.[27] While this may be so, what does not occur is a straightforward return to Realism, but rather a form of narrative that incorporates certain postmodernist traits, while still managing to tell stories.[28] Thus, such literature also frequently includes a certain amount of some of the defining characteristics of postmodernist narrative as theorised by Linda Hutcheon (with reference to Latin American as well as Anglophone literature), in particular the simultaneously complicitous

---

Linda Hutcheon, *The Politics of Postmodernism* (London: Routledge, 1989), pp. 23–29, 62–70.

26 For the middle-class nature of contemporary travel writing, see Patrick Holland and Graham Huggan, *Tourists with Typewriters: Critical Reflections on Contemporary Travel Writing* (Ann Arbor: U of Michigan P, 1998), p. 20.

27 González Echevarría, *La ruta de Severo Sarduy*, pp. 251–52.

28 González Echevarría's definition of Latin American postmodernism coincides almost exactly with Shaw's description of the characteristics of the Post-Boom in Latin American literature (Shaw, *The Post-Boom in Spanish American Fiction*, especially pp. 2–20) rather than with Williams's association of postmodernism only with the more experimental literature being produced in contemporary Latin America (Williams, *The Postmodern Novel*). Nevertheless, Shaw himself is rather circumspect about whether Post-Boom works can be termed postmodernist and, indeed, finds them closer to postcolonialism than postmodernism (pp. 167–78).

and critical nature of postmodernist writing, and its propensity for continuing to use certain features typical of high modernism (such as the self-referential metatext) while, at the same time, undermining and ironising (in a particularly postmodern fashion) the function of such features.[29] For Hutcheon, postmodern irony is the kind of irony where the critical distance necessary for standard (modernist) ironic discourse is not rigorously maintained: 'It is the function of irony in postmodern discourse to posit [a] critical distance and then undo it'.[30]

In the event, postmodernism in Mexico is both a continuation and a rupture with modernism, simultaneous or alternating; a development and up-dating of some of its features and a re-evaluation of other less modern literary strategies. In general postmodernism is characterised by its extreme heterogeneity of styles and subjects. Nevertheless, the majority of prose being published in Mexico today would seem to err on the side of the nuanced rupture with modernism detailed above. Thus all seems well for the survival of the travel chronicle as a literary genre in late twentieth century Mexican culture: the author's task is to explore facets of a more heterogeneous Mexican postnational identity, possibly including a more or less overtly political commentary on the effects of globalisation in the region, and on the relations between self and other, and then he/she should seal the resultant text with his/her literary fingerprint, including an apposite (ie. not too heavy) dose of the right kind of metatextuality and/or other postmodernist narrative features.[31]

---

29   Hutcheon, *The Politics of Postmodernism*, pp. 1–29. González Echevarría finds that the postmodernist text displays a distinct lack of metatext. Nevertheless, Hutcheon's description of the use of metatextual features to undermine confidence in their validity seems a plausible refinement of González Echevarría's definition.

30   Hutcheon, *The Politics of Postmodernism*, p. 15.

31   With respect to the question of metatextuality in particular, Patrick Holland and Graham Huggan have also noted the prevalence of metatextual play as a technique used in postmodernist travel writing, citing texts by Italo Calvino, Roland Barthes, Umberto Eco and Jean Baudrillard as examples: 'When postmodernism impinges on travel writing [...] it usually does so obliquely, under the sign of "meta": metatravel, metahistory, metageography, metafiction. Postmodernist travel books are almost invariably metanarratives, reflecting on their own status as texts – as *theoretical* texts – on travel' (Holland and Huggan, *Tourists with Typewriters*,

Nevertheless, as Patrick Holland and Graham Huggan have noted on the subject of Anglophone travel writing, although conditions seem to be right for postmodern travel writing, very little travel writing has actually achieved a fully postmodernist form even if it charts the changing faces of postmodernity in terms of its subject matter: 'The typical travel book (insofar as it can ever be agreed upon that such a creature exists) continues to cleave to modern realist conventions'.[32] The same is true in Mexico. The vast majority of travel writing published since the late 1980s continues to be written in an unproblematised, Realist mode, simply updating its subject matter to explore contemporary, partially postmodern, society. Nevertheless, some key travel chronicles have responded to postmodernism in terms of their formal composition, and it is to those works that I shall turn my attention in the remainder of this study.

The key feature that has changed in more fully postmodernist Mexican travel writing is the basic chronotope. This is both in response to key changes in forms of travel (more short trips for leisure purposes) and sensibilities (less clear sense of a goal or purpose), and to the desire for formal innovation with respect to the hackneyed model for traditional travel writing, and it is also, subsequently, the root cause of other changes in the way that postmodernist travel chronicles are written (the amplification of the same structuring principle at all levels of the narrative), and what they may hope to achieve in political terms. Postmodernist Mexican travel chronicles are often written following what, in a reworking of Bakhtin's terminology, I choose to call the 'chronotope of the net' or 'the web' rather than that of the road.[33] In very simple, pragmatic terms, this chronotope eschews traditional, linear, goal-orientated travel, as the narrative opts to cover a series of short trips branching out from a focal point, or a web of criss-crossing journeys, or more circuitous, spiralling journeys, often motivated by the pursuit of a random set of off-beat and often irrelevant goals. However,

---

p. 158). See also Alison Russell's reference to the existence of 'meta-travel writing' in her *Crossing Boundaries: Postmodern Travel Literature* (New York: Palgrave, 2000), p. 19.

32   Holland and Huggan, *Tourists with Typewriters*, p. 158.
33   See Chapter 1.

the 'chronotope of the net' also encompasses more metaphorical, virtual and subjective conceptions of travel, including intertextuality as a form of travel in itself. And in its most extreme form, it encompasses journeys through an 'archive' of past travel writing rather than real journeys in recognisable time and space, in line with Roberto González Echevarría's theorisations about the turn to 'archival fiction' in late twentieth century Latin American narrative.[34] Most importantly, the 'chronotope of the net' avoids the tendency to produce the essentialising and exoticising definitions of the 'Other' that were so closely associated with Bakhtin's 'chronotope of the road' model, since it has the potential to facilitate a more flexible exploration of group identity conceived as the result of a network of non-hierarchical relationships rather than a construct articulated by one individual as the result of the fortuitous and fleeting crossings of his/her path. It is thus most suitable for the exploration of postmodern subjectivities. (Of its postcolonialist potential, more later.)

To grasp the ramifications of the 'chronotope of the net' in more detail, let us turn to a consideration of what other critics, working in a predominantly Anglophone context, have had to say on the subject of postmodernist travel writing. In 'Departures: Travel Writing in a Post-Bakhtinian World' (1992) Sarah C. Blanton summarises the characteristics of what she chooses to call 'post-Bakhtinian', and implicitly postmodernist, travel writing, using as her models the works of Bruce Chatwin, Ryszard Kapuściński, V.S. Naipaul and others.[35] She finds that these travel writers no longer feel that their own journey is

---

34   Roberto González Echevarría, *Myth and Archive: A Theory of Latin American Narrative* (Cambridge: Cambridge UP, 1990), pp. 142–86. For more on González Echevarría's theory of 'archival fictions', see Chapter 6 in this study.

35   Sarah C. Blanton, 'Departures: Travel Writing in a Post-Bakhtinian World' (unpublished doctoral thesis, University of South Florida, 1992), pp. 63–4. Blanton makes it clear that 'post-Bakhtinian' travel writing also responds to the conditions of postmodernity.

I should also like to acknowledge here my debt to Blanton's thesis in the elaboration of my own argument regarding the 'chronotope of the net'. Blanton's work views postmodern travel writing through the prism of Bakhtininan thought in general – questions of dialogism, carnival and also chronotope – in order to explore the representation of self and other in such work. However, although

substantial enough to be classed as travel writing *per se*. Other more recent critics of postmodernist travel writing such as Patrick Holland and Graham Huggan, and Alison Russell reiterate this feeling – the postmodern travel writer tends to express a loss or dissolution of self and a sense of exhaustion, both literal and metaphorical.[36] In terms of what postmodernist travel writing actually consists of, as a result of the diminished role and destabilised identity of the active first-person narrator, such travel writers, according to Blanton, tend to turn to the more subjective, 'circular', inner journeys of dream and memory, to imaginative journeys in time, and to the establishment of a dialogue with other narratives (history and fiction) to flesh out their accounts. In the present tense of their journey they tend to establish a dialogue with other real subjects, or at least an exchange of gazes.

Increased focus on issues of subjectivity, Blanton continues, also leads to a breakdown in the need for chronology, and the dependency on other people's stories, relayed via dialogue, quotation or paraphrase, further destabilises chronological ordering. These travel books also display a degree of uncertainty in their presentation of material, blurring the borders between fact and fiction: there is no desire to produce a 'totalising', coherent, authoritative narrative. Using Bakhtinian terms, Blanton asserts that this kind of travel writing is 'carnivalised' and she concludes that in this topsy-turvy genre, self and other are no longer discrete, diametrically-opposed entities, with the latter subjected to the former's gaze of 'Western authority' only.[37] Rather, authors of such texts are in a better position to demonstrate the 'interconnectedness' of self and world, and respond more closely (even if not in a literal fashion) to the shifting boundaries and identities of the postmodern world.[38] (And, although Blanton does not spell this out, this postmodern world is also quite clearly a postcolonial one.)

---

    she discusses the 'chronotope of the road' model, she does not identify the 'chronotope of the net' as such.

36   Holland and Huggan, *Tourists with Typewriters*, pp. 158, 202; Alison Russell, *Crossing Boundaries*, pp. 8–9.

37   Blanton, 'Departures', p. 68.

38   See also Russell, *Crossing Boundaries*, p. 11.

On the level of the text, such postmodernist travel narratives acknowledge the inevitability of intertextuality, and aim simply to explore this sense of a 'web' of intertextual relationships in their work.[39] And it is here that this definition of 'post-Bakhtinian' travel writing coincides perfectly with the 'chronotope of the net' paradigm for postmodernist travel writing advanced above – postmodernist travel writing is defined by its literal and metaphorical exploitation of 'nets' and 'webs' as devices for advancing the narrative and revealing the workings of the contemporary (postmodern for some; postcolonial for most, albeit in different ways) world.[40] As Iain Chambers in his *Border Dialogues: Journeys in Postmodernity* (1990) has put it,

> Innocence has been replaced by the ironic mode, induced by the challenge of complexity; my sense of place and position has given way to the uncertainties of an ex-centred voice. Within that limit I acquire a certain freedom. For although the speaking subject may well now be decentred it is certainly not dismissed. On the contrary, more aware of my limits, I become more self-conscious, more situated, more sensitive to my particular place in a differentiated world. No longer able to speak in the name of the 'others', to assume their voices and experiences and reduce their histories to mine, a previous monologue, spoken in the name of reason, theory, politics or 'mankind' (*sic*) is transformed into the diverse possibilities of dialogue. Cast into the uncertain outcome of this worldly exchange, an assumed intellectual unity – political, cultural, ethnical, patriarchal, Eurocentric – shatters against the complex structures, networks, cultures and societies in which different voices, histories and languages seek connections, sense, hope, a future, an existence.[41] (author's editorial comment)

---

39   Blanton, 'Departures', p. 64.
40   Donatella Mazzoleni has also examined the figures of the 'web' and the 'spiral' as the most appropriate means for approaching the diaphanous body of the (post-) metropolis ('The City and the Imaginary', trans. by John Koumantarakis, in *Space and Place: Theories of Identity and Location*, ed. by Erica Carter, James Donald and Judith Squires [London: Lawrence & Wishart, 1993], pp. 296–300).
41   Iain Chambers in his *Border Dialogues: Journeys in Postmodernity* (London: Routledge, 1990), p. 104.

The Postmodern and the Postcolonial

Much of the above analysis of Mexican/Latin American postmodernism seems to hint at a possible postcolonialist compatibility. In particular, the general tendency in Mexican postmodernism to favour a return to story telling, particularly to stories from the margins, and the avoidance of totalising, authoritarian projects and values sit comfortably with the political project of a Latin American postcolonialist sensibility that also wants to give voice to the subaltern and to challenge Western rationality and hegemony. Nevertheless, the use of such features as postmodern irony might seem to hamper the more clearly political agenda of postcolonialist writing. How then might postcolonialism and postmodernism work together in a productive manner?

For some critics, the two –isms are antithetical. As Ato Quayson argues in his authoritative essay, 'Postcolonialism and Postmodernism', for critics such as Kumkum Sangari or Helen Tiffin 'the postmodern is part of an ensemble of the hierarchizing impulse of Western discourses, and [...] even though it hints at pluralism and seems to favor an attack on hegemonic discourses, it is ultimately apolitical and does not feed into larger projects of emancipation' such as those that postcolonialist discourse might seek to endorse.[42] Thus, any suggestion that the two might combine would 'disempower the postcolonial'.[43] Furthermore, postmodernism tends to focus on the superficiality of image culture and multiple subject positions, whereas postcolonialism's main dimension is the question of agency and representation.[44]

Nevertheless, other critics do concede that the postmodern and the postcolonial may work together towards similar objectives, and that this has occurred most notably in the field of literature, for example in works of magical realism. Quayson notes the work of Linda Hutcheon and Steve Connor in this respect,[45] and his own conclusions

---

42   Ato Quayson, 'Postmodernism and Postcolonialism', in *A Companion to Postcolonial Studies*, ed. by Henry Schwarz and Sangeeta Ray (Oxford: Blackwell, 2000), p. 87.
43   Quayson, 'Postmodernism and Postcolonialism', p. 87.
44   Quayson, 'Postmodernism and Postcolonialism', pp. 100–01.
45   Quayson, 'Postmodernism and Postcolonialism', p. 88.

also point towards the productive combination of the two -isms: postmodernist aesthetics and narrative strategies put at the services of a postcolonialist political agenda.[46] In Latin America, one might add, such a postcolonialist political agenda might specifically single out postmodernism/postmodernity as something to resist, all the while making use of postmodernist literary strategies in which to couch the terms of its dissent.

If we thus allow that the combination of the postmodernist with the postcolonialist may exist in Latin American literature, with respect to the current study of Mexican travel writing, what we need to explore is how postmodernist travel chronicles – ones that follow the 'chronotope of the net' model – use that same chronotope to express a more or less postcolonialist stance. If we look back at the characteristics of the 'chronotope of the net' listed above, it is quite clear that such postmodernist travel writing does have postcolonialist applications. In addition to the postcolonialist potential of Mexican postmodernist writing in general (the privileging of voices from the margins of society and the lack of totalising, authoritarian projects and values), one should particularly note the 'chronotope of the net''s ability to avoid producing imperialist essentialising and exoticising definitions of the 'Other' in preference for the exploration of more egalitarian networks of relationships based on dialogue and the exchange of gazes.

Nevertheless, it should also be noted that the vast majority of the references from the above section on postmodernist travel writing were taken from criticism of Anglophone travel writing – the work of Blanton, Holland and Huggan, Russell and Chambers. But does this mean that Mexican postmodernist travel writing is just the same as that produced in the English language and that its postcolonialist applications are identical? Surely the way that a postmodernist/postcolonialist Mexican travel writer approaches the genre cannot be the same as that of someone such as Bruce Chatwin or Paul Theroux? It is true that there is nothing inherent in the 'chronotope of the net' model that prevents a metropolitan writer from using it, and, indeed, some metropolitan writers do wish to express postcolonialist sensibilities (see

---

46 Quayson, 'Postmodernism and Postcolonialism', pp. 106–08.

Iain Chambers' comments quoted earlier in this chapter).[47] However, what I want to argue here is that technically 'postcolonial' writers – in this case Mexican ones – choose to use this particular chronotope's ability to combine the postmodern and the postcolonial in order to reconcile themselves with such a pervasive and persuasive vehicle for imperialist discourse – it allows them to produce travel writing without feeling that they have become apologists for imperialism in the process. The remainder of this study is dedicated to examining in detail three examples of postmodernist travel chronicles in order to explore the different approaches that these writers take – the different ways in which they conform to the model of the 'chronotope of the net' – and the different ways in which their work combines the postmodern and the postcolonial.

47 It is also true that there are Anglophone writers from the now decolonised nations of the British Empire who might undertake to produce travel writing ('countertravel writing') that is, indeed, almost identical in form and purpose to that produced by contemporary Mexican writers (Holland and Huggan, *Tourists with Typewriters*, especially section entitled 'Countertravel writing and postcoloniality', pp. 47–65).

CHAPTER 4
Postmodernist or Postcolonialist?
Juan Villoro's *Palmeras de la brisa rápida*

> The literature of travel has become measly, the standard opening that farcical nose-against-the-porthole view from the plane's tilted fuselage. The joke-opening, that straining for effect, is now so familiar it is nearly impossible to parody. [...] There is nothing much to say about most aeroplane journeys. Anything remarkable must be disastrous, so you define a good flight by negatives: you didn't get hijacked, you didn't crash, you didn't throw up, you weren't late, you weren't nauseated by the food.[1]

> In fact the conception of a trip without any objective and which is, as a result, endless, only develops gradually for me. I reject the picturesque tourist round, the sights, even the landscapes (only their abstraction remains, in the prism of scorching heat). [...]
> The only question in this journey is: how far can we go in the extermination of meaning, how far can we go in the non-referential desert form without cracking up and, of course, still keep alive the esoteric charm of disappearance? A theoretical question here materialized in the objective conditions of a journey which is no longer a journey and therefore carries with it a fundamental rule: aim for the point of no return.[2]

When acclaimed writer and journalist Juan Villoro (né 1956) was commissioned in 1988 to write the first travel chronicle for Alianza Editorial Mexicana's new series of travel literature, he felt that he was being asked to reinvent the travel chronicle *ab ovo*.[3] The metatext of his chronicle, *Palmeras de la brisa rápida: un viaje a Yucatán* (1989), gives a full account of the paucity of valid role models as well as other

---

1   Paul Theroux, *The Old Patagonian Express: By Train through the Americas* [1979] (Harmondsworth: Penguin, 1980), pp. 12–13.
2   Jean Baudrillard, *America* [1986], trans. by Chris Turner (London: Verso, 1996), pp. 9–10.
3   The commissioning editors obviously saw an opportune moment for the revival of the travel chronicle, even if individual authors did not.

problems encountered with respect to both form and content. This also includes a significant number of comments about what, for him, is the problematic role of intertextuality as subject matter in contemporary travel chronicles. Nevertheless, features such as Villoro's use of metatext and intertext, together with the remaining subject matter of the chronicle (tourism in the Yucatan Peninsula and its effects on Yucatecan daily life), combine to produce a seminal example of what a postmodernist Mexican travel chronicle might be.

What follows in this chapter is a detailed exploration of how Villoro reinvents the Mexican travel chronicle in the late 1980s: how what he comes up with fits with – even sets a precedent for – the 'chronotope of the net' model and how it responds to the postmodern in both form and content. Indeed, it was originally conceived of as a piece that was exclusively interested in the question of postmodernism as it relates to Villoro's work and that studied Villoro as really just another travel writer in the canon of world travel writing; a contemporary of Paul Theroux, Bruce Chatwin, Jean Baudrillard and others. However, in the context of the current study, I ask my reader to bear with me until the final section of the chapter for an exploration of the postcolonialist aspects of the work and how these might combine with the postmodernist ones.

¿El viaje a un estilo?: Metatextuality

Villoro intersperses his narrative with a metatextual discussion of what might reasonably be expected of a travel chronicle written in 'las postrimerías del siglo' (p. 30). After a circumlocutory introduction which establishes a putative reason for his journey, Villoro ostensibly drops the charade and offers a review of his real circumstances:

> Cuando René Solís y Sealtiel Alatriste me propusieron escribir un libro de viajes no me costó trabajo encontrar un destino emocional: Yucatán, el mundo de mi abuela y el lugar donde nació mi madre.[4] [...] Me entusiasmó tanto ir a ese

---

4   The sentimental grandmother connection is startlingly similar to Bruce Chatwin's introduction to *In Patagonia* [1977] (London: Picador, 1979), pp. 5–7. There

'país dentro del país' que olvidé pensar en los retos literarios del asunto. Sólo hasta el día de la partida reparé en que los Grandes Viajes son testimonios del coraje: ahí están los cuadernos congelados de Scott y la caligrafía de Magallanes, modificada por la humedad del naufragio en turno. Aun en pleno siglo XX el viaje literario supone un singular arriesgue: Graham Greene a punto de morir de disentería en Tabasco, Frigyes Karinthy tomando notas con el cráneo abierto[5] o Saul Bellow discutiendo todos los temas espinosos del Cercano Oriente. Así las cosas, un viaje a Yucatán parece demasiado plano. Como que faltan trincheras, enfermedades, zonas en disputa, el Ayatola iracundo, el terrible mosquito.[6]

This might be read as a red-herring set up to distract the reader's attention from the fact that Villoro took the travel grant and had a very nice holiday, but could not really be bothered to complete his assignment, all this achieved by paradoxically drawing the reader's attention to the fact. Or it might be the formulaic display of self-consciousness without which Villoro feels he will not be considered modernist, let alone postmodernist. However, these disruptive statements might genuinely be an honest acknowledgement that with the commission for a revived Mexican travel chronicle he has been set a nigh-on impossible task. Good, old-fashioned travels and adventures are increasingly difficult to find, especially when one's destination is within one's own country, and most renowned today for being a tourist's paradise, over-exposed to all those technological and sociological features of (post)modern society which have threatened the travel chronicle's existence.

Nevertheless, it is not just the content of the travel chronicle in a postmodern era (matters such as the journey's purpose, means of conveyance, itinerary, and the search for novelty, adventure or even reality) which gives Villoro trouble: spaced at intervals throughout the text he includes metatextual white flags to cover a number of the traditional base elements of the travel chronicle's composition:

---

    are other significant similarities with Chatwin's travel writing in Villoro's fragmentary structure and in his use of history.

5   Frigyes Karinthy wrote *A Journey Round my Skull* (1939), the narrative of a journey from Budapest to Stockholm to have a brain tumour operated on, without general anaesthetic.

6   Juan Villoro, *Palmeras de la brisa rápida: un viaje a Yucatán* (Alianza Editorial Mexicana, 1989), p. 29. All subsequent quotations are from this edition and are indicated parenthetically in the text.

the construction of the active first-person narrator's character; the description and/or reconstruction of people, places and events; and issues of interpretation and ascription of significance. This type of metatextual problem would appear to be a backed-up reaction to the modernist crisis in Realist representation.

Villoro's metatext ironically foregrounds problems concerning verisimilitude, authority, and the lack of meaningful sign systems in an attempt to address, if not overcome, the hurdles of modernism. With respect to verisimilitude he cites Carlos Castaneda's *The Teachings of Don Juan* (1968) as a circumspect example of how linguistic tropes (such as the expression of incredulity, or the stereotypical image or commonplace) can create the effect of believable, Realist narrative without necessarily conveying the truth (p. 110). Villoro, however, depicts himself as struggling to stick to the truth: 'el cronista va demasiado rápido, distingue un arquetipo antes que una gente' (pp. 40–41). He repeatedly shows his reader that he is at pains to keep the pace of his narration compatible with our expectations of Realist narrative, despite the antiquated notions of composition that this supposes: 'Desde que Joyce agobió a Leopold Bloom con un día que no resistiría ni un medallista de decatlón, la literatura sólo es moderna si tiene un desorden temporal. Volvamos al anticuado tiempo lineal' (pp. 51–52).[7]

As a source of authority in the text, Villoro queries his own certainties, and his ability to convey them through the medium of language: 'Parto de la base de que mi propia opinión es falible, insegura, y me burlo un poco de ella'.[8] He also does not feel that, for want of more substantial subject matter, he has the authority to offer himself as an interesting subject for the chronicle: 'La sensación de estar en una ciudad tan historiada reforzó mi idea de escribir un viaje literario, es decir personal. Sin embargo la personalidad no siempre es tan extensa

---

7   Nevertheless, it might also be argued that, '[t]he fictions of linearity and chronology function as the truth of travel narrative', or rather that what Villoro hangs onto as a guarantor of truth is simply another fiction (paraphrase of the ideas of Mary Louise Pratt, in David E. Johnson, '"Writing in the Dark": The Political Fictions of American Travel Writing', *American Literary History*, 7:1 [1995], 6).
8   Personal interview with the author, 19 February 1996.

como uno quisiera' (p. 57), particularly if one aspires to be a 'viajero sentimental' who tries not to seek out personal adventure, but to just let life happen (p. 40).⁹ Although, as he notes, 'A diferencia de las guías, las crónicas no proponen un estilo de viaje sino el viaje a un estilo' (pp. 57–58), he feels that the journey to a style of writing is dependent on his personality, and hence something to which he cannot aspire. Nevertheless, he immediately backtracks, hankering after a more old-fashioned type of travel writing, one less dependent on the personality of the author and more dependent on the role of the author as a figure of authority:

> Apenas me convencí de esto [escribir una crónica personal], opté por el recurso contrario. Ya no me importó que la ciudad estuviera mil veces descrita. ¡Al diablo la personalidad y sus vanidades! Pensé en las virtudes de los datos llanos, agua que corre sobre piedras lisas. (p. 58)

Finally, Villoro notes that 'el siglo XX ha inventado los símbolos vacíos' (p. 64): the ability to create and sustain meaning is permanently undermined. To accentuate this sense of emptiness and linguistic inadequacy that the metatext of *Palmeras* exudes, Villoro's favourite stylistic devices are the simile and the understatement. The simile displays a great suspicion towards the symbolic register (metaphor), and the transcendental nature of language that this implies, by keeping all interpretative options in a state of suspension, while also revelling in its own heavy-handed, pedestrian nature. Understatement, an ironic trope, puts a permanent check on the writer's power to utter clear statements and betrays an underlying inability to say anything. Nevertheless, Villoro's use of language is not a modernist *mise-en-abîme* of meaning: he has an irrepressible desire to tell stories, no matter how fraught the circumstances. The previous quotation ('Apenas me convencí...') also demonstrates his desire for a type of language which does hold meaning fast, and which can tolerate metaphor.

---

9   Villoro also chose not to return to the Yucatan after Hurricane Gilbert in September 1988, stipulating that, on a level of personal experience, his trip should be a 'viaje repetible' (personal interview).

In a few brief sentences, then, Villoro offers the epistemological crisis of modernism to his readers and largely dismisses it. The issue of representation is not so very problematic for Villoro; it is the reality of his circumstances which causes him most of his problems in writing a present-day travel chronicle. Other metatextual remarks attest to these more postmodern problems. He repeatedly comments that contemporary Yucatan has little to offer by way of novelty or adventure: it has already been 'done to death' by previous travel writers, and by the literature of tourism that its major industry generates. Furthermore, reality in the peninsula is compromised by this tourist industry that corrupts whatever it touches, turning everything into a spectacle of reality. Ironically exaggerating his lack of subject matter, Villoro notes that Yucatan is also a place of inherent inactivity: 'en el Paseo Montejo nada es tan vulgar como un suceso' (p. 67); the strength of the sun appears to impede his descriptions: 'el calor aconsejaba ahorrar palabras' (p. 36). Not even the cockroaches will oblige him with any activity: 'nunca he estado en el trópico sin tener escaramuzas con insectos; por lo visto escribir un libro es el mejor repelente' (p. 194). He concludes on the subject of elusive, unreliable reality by paraphrasing Nabokov: 'esta palabra ya sólo dice algo si va entre comillas' (p. 56).

The bottom-line when it comes to the purpose of the journey in *Palmeras* is that Villoro has been commissioned to write a travel chronicle of a literary nature. The sense of quest common to the vast majority of traditional travel writing the world over is thus replaced by that of a random selection of goals. Villoro recognises the fact of his literary commission on a number of occasions: 'No estaba ahí por gusto' (p. 40); 'No estaba en el mejor estado para iniciar la ruta Puuc, pero el libro no se podía detener en la página 107' (p. 107). In fact his references to the material conditions of publication are also a complicit nod to the fact that he cannot be a truly independent traveller since he is tied to the postmodern marketplace by a commission.[10] Villoro

---

10   Holland and Huggan also note the ironic complicity of postmodern travel books with the marketplace (Patrick Holland & Graham Huggan, *Tourists with Typewriters: Critical Reflections on Contemporary Travel Writing* [Ann Arbor: U of Michigan P, 1998], p. 198).

reacts by offering two other purposes for his journey: the personal quest (the traveller going in search of lost roots and personal identity), plus a complementary documentary travel motive (an up-to-date overview of postnational Yucatecan identity), including a literary-history travel option (travel in the footsteps of previous travel writers). Among so many motives for travel, any *leitmotif* of quest will necessarily be obscured. The reader is lost in the random selection of Yucatecan daily life, and this is intentional. There is deliberately no strong sense of progression to a goal, material or abstract, but to a whole network of off-beat goals.

Furthermore, Villoro's trip, like those made by so many contemporary Mexican travel chroniclers, consists in a plane journey to another urban centre outside of the Federal District, followed by a series of short trips (by car or bus) out from that point. And it is not only the structure but the mode of transport which poses a problem for a traditional, linear, quest-orientated travel narrative: plane travel is not considered worth narrating, and the ensuing trips constitute more of a network or web than an itinerary.[11] With no sense of progression towards a goal, be it a recondite place or the completion of a personal feat, the chronological narration of the chronicle becomes arbitrary or irrelevant, and the point of continuing to narrate the journey suffers an equal fate. The structure of the chronicle tends towards the assemblage of fragments of narrative with little or no link between them.

Villoro's comments on the pointlessness of narrating plane journeys echo those of Paul Theroux in *The Old Patagonian Express* (1979) quoted as the first epigraph to this chapter:

> En los antiguos viajes el medio de transporte era un primer acceso a la aventura: el barco a punto de zozobrar, el tren descarrilado, el asalto a la diligencia. Para quien viaja en avión, la única posibilidad de combinar el riesgo con la supervivencia

---

11 One particularly perceptive reader review of Villoro's text posted on Amazon.com's website comments that 'es un viaje que siempre se desvía del sitio a donde al parecer pretende llegar. Narra una red, no un itinerario' (Fabrizio [Mexico], 30 April 2000, http://www.amazon.com/exec/obidos/tg/detail/-/9686001948/qid=1108128196/sr=8-2/ref=sr_8_xs_ap_i2_xgl14/104-1683169-0902342?v=glance&s=books&n=507846, accessed 12 March 2005).

> es el aerosecuestro. Pero entonces el libro ya sólo puede tratar del secuestro. El rehén es un personaje excesivo que pierde interés apenas lo liberan. ¿A quién le interesa que luego visite una pirámide? (p. 29)[12]

And the conception of Villoro's travel chronicle is only slightly more purposeful and meaningful and the structure only slightly more chronologically orientated than that of Jean Baudrillard's extreme experience of Los Angeles' 'network of thoroughfares' in *America* (1986), quoted as the second epigraph to this chapter. As Villoro has commented, 'La estructura es totalmente fragmentaria de manera que tú no puedes trazar una historia; no hay una historia real en el libro [sino] un sentido de unidad y de conjunto [que se consigue] por el tono, por la atmósfera'.[13] He clutches at scraps of narratable reality in order to create 'un álbum de imágenes dispersas' (p. 54), a new non-authoritarian collage of the imagined community of the Yucatan Peninsula. Villoro's text thus displays many of the basic characteristics of the 'chronotope of the net', as discussed in Chapter 3.

Villoro also constantly mediates his experience and knowledge of Yucatecan reality through other genres and media. He only gets up steam for some good old story-telling when he is telling other people's (hi)stories; that is to say, when narrating an already mediated reality, related to him by other, more qualified, chroniclers of Yucatan whose names he withholds until the end of the chronicle. Furthermore, he repeatedly offers these (hi)stories as narratable through lens of another (mass) medium – the cinema, the popular press, or photography – thus diminishing the sense of his appropriating them as material for a travel chronicle. (Again, this show of abdication of authorial control is consistent with the possibility afforded by the 'chronotope of the net' for facilitating the exploration of group identity as a network of

---

12   The similarities between Theroux's and Villoro's writing are also extensive. For a perceptive overview of Theroux's self-reflexive literary travel writing see Terry Caesar's 'The Book in the Travel: Paul Theroux's *The Old Patagonian Express*', *Arizona Quarterly Review*, 46:2 (1990), 101–10; and Elton Glaser's 'The Self-Reflexive Traveler: Paul Theroux on the Art of Travel and Travel Writing', *The Centennial Review*, 33:3 (1989), 193–206.

13   Personal interview.

non-hierarchical relationships.) And finally, Villoro tries to distance himself from what reality he encounters; a choice which is also clear in his stance as a passive 'viajero sentimental'. If reality is going to be evasive, Villoro will react by evading it.

With reference to questions of stylistics, Villoro's metatext seems to hanker for a pre-modernist type of travel chronicle, albeit without dropping the modernist recourse that is the metatext itself. Nevertheless, with reference to the material conditions of the journey, the metatext acknowledges a certain postmodernity at play; a postmodernity that has consequences for the way the journey can be narrated. Yet it is precisely the conflicting nature of the metatext's comments which makes it into a postmodernist metatext – it does not offer a stable position from which self-referential criticism of the genre may be made. Instead, it highlights the lacunae of the text and duplicitously attempts to stand in for them; it offers a critique of what a contemporary travel chronicle should be and then makes a show of opting not to follow its own advice; and it destabilises the narrative without ceasing to tell stories.

¿*Un estilo de viaje?*: Intertextuality

Villoro's treatment of intertextuality complements these observations on his use of metatext. Villoro comments in his metatext that he wants to find a new style in which to write travel chronicles, rather than suggest a style of travel for his reader to emulate. Nevertheless, the intertextual practice of travelling in the footsteps of previous travellers and travel writers seems to be a permanent imposition of 'un estilo de viaje'; one which also places limitations on the author's search for a new style of travel writing.[14] Where can a contemporary travel writer go to avoid the footsteps of his predecessors? And how can he or she describe and narrate the experience in terms which are substantially different from those of previous travel chronicles? Intertextuality, then, would appear

---

14   In interview Villoro contradicted himself, claiming that his chronicle offered both a 'viaje a un estilo' and 'una propuesta de un tipo de viaje'. This reversibility of positions is perhaps yet another indicator of the postmodernist nature of the text.

to pose one of the most serious hindrances to the creation of radically new travel chronicles, threatening to deprive them of both original style and content.

It is, however, inevitable that intertextuality should remain a part of the travel chronicle as the generic definition of the practice becomes more diffuse: it has always been one of the defining characteristics of the *literary* travel chronicle. Villoro thus selects intertextual relationships which give him some critical leverage on his sense of lack of real experience; and which, although at times threatening to swamp the new chronicle, help provide it with the means to define itself in a new era.

For Villoro, intertextuality is a game. Moreover, literature in general is a game. In '¡Hombre en la inicial!', his brief chronicle on how he became a writer, Villoro plays on an extended metaphor between baseball, voyages of discovery and literature, asking, '¿Cómo pasamos de un libro a otro, quién tiene el mapa de todo el archipiélago, las bases dispersas que forman nuestro juego?'[15] His use of intertextuality is at once a voyage of discovery and a game of literary dexterity.

Villoro comments in his metatext on his desire to avoid what has already been written (pp. 57–58), yet faced with a lack of anything more interesting, more personal to narrate, the 'estilo de viaje' of nineteenth-century archaeological travel writers such as John Lloyd Stephens proves inescapable. After his discussion of the writing of 'grandes viajeros' worldwide which occupies him on his way to Benito Juárez airport (p. 29), he goes on to say that, 'En ese momento en que la gente bebía cafés desteñidos en la sala de espera, mi mayor problema se llamaba John Lloyd Stephens' (p. 30). Villoro then outlines the adventures, discoveries and general heroism of Stephens and the artist Frederick Catherwood on their journeys to explore the archaeological sites of the Yucatan Peninsula, recorded in *Incidents of Travel in Yucatan* (1843), and indicates that as a 'cronista posterior' the best he can hope for is to look for traces of Stephens (and Catherwood) in Yucatan, rather than of the ancient Maya themselves:

---

15 In Juan Villoro, *Los once de la tribu: crónicas* (Aguilar, 1995), p. 20.

> De las muchas cosas que vio [Stephens], la que más le intrigó fue una pequeña mano roja que se repetía en grutas, templos, casas y pirámides. Acaso por ser una marca tan modesta, la mano roja le hacía pensar en la grandeza de los antiguos moradores de Uxmal, Labná y Chichén Itzá. Yo iba a viajar con la misma sensación de desmesura. Entre las manos rojas de los mayas siempre vería la sombra de Stephens. (p. 31)

Just as Stephens imagined the images of the red hands as 'welcome' signs which brought the past into contact with his present, Villoro finds the mass-produced copies of Catherwood's engravings as welcome signs in his hotel bedroom in Mérida (p. 35); a ubiquitous icon of a past age of adventure travel in Yucatan.

As a 'cronista posterior' to Stephens and Catherwood, and to the many illustrious travel writers who have written on Yucatan since (Sir Eric S. Thompson and others), Villoro formats his descriptions of places of interest as a commentary on previous texts and drawings. Typically, these places of interest rarely live up to the expectations created by the 'grandes viajeros': 'Las delicadas configuraciones que había visto en los grabados de Catherwood carecían de relieve bajo el sol acuchillante' (p. 115). Reality is continually mediated or displaced by these authoritative texts and images. Villoro does not even see the monuments themselves so much as their on-going circulation as simulacra:

> En Sayil presencié una escena que captura la situación de los mayas actuales. Un artesano tallaba algo que anunció como caoba y parecía triplay, pero lo sorprendente no era el material sino el modelo que usaba: ¡una reproducción en un libro de Sir Eric S. Thompson! Supongo que así se cierra el círculo antropológico: el estudioso como objeto de estudio de los estudiados. (p. 112)

For Villoro the interplay of texts and engravings is the reality of contemporary Yucatan.

Villoro is not *overtly* critical of Stephens. Indeed, Stephens's account of Yucatan is well-informed on an encyclopaedic range of subjects concerning the peninsula, and, all things considered, it is also reasonably liberal. He is admittedly complicit with on-going colonial practices and privileges in the region in that he uses the indigenous Maya to carry both himself and his luggage, and he also witnesses scenes of peons being disciplined with anthropological *sangfroid*, but he does record the situation, and the massive success of his writing did contribute to knowledge and action on human rights abuses in nineteenth-century Yucatan. Certainly Justo Sierra O'Reilly's almost immediate translation of the chronicle (published in 2 vols, 1848 and 1850 respectively) was at pains to try to cover up Stephens's revelations of the darker side of life in the Yucatan (*Palmeras*, p. 71).

Villoro also uses the example of the annotated text (Sierra O'Reilly's translation of Stephens) to underscore the transitory and only partial authority of all travel chronicles, his included ('De manera semejante, estas crónicas podrían estar enmendadas por algún parroquiano del Express' [p. 72][16]). There is a process of transculturation at work: the Yucatecans simultaneously absorb and distort the texts of their reality. Furthermore, the intertextual presence of Stephens and Catherwood in Villoro's travel chronicle reveals the constructed nature of all claims to knowledge and reality, and it underscores Villoro's desire not to offer his reader an authoritarian, 'totalising' form of narrative, thus revealing the postmodernist objectives of his intertext.[17]

This travel in the footsteps of previous travel writers is Villoro's 'estilo de viaje'. It does not take the form of an historically accurate reenactment of Stephens's journey or of a conscientious chronologically-ordered retracing of steps with a view to discovering fresh data about the traveller or his circumstances. Instead, Villoro's actual style of travel is informed by Stephens's in its acknowledgement of its shortcomings: the potential drama of running out of petrol on the road to Teabó, the potential torch-light exploration of the caves at Loltún, the potential encounter with the cockroach in Mérida.[18] These shortcomings have a parallel function to that of the lacunae highlighted by the metatext. Villoro's literary style is more obviously informed by Stephens's in its plea for linear temporality, a narrative style which advances apace with displacement, and good old story-telling, although, as noted previously, he reserves the right not to follow his

---

16 El Express is a popular café in downtown Mérida.
17 Linda Hutcheon, *The Politics of Postmodernism* (London: Routledge, 1989), p. 24.
18 The reader's review on Amazon.com's website mentioned above also picked up on the fact that Villoro 'se sirve de las ausencias, de su acuciosa percepción de ellas' (Fabrizio (Mexico), 30 April 2000).

own advice. In so doing, his intertext reveals a sense of resignation and an embedded post-consciousness within the contemporary chronicler; at the same time as an awareness that the real journey, the real game, is indeed through literature, not reality. It is a nod to the impossibility of completely original contemporary travel writing. Nevertheless, Villoro also attempts to counterbalance the weight of such grand intertexts of travel writing with his own historiographical reconstructions of the itineraries of undervalued Yucatecans; Yucatecans who demonstrate their adaptability to newer, more postmodern circumstances.

Postmodernity, Post-Tourism and Postmodern Irony

Villoro's intertext offers an illustration of what options are not open to him. If metatext and intertext were all this travel chronicle had to offer, we would have reached the *reductio ad absurdum* of the genre: it suggests a lack of real, first-hand content; a lack of novelty, authenticity, reality. At worst the main body of this text advertises itself as an unhinged series of lightning character sketches, non-events, pseudo-events, personal trivia, and frivolous commentary to fill in the gaps. At best, however, this chronicle may be seen as a collage of different texts, genres, styles, registers, and languages, clearly trademarked as postmodernist writing. It uses and abuses its sources, acknowledging the tradition of travel writing and accepting the challenge in its use of irony, parody and pastiche; it blurs the divisions between fact and fiction; and it renders problematic the telling of stories (the role of the teller) without stopping telling them.[19] As a storyteller Villoro also acknowledges that he is inextricably bound up with postmodernity in his condition as a leisured traveller (a tourist) and hence is limited to an

---

19   See Hutcheon's analysis of postmodern storytelling, *The Politics of Postmodernism*, pp. 47–61. Villoro also deliberately blurs the boundaries of fact and fiction in a particularly novel and destabilising way in his 'imaginary chronicles' (*Tiempo transcurrido: crónicas imaginarias* [FCE, 1993]).

experience of reality which corresponds to his condition. He inevitably finds the postmodern subject on his travels.

Villoro's destination bodes well for an enquiry into the postmodern: Yucatan is a border zone where processes of transculturation and demographic movement are escalated to extreme levels. Because of its long-term isolation from highland Mexico and its consequent openness to foreign influence; because of its nineteenth-century boom in sisal hemp production which attracted international investment to the area; and because of its late twentieth-century experience of 'maquiladoras', 'se ha convertido en una economía fronteriza, como si colindara con los Estados Unidos' (*Palmeras*, p. 178). It is a 'frontera portátil', a 'travelling metaphor' of the Mexico–United States border.[20] In this region, mass tourism and migration are significant forces of postmodern influence, promoting the interaction of different cultures.

Villoro does attempt to seek out the sectors of Yucatecan society ostensibly least exposed to postmodernity: the indigenous Maya communities in remote areas of the peninsula. Nevertheless, even here, he comments only on the superficially postmodern transformations of these people. Maya children beg in three languages and ask the soft-drinks seller, 'Diet coke, ¿ba hux?' ('Have you got any Diet Coke?') (p. 111). Villoro spends rather more time studying the elements of Yucatecan society most exposed to the heightened syncretisms of postmodernity, writing an 'anecdotario' of their (hi)stories, past and present: the itinerant lives of the rock musician Gabriel Ocampo, the once famous chess-player Carlos Torre Repetto (a distant relative to boot), and the transnational businessman Luis Iturbe. He also includes accounts of recent settlers in Yucatan (the Lebanese, ex-residents of Mexico City, and others). Past contact between Yucatecans and the residents of New Orleans and Miami is offered as a positive sign of Yucatan's openness to foreign influence: John Lloyd Stephens and John Kenneth Turner, both United States citizens, made their way in Yucatecan high society with very little difficulty. In present times, the movement

---

20   Villoro, 'La frontera de los ilegales', *Biblioteca de México*, 36 (November-December 1996), 17; and John Kraniauskas, 'Border Issues', *Travesía: The Border Issue*, 3:1–2 (1994), 5.

between Yucatan and Los Angeles of Luis Iturbe in his commercial enterprises, or Gabriel Ocampo in his musical itinerary are viewed positively: they are both enterprising, postmodern Yucatecans. Again, the architecture of the Paseo Montejo or of the henequen estates belongs to a past era of wildly eclectic transculturations: Villoro appreciates the effect, as well as his local guide's ingenuous interpretations. The vernacular architecture of the assembly plant buildings and of the Hotel María Nefertiti in Río Lagartos is an example of Yucatecan syncretism (p. 151), of the local ability to absorb and subvert outside influence. This is postmodernism in a positive sense: Mexican postmodernism; something that Villoro seems particularly predisposed to take in.

Nevertheless, even if Villoro had wanted to avoid postmodernity in the Yucatan peninsula, he suggests that this would have been impossible. He sees the vast majority of Yucatecans as being irreparably altered by the impact of mass tourism on the area. Certainly as a result of exposure to tourism, the ubiquitous hammock sellers in Mérida, the Yucatecan minibus-driver with his 'don de lenguas' (p. 97), the guide to the Hacienda Yaxcopoil, and the Maya who makes reproductions of Thompson engravings all betray signs of adapting to tourism in a way that Villoro finds partly fascinating, partly frustrating. The Yucatecans might be a hotchpotch of multicultural influences but Villoro at least hoped to be able to see them without the imposition of implicitly United States influence. He also slates constructions such as those of the Holiday Inn chain, which no matter how much they might be tailored to suit the individual location, reek of United States imperialism, not of any stimulating postmodern intercultural contact.

The worst example of adaptation to United States tourism has implications for Mexico as a whole. In a café in Mérida local men try to seduce United States tourists, and in so doing, turn themselves into national stereotypes of the type created by generations of foreign or 'extranjerizante' writers and travel writers:

> Era difícil no ver a esos ultralatinos con ojos de D.H. Lawrence, Malcolm Lowry o Carlos Fuentes: se reían como mexicanos, miraban como mexicanos, ligaban como mexicanos, sus pies ya se mezclaban con las sandalias arenosas y las alpargatas griegas; para seguirlos viendo hubiera sido necesario cambiar de pasaporte; eran tan insoportablemente mexicanos como zapatistas con ates de Morelia en las cananas. (p. 42)

These Mexican men actually appear to be experiencing a form of post-national identity, in Monsiváis' terms, or of hyper-Mexicanness in Baudrillard's (they are 'the ecstatic membrane that has come away from the real object', like a Polaroid photo of real Mexicans).[21] However, Villoro laments this as a loss of identity caused by the presence of United States tourists, rather than as a positive postmodern adaptation of national identity under the pressures of globalisation.[22]

If Villoro's study of his target culture generally reveals a positive attitude to the 'autochthonous' postmodernity he uncovers, the fact that a considerable amount of this postmodernity is propelled by the tourist industry provokes him to offer quite a different image of tourists. Villoro displays throughout a consciousness of Yucatan's current vocation:

> Para quien viaja en grupo, Yucatán es el avión, el Holliday Inn (*sic*) decorado con los mejores muebles de plasticuero y terciopana, la cafetería que ofrece la jugosa hamburguesa con tocino y queso amarillo, el camión con aire acondicionado para ir a las ruinas, es decir, todo lo necesario para que uno se sienta como en Florida sólo que con pirámides. (p. 35)

'Quien' here refers implicitly to citizens of the United States, and Villoro underlines the fact that when United States citizens travel *en masse* they take their lifestyle with them; a lifestyle that Baudrillard has pointed out as being the crux of (United States) postmodernity. Villoro sees this kind of postmodernity as an imperial imposition in Mexico.

Fighting back against this imperialism, Villoro targets these US tourists as the butt of his humour: the fat woman on the bus to Chichén Itzá who claims that the lack of air conditioning is '*the only real thing*' (p. 96, author's italics); the multi-culturally dressed girls in the Café Express; the recently-operated plastic surgery patients in the Museo de Antropología; the sunburnt woman in the large black smock at a concert

---

21   Baudrillard, *America*, p. 37.
22   See Daniel Cooper Alarcón, *The Aztec Palimpsest: Mexico in the Modern Imagination* (Tucson: University of Arizona Press, 1997) for a perceptive study of the way in which contemporary Mexican national identity has been shaped by foreign travel writers working within the 'Mexico as infernal paradise' paradigm, and more recently by the adaptations to that paradigm of the tourist industry.

of popular Yucatecan music are the exclusive subjects of Villoro's use of the grotesque:

> La norteamericana sentada frente a mí llevaba el único huipil negro que vi en Yucatán. Su atuendo luctuoso era ideal para quien padece una maldición, y ella la padecía. Su piel estaba aquejada de mal de pinto y de una alarmante proliferación de pústulas y llagas. (p. 77)

And Villoro's negativity towards United States tourism is subsequently extended to include a rejection of postmodernity as a United States imposition, too:

> Al terminar [el concierto] hasta los turistas posmodernos que llegaron con miradas de fin de milenio, vestidos en todos los tonos del negro, tenían los ojos arrasados de lágrimas. Se fueron de prisa, como si hubieran sido víctimas de una traición emocional, en busca de algo que los hiciera reconciliarse con una vida sin sentido. (p. 79)

Nevertheless, even though Villoro is critical of tourism's potential for cross-fertilisations of United States postmodernity, he is also very aware that, in his condition as a traveller writing a chronicle about travel primarily because he has been commissioned to do so, he is indistinguishable from other tourists, whether he likes it or not. Visiting other Mexican communities does not help Villoro to overcome the tourist barrier: the world is, of course, not divided into Mexicans and tourists as he has ironically claimed.[23]

Distressed by the lack of opportunities for action on his post-Stephens trip, Villoro begins protesting that, 'Según todas las probabilidades yo visitaría Yucatán sin operar a nadie de estrabismo ni descubrir sitios arqueológicos; pero si la aventura era imposible, al menos podía viajar sin hacer "turismo"' (p. 35). Yet only hours later, after a preliminary stroll around Mérida and a few observations of other tourists in cafés around town, he returns to his hotel room thinking the opposite:

---

23 Juan Villoro, 'Todos somos gondoleros', *LJS*, 17 May 1998, p. 15.

> Los viajeros aéreos llegan con tobillos de paracaidista. Ya no sabía adónde conducir mis pasos inseguros. Regresé, sintiéndome progresivamente turista. Había caminado con la prisa de otra ciudad; ningún propósito tropical requería esa desmesura. Pensé esto al ver los pasos económicos de los demás paseantes. ¿Adónde podía conducir mi empapada celeridad? A comprar hamacas. Al menos esto juzgó el tercer vendedor que me salió al paso. (pp. 38–39)

He looks like a tourist, despite being Mexican, hence he is one.[24] His choice of writing his journey hardly exempts him from the classification when taken alongside the reading and writing of other tourists in the cafés he visits.

The problem is that travel in the late twentieth century is inseparable from tourism. Being a professional observer of tourists does not look significantly different from being a common or garden sort of tourist, dedicated to life on the pleasure periphery. This is especially true in these days of specialised tours, where all variations on the theme of travel are valid tourist options; where 'A trip to Chichen Itza may be experienced simultaneously as pleasure, education, work, adventure, and time travel'.[25] Grudging acceptance, or even enjoyment, of this situation is what recent sociologists have defined as the post-tourist approach, and this is perhaps the heading under which we can classify Villoro's form of tourism.[26]

---

24 Villoro's healthy, albeit ironic, acknowledgement of his tourist status is unfortunately lost in later chronicles where he attempts to reinstate a clear barrier between the traveller/writer and the tourist (see 'Nada que declarar: Welcome to Tijuana', *Letras Libres*, 17 [May 2000], http://www.letraslibres.com/interna.php?num=&sec=3&art=6314&pag=0, and 'Días robados: delitos crónicos', *Letras Libres*, 34 [October 2001], http://www.letraslibres.com/interna.php?sec=5&art=7047, both accessed 12 March 2005).

25 Cooper Alarcón, *The Aztec Palimpsest*, p. 182.

26 The sociological post-tourist debate starts in Maxine Feifer, *Going Places: The Ways of the Tourist from Imperial Rome to the Present Day* (London: MacMillan, 1985), and is taken up again, with few changes, in John Urry, *The Tourist Gaze: Leisure and Travel in Contemporary Societies* (London: SAGE Publications, 1996). Paul Fussell's post-tourist classification in his anthology of travel writing *The Norton Book of Travel* (New York: Norton, 1987) is a literary boundary post and he makes no reference to Feifer's earlier uses of the term. Fussell's term does not strictly adhere to the limits of what, in other genres and media, has been

The post-tourist firstly 'does not have to leave his or her house in order to see many of the typical objects of the tourist gaze', because they are available through mass media, thus redoubling the framing of the tourist's gaze. Secondly, 'the post-tourist is aware of change and delights in the multitude of choice': he/she may swap from sun bathing to educational museum visits in an instant, and his/her souvenirs may be simultaneously valued as 'pieces of kitsch' and 'socially revealing artefacts'. And thirdly, the post-tourist 'knows that they (*sic*) are a tourist and that tourism is a game, or rather a whole series of games with multiple texts and no single, authentic tourist experience'. He or she 'is above all self-conscious, "cool" and role-distanced'.[27]

The post-tourist's multiple framings of his or her raw material is evident in Villoro's filtering of his text through the prism of other media. The post-tourist's interest in multiple choice and variety translates into Villoro's use of fragmentation and unstable interpretations. The post-tourist's self-consciousness which allows him or her to acknowledge both complicity with, and distance from, tourism reinforces Villoro's need for a metatext. And the post-tourist's awareness that tourism is a game prompts Villoro's use of intertextuality, and, in terms of content, ratifies his narration of futile searches for authentic local culture, and the consequent turn to 'playing the tourist game' where he becomes a tourist of tourism. Alongside, and contradicting, his search for real Yucatecan culture, Villoro chooses at times to 'follow the crowd', to go on an organised tour of Chichén Itzá, for example (pp. 95–103).

But, of course, if Villoro is a post-tourist, so too are some of the tourists whom he comes across on his travels. The fat woman on the bus on the way to Chichén Itzá knows that she is not about to get an authentic, unmediated experience in the ruins. Such tourists might not all be 'cool' or indulge in irony – although the fat woman's comments

---

termed postmodernism, tracing his post-tourists back to the 1920s. In fact the literary histories of 'Touristic Tendencies' and 'Post-Tourism' appear to run apace in Fussell's view: what he actually understands by post-tourism, made manifest in these parallel histories, is anti-tourism. While anti-tourism is no doubt a part of the post-touristic attitude, it is not the whole story according to the sociologists.

27   Paraphrased from Urry, *The Tourist Gaze*, pp. 100–01. This is a summary of Feifer's definition.

about the lack of air conditioning are, in essence, ironic – but they are all undoubtedly aware that they are tourists and that tourism is a game. The difference between tourist and post-tourist is a question of degree, not of mutual exclusivity. It is perhaps an indication of Villoro's brand of irony that he is capable of still being ironic despite the fact that he knows that not even this access to irony will really distinguish him from the tourists who surround him; that there is no sustainable possibility of critical distance.

For better or worse, the mood of postmodernism is ironic:

> In general terms [postmodernism] takes the form of self-conscious, self-contradictory, self-undermining statement. It is rather like saying something whilst at the same time putting inverted commas around what is being said. The effect is to highlight, or 'highlight,' and to subvert, or 'subvert,' and the mode is therefore a 'knowing' and an ironic – or even 'ironic' – one.[28]

Postmodernism is 'knowing'; that is, it somehow needs to display a consciousness of its postmodern status. Even when no irony is apparent, straightforward 'reading for the facts' has ceased to be an option. Postmodernism is a critique of postmodernity which is aware that it cannot entirely separate itself from the postmodernity of its own circumstances of production:

> Postmodernism's distinctive character lies in this kind of wholesale 'nudging' commitment to doubleness, or duplicity. In many ways it is an even-handed process because postmodernism ultimately manages to install and reinforce as much as undermine and subvert the conventions and presuppositions it appears to challenge.[29]

Villoro is inextricably attached to the postmodern in his personal circumstances: his destination, his commission, his status as (post-)tourist. Through irony he provides a critique of postmodernity, challenging it in his parodies of the figure of the United States tourist. Yet, in the instances in which Villoro reveals his complicity with his postmodern circumstances, his irony also reveals itself as postmodernist: it undoes

---

28 Hutcheon, *The Politics of Postmodernism*, p. 1.
29 Hutcheon, *The Politics of Postmodernism*, pp. 1–2.

that critical distance. In so doing this travel chronicle proposes 'un viaje a un estilo posmoderno', one which both emulates and critiques the new cultural paradigm.[30]

The Possibility of a Postcolonialist Reading

Reading Villoro's *Palmeras de la brisa rápida* for signs of postmodernism in form and content is all very well – the postmodern is explicity present in Villoro's text –, but, in focusing only on the postmodern, such a reading obscures another way of reading the chronicle – as a postcolonialist, or more specifically postimperialist, critique of the genre of travel writing as well as of life in late twentieth-century Mexico. Villoro targets both the imperialist tendencies of travel writing and its major exponents in

---

[30] Villoro's travel chronicle, despite causing quite a furore in the Yucatan on account of its (postmodern) irony, has been well received in the literary circles of the capital (see positive reviews by Noé Cárdenas, '"Toma el Llavero, Abuelita"', *Textual*, 2 [June 1989], 52–53; Alberto Román, untitled, *Nexos*, 141 [September 1989], 64–65; Fabrizio Mejía Madrid, 'Diet Coke, ba hux?', *Nexos*, 146 [February 1990], 73–74; and, later, Álvaro Ruiz Abreu, 'Novela de la crisis y crisis de la novela', *Nexos*, 241 [January 1998], 191). The metaphor of the book's title has been taken up and reworked by one critic (Fabienne Bradu, review of Nathalie de Saint Phalle's *Hoteles literarios, viaje alrededor de la tierra*, *Vuelta*, 208 [March 1994], 44); and Villoro's metatextual definition of the travel chronicles of the 'Grandes Viajeros' has been quoted verbatim by another (Jesús R. Cedillo, 'Viajeros en el norte de México', in *Ensayistas de Tierra Adentro*, ed. by José María Espinasa [Fondo Editorial Tierra Adentro (CNCA), 1994], p. 201). And among publishers, the book achieved what its editors had set out to do: revive the tradition of travel chronicling in Mexico. As mentioned earlier in this study, on the basis of Villoro's book, the editors at the CNCA were inspired to commission the works produced in their 'Cuaderno de viaje' series.

Palmeras was reedited by Alfaguara in 2000 although curiously relaunched as if the previous edition had never existed (see anonymous reviews published in *El Informador*, 23 May 2000, http://www.informador.com.mx/lastest/2000/mayo/23May2000/23aro3b.htm and in *Publi.com*, [no date], http://www.publi.com/news/2000/0409/a15.htm, both accessed 12 March 2005).

Mexico and the neo-imperialist nature of globalisation as seen in the workings of the tourist industry in the country.

With respect to his attitude to travel writing as a genre, Villoro's comments in the opening pages of his account concerning the challenges of writing a contemporary travel chronicle reveal some of the same unease with the genre that José Emilio Pacheco expressed when he defined travel writing as 'un género del Norte'.[31] For Villoro, travel writing is typically about 'los Grandes Viajes' which neither he as Mexican writer can aspire to emulate, nor his late twentieth-century, partially (post)modernised country to provide. While such an expression might be considered an example of the trope of 'belatedness' seen in so much contemporary Anglophone travel writing where the lament for real travel is a conservative expression of imperialist nostalgia,[32] Villoro's lament should really be read as ironic. Mexicans, he implies with his list of names of great travellers, were never part of the club, so it is hardly the case that he is too late to be one. Rather Mexico has always been, and – with the rise of mass tourism – still is, the object of the traveller's gaze and Mexicans' view of their country, their ability to know themselves, is still obscured by the views of foreigners. This kind of comment, then, has a postcolonialist agenda. However, the ironic reading that I proposed above is arguably dependent on knowing who Villoro is and what his politics are – otherwise it is simply not ironic. As a Mexican writer who is intensely aware of Mexico's position with respect to the West, he is hardly going to be expressing imperialist nostalgia for the Great Voyages made by Europeans and United States citizens. This is thus a postcolonialist critique of travel writing, but one that is filtered through – perhaps obscured by – the double prism of postmodern irony.

---

31 See the introduction to this study.
32 The term is borrowed from the work of the Latin American anthropologist Renato Rosaldo, glossed by Holland and Huggan in their *Tourists with Typewriters*, pp. 29–30.

Regarding Villoro's travel-writing predecessors in the Yucatan, it is significant that he does not focus on the numerous works of travel writing by other Mexicans who had travelled in the region – José Vasconcelos, Martín Luis Guzmán, Salvador Novo, Octavio Paz, Fernando Benítez, José Revueltas (who had stayed in the same hotel as Villoro in Mérida) or even Mónica Mansour (who had stayed in the same eccentric hotel as him in Río Lagartos).[33] Instead, he deliberately selects John Lloyd Stephens; a travel writer who, although inspired by Humboldt's spirit of scientific enquiry, was also quite clearly part of the 'capitalist vanguard', looking for ways to justify United States imperialist designs in the region.[34]

Villoro repeatedly refers to himself as a 'cronista posterior [a Stephens]'and flags up the 'sensación de desmesura' (p. 31) that he experiences in his travels because of Stephens's works of imperialist adventure and discovery. Although, as I mentioned earlier, Villoro is not *overtly* critical of Stephens, the very fact that he mentions a writer such as Stephens so often is indicative of the way in which he hopes to nudge his reader towards a critical position. Thus, to rework Kwame Anthony Appiah's neat formulation, the post- in 'posterior' is the post- in postcolonial as least as much, if not more so, than it is the post- in postmodern.[35] Furthermore, Villoro's frequent expression of the trope of disappointment, so common in the works of the 'capitalist vanguard' as

33 See bibliography for references to works by these Mexican travel writers. In particular, for José Revueltas's account of the Posada Toledo see his *Obras completas*, 26 vols (Era, 1978–1987), XXV: *Las evocaciones requeridas: memorias, diarios, correspondencia, 1*, prol. by José Emilio Pacheco (1987). p. 291; and for Mónica Mansour's account of the Hotel Nefertiti, see her 'Reconózcase quien pueda', in María Luisa Puga & Mónica Mansour, *Itinerario de palabras* (Folios, 1987), pp. 76–77.

34 Daniel Cooper Alarcón, 'The Ruins of Manifest Destiny: John L. Stephens's *Incidents of Travel in Central America, Chiapas, and Yucatan*', in *A través del espejo: viajes, viajeros y la construcción de la alteridad en América Latina*, ed. by Lourdes de Ita Rubio and Gerardo Sánchez Díaz (Morelia: Instituto de Investigaciones Históricas, Universidad Michoacana de San Nicolás Hidalgo, 2005), pp. 333–42.

35 See Kwame Anthony Appiah, 'Is the Post- in Postmodernism the Post- in Postcolonial?', *Critical Inquiry*, 17:2 (1991), 336–57.

part of the way they managed to discursively construct Latin American as in need of an imperialist overhaul, is more pointedly critical.[36] His account, as I mentioned earlier, is styled on that of Stephens in terms of its expression of its shortcomings and failings – the fact that, for example, certain Mayan ruins did not live up to the clarity of their depiction in Catherwood's engravings – and we should not take such comments at face value – Villoro makes such comments ironically, in order to alert us to the politics of the kind of writer who typically makes such comments. However, the postmodernist flippancy with which Villoro expresses such disappointment also complicates the pontentially postcolonialist critique he is advancing.

With respect to tourism, although Villoro seems to be receptive to what might be identified as an autochthonous kind of Mexican postmodernism, as seen in the wild syncretisms of Mexican culture past and present, and to the postmodern lives of some of the Yucatecans he meets during his trip, he also conflates the practice of tourism, the term 'postmodern' and the United States in a way that suggests that he finds postmodernity and postmodernism of specifically United States provenance and brought to Mexico in the suitcases of United States tourists. This he posits as something to be resisted – for Villoro tourism and postmodernism are both forms of neo-imperialism – and it is this resistance that is essentially postcolonialist, even if, it is also complicated by its postmodernist playfulness, where Villoro recognises his own complicity in such dynamics in his status as (post-)tourist.

More might perhaps be made of other postmodernist aspects of Villoro's chronicle which more clearly help him to achieve a postcolonialist effect. His flaunting of his lack of authorial authority and his presentation of an 'album de imágenes dispersas' both suggest new ways of positing the relationship between traveller and world that are consistent with both postmodernist and postcolonialist positions. There is, thus, clearly a way to read this chronicle that finds Villoro to be producing a postcolonialist critique of imperialist travel writing and of the effects of globalisation, of United States postmodernity,

---

36 Mary Louise Pratt, *Imperial Eyes: Travel Writing and Transculturation* (London: Routledge, 1992), pp. 146–55.

as experienced in Mexico. Nevertheless, the playfulness, the double irony of postmodernism, does threaten at times to obscure the more postcolonialist nature of Villoro's chronicle, thus fuelling concerns expressed by some critics that postmodernism will hamper the political objectives of postcolonialism.

Chapter 5
Virtual Journeys:
Héctor Perea's *México: crónica en espiral*

'Uno – escribió el gran poeta Wallace Stevens – no vive en una ciudad sino en su descripción'. Si esto es cierto poética y sociológicamente, uno se domicilia en el trazo cultural y psicológico integrado por las vivencias íntimas, el flujo de comentarios y noticias, los recuentos de viajeros y las leyendas nacionales e internacionales a propósito de la urbe. También, uno se mueve en el interior de las conversaciones circulares sobre la ciudad, sus virtudes (cuando las hay) y sus defectos (cuando se agota con rapidez la lista de las virtudes).[1]

Igual que las urbes invisibles de Italo Calvino, México es una ciudad imaginaria, cuya historia, más que palparse, se adivina [...]
  De los pasados esplendores de la ciudad de México persisten, empero, las voces de quienes la cantaron, con líricos acentos, cuando era la región más transparente del aire; de quienes la describieron, azorados, cuando a ella llegaron allende el mar océano o la establecieron en lengua latina para darle cabida en las ciudades del mundo o la magnificaron con palabras hiperbólicas y artificiosas; de quienes la puntualizaron en términos científicos; de quienes la liberaron con sus discursos cívicos y sus artículos combativos y la relataron en sus costumbres y sucesos; de quienes hoy la registran, la definen, la inventan y la salvan de la destrucción merced a la palabra. Las voces, en suma, que la han construido letra a letra en la realidad perseverante de la literatura. La nuestra es una ciudad de papel.[2]

The contemporary travel writer who decides to approach Mexico City as the setting for a travel book faces an even more impossible set of problems than those described by Villoro; problems with the genre itself and how it should respond to contemporary times and literary practices, as well as a substantial intensification of the problems associated with the location itself. It is not that 'real' travel is impossible in a specifically urban environment. That major physical displacements constituting

---

[1] Carlos Monsiváis, 'Apocalipsis y utopías', *LJS*, 4 April 1999, p. 2.
[2] Gonzalo Celorio, *México: ciudad de papel* (Tusquets, 1997), pp. 16–17.

travel within an ever-expanding megalopolis such as Mexico City are not only possible but daily necessities for the vast majority of the resident population is something that has already been adequately established by sociologists and anthropologists, chroniclers and historians, novelists and poets. An overview of the multiple faces of travel in the Federal District is provided in the book *La ciudad de los viajeros: travesías e imaginarios urbanos, México, 1940–2000* (1996). In the introduction, Néstor García Canclini makes it clear that, 'La ciudad moderna no es sólo lugar de residencia y de trabajo. Se ha hecho también para viajar: a ella, desde ella y a través de ella'.[3] Indeed, for some commentators, travel is the defining feature of the postmodern megalopolis.[4]

The real problem is that Mexico City is the 'lettered city' *par excellence* and has been the site of intensive chronicling and travel chronicling since the time of the Conquest onwards. The city itself has had an official chronicler since the mid-sixteenth century, and since 1987 the role has been fulfilled by the Consejo de la Crónica de la Ciudad de México, a whole committee of chroniclers. Even in the early days of the *Colonia*, Mexico City was a place where travel to, from, and across the city was an important daily concern. One of the earliest chronicles of the city, written in 1554 by the Spaniard Francisco Cervantes de Salazar, took the format of a tour given by two locals to a visitor from Spain.[5] Almost four centuries later, Salvador Novo's prize-

---

[3] Néstor García Canclini, 'Los viajes metropolitanos', in *La ciudad de los viajeros: travesías e imaginarios urbanos, México, 1940–2000*, ed. by Néstor García Canclini, Alejandro Castellanos and Ana Rosas Mantecón (UAM-Iztapalapa/ Grijalbo, 1996), p. 11.

[4] Juan Villoro notes that, 'Estamos en la *transciudad* que renunció a ser un espacio fijo – la morada, el hábitat, la plaza pública – para admitir el caos como único motor de crecimiento y transformarse en el escenario inabarcable que los topógrafos aéreos llaman "mancha urbana"' ('La ciudad virtual' *LJ*, 28 April 1996, p. 27 [author's italics]). And in another article, basing his argument on those of Klaus R. Scherpe and Paul Virilio, he comments that in Mexico City, 'el paisaje nos excede en tal medida que la única forma de cohesionarlo, de darle sentido, es ir de un lado a otro: funciona *porque* es atravesado' ('La ciudad es el cielo del metro', *Lateral* [March 1995] 17 [author's italics]).

[5] See José Iturriaga de la Fuente, *Anecdotario de viajeros extranjeros en México, siglos XVI–XX*, repr., 4 vols (FCE, 1993–94), II, 52–58.

winning *Nueva grandeza mexicana: ensayo sobre la Ciudad de México y sus alrededores en 1946* gave new vigour to Cervantes de Salazar's format. Once again, the narrator is a local giving a tour of the city to a friend from the provinces:

> Yo iba a disfrutar, durante una semana, el privilegio de servir a mi amigo como guía de turistas; de llevarlo por la ciudad, mostrársela, exhibir mi pericia y mi conocimiento de todos sus secretos frente al asombro de un provinciano que por primera vez la visitaba. Y al propio tiempo, iba yo mismo a paladear la añoranza de la ciudad que recordaba desde hacía muchos años, con el fervor inédito con que mi amigo descubriría – muchas veces al unísono conmigo – su desarrollo, su transformación, su crecimiento.[6]

Since 1946 there have been numerous chroniclers who have situated their narratives in contemporary Mexico City. There are those who seek to recreate lost images of the city through memory (Octavio Paz, Gonzalo Celorio, José Emilio Pacheco and many of the older generation), others who stick firmly to the findings of their investigations (journalists such as Fernando Benítez, Carlos Monsiváis and José Joaquín Blanco), and still others – the youngest of the bunch – who speculate on the future faces of one of the most populous urban centres in the world (Óscar de la Borbolla and Fernando Curiel, for example). And among these chroniclers there are a number who, like Novo, have selected the theme of travel as the most efficient way to approach such a large and idiosyncratic city.[7] There are, indeed, so many chroniclers

---

6   Salvador Novo, *Nueva grandeza mexicana*, intro. by Carlos Monsiváis (CNCA, 1992), p. 21.
7   Recent chronicles of Mexico City which include a travel element are Jorge Ibargüengoitia's 'Misterios del Distrito Federal' (1969–76) in *La casa de usted y otros viajes* (1991); Fernando Benítez's *Viaje al centro de México* (1975); Roberto Vallarino's chronicles of Nezahualcóyotl (1982), in his *Crónicas cotidianas* (1984); Rafael Ramírez Heredia's *En un lugar de la mancha... urbana: Iztacalco* (1993); Fabrizio Mejía Madrid's 'Insurgentes en días lluviosos' (c.1994), in his *Pequeños actos de desobediencia civil* (1996); and Gonzalo Celorio's *El viaje sedentario: varia invención* (1994), this last a deliberately passive travel chronicle, in the style of Xavier de Maistre's *Voyage autour de ma chambre* (1795). A good anthology of contemporary (travel) chronicles of the Federal District is Jaime Valverde Arciniega and Juan Domingo Argüelles's *El fin de la nostalgia: nueva*

and travel chroniclers of Mexico City as to make one wonder how and why any writer should go about producing another chronicle of the city, with or without travel as a leitmotif: 'Escribir una crónica de la Ciudad de México es ya una tarea imposible', as the critic Noé Cárdenas has noted.[8]

But if, as Carlos Monsiváis notes in the first epigraph to this chapter, our primary experience of the city he is describing (implicitly Mexico City) is through literary descriptions and spiraling conversations, ultimately, the most innovative option for travel writing is to recognise Mexico City's textual, mediated nature, and to write a travel chronicle which advocates experiencing the city through a combination of literature, art and the imagination, travelling through the spaces of dreams and memories, fiction and poetic imagery, museums and art galleries, academic speculation and virtual reality. Not all of these additional dimensions to the travel experience are novelties for the travel chronicle. Indeed, Héctor Perea's analysis of Alfonso Reyes's chronicle of Mexico City, *Visión de Anáhuac: 1519* (1915), focuses on Reyes's ability to '*crear* una realidad partiendo de otra sólo existente' (author's italics), and his collation of the different perspectives available of a specific place – foreign and indigenous, contemporary and ancient, fictitious and historical, virtual and real – in order to create a collage of 'los mundos posibles' that are accesible in 'un espacio desplegado

---

crónica de la ciudad de México, prol. by Carlos Monsiváis (Nueva Imagen, 1992). Also see *Nexos*, 150 (June 1990) and *Blanco Móvil*, 69 (1996), dedicated to 'Crónica de un día cualquiera: Ciudad de México' and 'Literatura de la Ciudad de México: crónicas y cuentos' respectively.

Ignacio Corona's 'Contesting the Lettered City: Cultural Mediation and Communicative Strategies in the Contemporary Chronicle in Mexico' provides an excellent critical analysis of the practice of writing chronicles (although not specifically travel chronicles) of contemporary Mexico City (in *Latin American Literature and Mass Media*, ed. by Edmundo Paz-Soldán and Debra A. Castillo [New York: Garland, 2001], pp. 193–206).

8   Noé Cárdenas, 'Otros tiempos y lugares', H. Perea, *México: crónica en espiral*, review, *Nexos*, 233 (May 1997), 99.

en la imaginación'.[9] Much more recently Gonzalo Celorio has also selected a speculative, intertextual approach to Mexico City in his *México: ciudad de papel* (1997) (quoted in the second epigraph to this chapter). Nevertheless, a text which is contemporaneous with Celorio's and penned by the same writer who so astutely analysed Reyes's vision of the capital, offers the most diverse, speculative, 'hypertextual'[10] approach to the city, consistent with the features of the 'chronotope of the net' discussed in Chapter 3. That text is *México: crónica en espiral* (1996) by the prize-winning academic, writer and journalist Héctor Perea (né 1953).

This chapter will examine Perea's problems with and solutions to the conundrum of writing a contemporary travel chronicle of Mexico City, tracing in detail his preference for a more metaphorical, virtual approach to travel writing in order to compensate for the lack of personal travel narrative. In particular it outlines six alternative 'dimensions' to the traditional travel narrative that may be found in Perea's account, culminating in an exegesis of how even the personal is rendered through the dimension of intertextuality in Perea's text. It then goes on to explore the possibility of a specifically Mexican 'postcolonialist' reading to be found in the way the chronicle handles the complex relationship between Mexico and Spain, Mexico City and Madrid. (As an aside, it should be noted that, for reasons of space, the postmodernist nature of travel chronicles that follow the 'chronotope of the net' model is taken for granted here.)

9   Héctor Perea, *La rueda del tiempo: mexicanos en España* (Cal y Arena, 1996), pp. 351–52.
10 I use the adjective 'hypertextual' here to refer to an intense, elliptical form of intertextuality which actually requires reading the primary text side-by-side with other texts/images to complement and even to make sense of it, as well as requiring the reader, on occasion, to jump from one part of the primary text to another rather than read it in a strictly linear fashion.

Las estancias de Perea: The Unsatisfying Vestiges of the Traditional Travel Narrative

Although Perea does not foreground his problems with the traditional travel chronicle genre in quite the same metatextual manner that Villoro does, traces of the difficulties he experienced are evident in the rather awkward coexistence of vestiges of the standard features of the genre with a much more metaphorical conception of travel and travel writing. In fact, from a purely textual point of view, Perea is barely able to convince his reader that he has made any real and/or specific journey(s) at all in order to write his chronicle: the text by and large lacks active first person narrative, a sense of temporality and causality, and a clear itinerary, albeit spiral, as suggested by its title. In sum, it lacks verisimilitude.

But what Perea wanted was a 'synthetic' form of travel chronicle which would express his 'synthetic' experience of the city. Perea was born in Mexico City; however, his long periods of residence in Madrid during the 1980s mean that his experience of travel in the Mexican capital is heightened: some of the personal episodes which he narrates are events drawn from his memories of a series of return journeys which he made to the capital from his then base in Madrid.[11] This need to rediscover a city capable of changing beyond recognition in the space of one or two years pervades the whole of Perea's chronicle, regardless of whether the incident narrated is taken from his memories of childhood and of his return journeys from Madrid, or from more recent exploratory rambles undertaken to search out material for this particular project:

> La ciudad más grande del mundo, la más contaminada, la más llena de historia de América, celosa como pocas, puede cobrar, y de hecho la hace con saña, su tributo de atención. Tributo prehispánico, colonial, cotidiano. Abandonarla por mucho tiempo significa perderla. Gracias al moderado tiempo de desarraigo, yo, si así lo deseaba, me dijo JEP [José Emilio Pacheco], podía volver: México-Tenochtitlán sería benigno con mis sentidos.[12]

---

11   Cárdenas, 'Otros tiempos y lugares', 99.
12   Héctor Perea, *México: crónica en espiral* (CNCA, 1996), p. 57. All further quotations are from this edition and will be given parenthetically in the text.

His experience of Mexico City, then, is of a permanent struggle to reconstruct, remember, replace the lost faces of the city with the ones he remembers from his childhood, adolescence, and studies in and of the city. Perea knows what should be there, what used to be there, or even what might have been there, and faced with its absence, partial or total, he narrates these lacunae, thus creating his own composite vision of Mexico City, which collates the submerged memory of the lake of México-Tenochtitlán with the virtual images of the city floating in cyberspace, and with a thousand 'espejismos', 'ilusiones' and 'cuentos de aparecidos' in between (p. 29). His synthesis of the city is one in which these different faces of the city can coexist without danger of destruction; one which corresponds to his experience and knowledge of the city, rather than to the reality that a reader retracing his footsteps might perceive.

Complementing his desire to narrate a composite vision of Mexico City, Perea opts for a narrative that integrates his multiple journeys through the city, collating the fruits of the full range of his personal experience of the city in a superimposed itinerary which purports to describe the figure of a spiral; a novel format in the history of Mexican travel writing. But can readers tell that the thread of the active first-person narrative is a fictitious construct, and does it matter if they notice? The average reader would certainly be aware that that this spiral journey is not the main focus of interest in the text, that there is very little sense of a succession of events, and that, plotting the course of the journey on a map of Mexico City, the figure of the spiral in two dimensions tends to be rather diffuse.

The use of active first-person narrative in Perea's text is barely enough to situate the reader in time and space. After only a sentence or two of orientating narrative, Perea switches to a more essayistic type of prose: 'Cruzo la calle de Durango y me planto frente a una construcción que sigue pareciendome fabulosa, aunque me haya topado con ella miles de veces' (p. 72). There follows an extensive quotation from Sergio Pitol's *El desfile del amor* (1984), and then a discussion of the architectural styles of the Colonia Roma. An even briefer example comes only pages later: 'De vuelta en Coyoacán. La estampa de Landesio pareciera una más de esas cincuenta y tres estaciones de Hiroshigué' (p. 79). Many more examples of first-person narrative are sustained only by the words 'recuerdo' or 'repito'. These memories and repetitions lend an oneiric quality to Perea's presence in the text.

In addition to this lack of active first-person narrative, there is also a lack of temporality and of causality between events. Although specific places are clearly identified, there is practically no attempt to provide temporal links between 'visits'. The 'today' and 'now' of the narrative of *Crónica en espiral* are more likely those of its moment of composition at the writer's desk, or of the non-specific discursive present of 'nowadays', than temporal markers referring to the actuality of the excursions themselves ('Hoy inicio esta "Crónica en espiral" ... ' [p. 5]). Rarely is there reference to a concrete 'tomorrow' or 'yesterday', to a sense of relativity in this non-specific present of writing. The few events narrated might have taken place in the space of four of five days, in an uninterrupted itinerary along the route of the spiral. It is more probable, however, that they are drawn from the six-month period during which Perea wrote the book, and then inter-spliced with earlier episodes. Hence causality from one event to another is flimsy.

Finally, the succession of locations detailed in Perea's text forms only the roughest semblance of a spiral shape: starting in the Centro Histórico he describes a route through the city which spirals out from this point to reach areas such as Coyoacán and San Ángel, Texcoco and La Noria, but many interconnecting areas are missed out, presumably because they do not interest the author. Although boredom is one of the contingencies of travel, it admittedly does not have to be re-enacted in a travel account, yet with such large tracts of the itinerary of the spiral un-narrated, the design of the chronicle seems flawed. There is also little sense of any real means of conveyance between Perea's isolated locations. At best he offers this description of a short walk in the Centro Histórico, 'Hace un calor de espanto. Y lo sentimos mucho más por venirnos andando desde San Ildefonso' (p. 26). And at worst, this fanciful return journey from Mixcoac to Coyoacán: 'El sendero líquido, entubado, me devuelve otra vez a Coyoacán, donde reinicio el alejamiento a contracorriente' (p. 84).[13]

---

13 However, Perea does also use this 'form of travel' to remind the reader of the original waterways of Mexico City.

The overall impression given by Perea's presence in his narrative, then, is of a lack of verisimilitude. There are, however, other ways of looking at Perea's 'character', which render him a more robust participant in the economy of the text. Despite his secondary importance in terms of the space accorded to him in the text, Perea, the character, reappears at regular intervals throughout, particularly at the beginning and end of chapters. Moreover, a sense of personal presence, albeit that of the writer at his desk, permeates the entire text, suggesting a much closer link between active first-person travel narrative and impersonal chronicling than one might think. The spiral journey structure is not so much an appendix as a vestigial early plan designed to be integral to the chronicle as a whole but which was found not to be sufficiently flexible for the finished product.[14]

Again, the reference to the spiral-shaped itinerary in the title is misleading as it suggests a continuum, a uniform displacement in time and space which is manifestly not narrated. Such a lack of continuity in the narrative of physical displacement does not necessarily disqualify Perea's text as a postmodernist travel chronicle. However, even postmodernist travel writing still generally requires the conveyance of a sense of being there, of personal experience and of the contingency of daily life in the world as we presently know it.[15] There is, admittedly, very little in terms of personal action in the text – nothing particularly idiosyncratic, no interviews, no chance meetings with the man in the street. Instead, Perea comes across as a very aloof spectator of the city who accords a sense of protagonism to the city at the expense of its living inhabitants. He situates and directs his reader's gaze from a room on the third floor of the Gran Hotel de la Ciudad de México, adjacent

---

14   Perea admitted the shortcomings of the spiral design in interview (personal interview with the author, 27 January 1997).

15   Alison Russell justifies the recent resurgence in Anglophone travel writing as being due to the 'readers' desire for writing that is responsive to the dramatic and complex ways in which the world has changed in the past few decades', and finds that specifically postmodernist travel writing, with one foot in the real world, and the other in that of aesthetic innovation and theoretical reflection, is in a more ideal position to offer such a response than other genres such as the novel, for example (*Crossing Boundaries: Postmodern Travel Literature* [New York: Palgrave, 2000], p. 2).

to the cathedral in the Centro Histórico; from the terrace bar on the roof of the Palacio de Bellas Artes, and from the elevated perspective of Bar Mata and Las Sirenas, all also in the Centro Histórico. However, this is not an up-dated but still imperialistic 'monarch-of-all-I-survey' type of gaze of the sort that Mary Louise Pratt identified in her seminal study of imperialist travel writing.[16] Perea is not trying to classify people or produce a totalising, utilitarian image of Mexican society from his elevated perches. He looks down not on the multitudes passing in the street below, but on the architectural vestiges of past epochs. He even imagines what might have been there for the spectator of the nineteenth century.[17]

No matter how flimsy and fleeting they may appear, these episodes of active first-person narrative are used to orientate the reader as quickly as possible: they are co-ordinates. Perea ultimately aims to access quite different terrain; terrain in which personal experience and contingency are encapsulated in the 'readings' he makes of the city. The fleeting appearances of Perea's character-narrator belie an extremely artful use of the narrator's role to direct a chronicle. Furthermore, Perea has produced a text which suggests that tracing a verisimilar journey 'in the first person' in a contemporary travel chronicle is an insufficient tool by which to establish the nature of the text. Perea, in interview, protested that the question of 'travel' in this kind of text should be viewed much more metaphorically: imaginative journeys, drug-induced 'trips', and audiovisual simulations are all valid ways of travelling: 'Piensa en el concepto del viaje según los años sesenta. El viaje no es solamente trasladarte a otro país, sino trasladarte a otra dimensión: el viaje del LSD, el viaje que te provoca la mariguana ...'. And indeed, the spiral shape of Perea's journey appears to require more dimensions than those offered by a town plan to chart its co-ordinates.

---

16   In *Imperial Eyes*, Mary Louis Pratt also updates her arguments, commenting that, 'In contemporary travel accounts, the monarch-of-all-I-survey scene gets repeated, only now from the balconies of hotels in big third-world cities' (*Imperial Eyes: Travel Writing and Transculturation* [London: Routledge, 1992], p. 216).

17   Juan Villoro also notes that, 'En 1994 Tokio o México son tan inabarcables que descalifican el intento de lograr un fresco totalizador. La crítica no se dirige hacia la ciudad como un paisaje externo; se ejerce dentro de ella' ('La ciudad es el cielo del metro', 18). This is precisely the function of Perea's 'penetrating' gaze.

La esfera de espirales: The Alternative Dimensions of Perea's Journey

As noted above, Perea displays a predilection for viewing the city from the rooftops, in a 'mirada giratoria' (p. 32). Elsewhere he also offers a brief aerial view of the city (p. 62). From these elevated vantage points he compares the perspective he presently has with that of previous spectators from similar positions, referring to engravings, murals, photographs and narrative accounts. Alternatively, his consciousness of sunken gardens, and of waterways and archaeological remains, securely buried under concrete and asphalt, offers an imaginary subterranean perspective.[18] These elevated and sunken perspectives constitute a third dimension in which the spiral of his travels might be plotted. Yet even here a degree of speculation is necessary for the reader to envision Perea's perspective and its correspondences.

A fourth dimension might be the extension of Perea's personal narrative to include an 'official' guided tour of Mexico City in cyberspace (pp. 52–5). García Canclini, in his essay 'Los viajes metropolitanos', asserts the 'reality' of travel through new media technologies as a way of taking on a city too big to be viewed knowledgeably in its totality by any single chronicler: 'Los "viajes audiovisuales" pasan a formar parte de las travesías por la urbe, de los modos de informarnos, situarnos y estar presentes en el vasto mundo, en la variedad de mundos que es nuestra propia ciudad'.[19]

---

18   It is perhaps ironic that Perea does not include the Metro, Mexico City's underground transport system, in his sunken perspective of the city. However, such an inclusion is more suited to Villoro's exploration of post-nationalist identities than Perea's less humanistic approach (see Villoro's 'La ciudad es el cielo del metro' for his exploration of issues of class and race associated with travel on the Metro).

19   García Canclini, 'Los viajes metropolitanos', p. 33. Claudio Magris has also insisted on the synthetic relationship of the new medium with older ways of travelling: there is always a virtual, speculative aspect to real journeys, and always 'la promesa, la nostalgia, la exigencia de la realidad' in virtual journeys ('El mundo según Internet', trans. by Héctor Abad Faciolince, *Nexos*, 237 [September 1997], 26).

Certainly Perea is aware of the limitations of his own vision of Mexico City and strives to include places in his itinerary which take him beyond 'la parte diaria y cotidiana' of the city.[20] He is also one of Mexico's most enthusiastic advocates of the World Wide Web and even intended his chronicle to resemble a 'paseo virtual' through the city.[21] However, in this central chapter where Perea attempts to explore the overview of the city offered by the Internet, he finds disappointment:

> Durante este recorrido virtual sobre el país y la ciudad de México voy extrañando cada vez más una visión extraoficial del asunto, algo más de acuerdo con la presunta libertad ilimitada del Internet. [...]
>
> Flota por el hiperespacio un México falso; o cuando menos, uno apenas entrevisto, muy, muy apretado y parcial. (p. 54)

The Internet in the early 1990s did not yet offer an integrated vision of the different perspectives, literal and metaphorical, political, aesthetic, historical and personal, available on the subject of Mexico City. Nevertheless, Perea does contrast this official vision of the city with a more discerning use of the Internet to access the city in the following chapter where he visits José Emilio Pacheco's chronicles at the magazine *Proceso*'s website (p. 56).

If the first three dimensions of Perea's spiral correspond to Euclidean geometry, and the fourth to the dimension of cyberspace, the remaining four 'dimensions' continue in his imagination. A fifth dimension is formed by his travels in time to capture the past faces of Mexico City and the speculative traits of the metropolis of the future. As García Canclini notes,

> Las travesías urbanas son también viajes por las relaciones entre el orden y el desorden, donde se activa la memoria de las imágenes perdidas de la ciudad que fue, y se imagina cómo será, por ejemplo en el 2000, la hipermetrópolis que se insinúa a nuestro alrededor. Se accede a través de los viajes a un imaginario sobre la ciudad posible, se construyen hipótesis – o se selecciona entre las disponibles – para explicar el sentido de los dramas urbanos.[22]

---

20 Personal interview.
21 Héctor Perea, personal email, 3 February 2005.
22 García Canclini, 'Los viajes metropolitanos', p. 24.

In the construction of Perea's text this dimension of time travel must be viewed in conjunction with a sixth possible dimension: that of his imaginary travels in space to trace the reflections of other cities found in Mexico City.

That these two dimensions are a deliberate part of the architecture of Perea's impossible spiral is without doubt. With reference to travel in historical time, for example, he writes, 'la historia no hace más que repetirse en una espiral ascendente en el tiempo' (p. 49). These historical repetitions are generated in spirals emanating from violent events which have taken place in La Plaza de las Tres Culturas in Tlatelolco in the first half of the book ('Tlatelolco es el lugar de retorno', writes Monsiváis; 'El lugar de partida de esta crónica y el lugar de vuelta en muchos momentos de nuestra historia: la de esta ciudad, la de nosotros mismos', adds Perea [p. 49]). In the second half of the chronicle, in a more diffuse sense, the historical repetitions are generated by the repercussions of the extremely destructive 1985 earthquake, particularly in the Condesa and Roma neighbourhoods. The two spirals are linked by the virtual explorations of Chapter 10; and, as a coda, the Tlatelolco spiral is reiterated with significant changes in the final chapter.

Many of Perea's accelerated travels in historical time are accompanied by brusque displacements to other cities with which Mexico City is associated, if only in Perea's imagination. Moving on from the traditional comparisons between Mexico City and Venice or Pompeii, Perea repeatedly compares the city with Madrid: the Museo San Carlos on the Puente de Alvarado transports him to El Prado ('Y viene el traslado en el tiempo y el espacio' [p. 44]); the Condesa de Miravalle's monument in Colonia Roma is a pastiche of La Cibeles (p. 73); and the backdrop of the Ajusco volcano reminds him of the Sierra de Guadarrama. However, his loci of comparison also stretch to the limits of the Iberian Peninsula: in other instances he refers to the churches of Andalucia,[23] the statues of La Reforma are the alter egos of statues in Lisbon (p. 34), and, in a more oblique manner he comments:

---

23   The comparison in question makes reference to the cathedral of Granada (p. 36), although Perea recognised in interview that he had really meant to refer to the mosque in Córdoba.

> Es extraña la sensación que produce el inventar una caminata por esta metrópoli del siglo XVII que en realidad podría haber sido otra. O que además, y de hecho, lo es con un poco de imaginación. Cualquier de las arterias peatonales – Motolinía, Palma, Gante – podría contener un ascensor de hierro que llevara a otro nivel de la ciudad... (p. 33)

This imaginary 'ascensor de hierro' must be inspired, at least in part, by the street escalator in Barcelona.

Perea uses the plasticity of 'un ascensor de hierro' as a metaphor for an imaginary 'traslado en el tiempo y el espacio': it is a bridge. Repeatedly in his chronicle he refers to the theme of bridges; bridges which are sometimes real ('puente auténtico' [p. 47]), sometimes also mythical (the Puente de Alvarado), and most frequently personal, imaginary ones between different historical epochs and places. The cupola of Santa Teresa church, for example, is 'un puente lanzado entre los distintos tiempos mexicanos' (p. 31). The maximum function of these bridges is to underscore both the plasticity and the abstraction inherent in Perea's spiral itinerary, and their specificity as a metaphor for travel in Mexico City.[24]

The spiral design also exists in a seventh dimension, in the movement between text and reader. It becomes an image of the light which allows reading to take place, and which has also traditionally symbolised Mexico City for Perea and so many other of its chroniclers. In the second chapter Perea quotes a passage from Martín Luis Guzmán's *La sombra del caudillo* (1929) which describes the play of sunlight on the heroine, Rosario, as she walks under the trees lining Avenida Insurgentes Sur with the mass of the Ajusco volcano dominating the horizon. Perea describes the scene: 'Ayer, anteayer y hoy, la ciudad ha sido otra vez de pura luz interior (Guzmán). México estaba encerrado ya en la esfera de espirales del primer encuentro de Rosario con Aguirre' (p. 17). The 'esfera de espirales' refers not only to the relationship

---

24   In the sixteenth century the term 'puente' was used in Mexico City to refer to 'cruceros en los que coincidían una calle de tierra y otra de agua', intersections of a road and a canal where the two ran parallel for a block or more ('México, Ciudad de', *Enciclopedia de México*, ed. by José Rogelio Álvarez, 14 vols [Encyclopaedia Britannica de México, 1993], IX, 5242).

between Rosario and Aguirre, but also to the cyclical movement of rays of sunlight, trapped in the circular valley of Mexico, and to the introspection that such a climate provokes.

Again, in the epigraph to Perea's chronicle – Octavio Paz's prose poem 'Valle de México' (1948) – the spiral is associated with the illuminating movement of the sun's rays and its battle with the countering 'gaze' of the valley (the earth, the lake, or the 'air'), where the poet is 'el afilado, quieto punto fijo de intersección de dos miradas que se ignoran y se encuentran en mí'. The sun is metaphorically cast as a bird of prey which attacks the poet; the rays of light as its wings: 'El sol me arranca los ojos. En mis órbitas vacías dos astros alisan sus plumas rojas. Esplendor, espiral de alas y un pico feroz' (*México: crónica en espiral*, p. 11). The Valley of Mexico for Paz is a crucible of light, defined by the transparency of its air, as it was for Reyes in 1915 and would still be for Fuentes in 1958. The loss of the clarity of the air in Mexico City, associated with the increasing invisibility of the volcanoes from the centre of town, is a point to which a nostalgic Perea returns repeatedly in the course of his spiral itinerary.

In both quotations, then, the figure of the spiral may be understood to represent the sun's rays, the path of light. The light is the protagonist. For Perea, too, it is the sun's rays which illuminate Mexico City, allowing the dialogue of seen object and seeing subject to begin its hermeneutic spiral of knowledge, and allowing the lines of a book to be read and reinterpreted. This spiral of the contemplative act is a recurrent image in Perea's work: *Océano de colores* (1996), his collection of essays concerning the relationship between art and literature, Mexico and Spain, is described on the fly-sheet as 'una crónica de la mirada: un recorrido por una galería de personajes que a su vez observan desde los puentes de la imaginación y la memoria los planos complejos de la imagen'.[25] In *México: crónica en espiral* it is Mexico City itself which has the ability to sustain and return the chronicler's gaze – it is a 'speculative' city –, and in so doing it creates the hermeneutic spiral of 'miradas' along which Perea travels.

---

25 Héctor Perea, *Océano de colores* (Aldus, 1996).

Finally, more than any other contemporary travel chronicler, Perea is dependent on his extensive knowledge of representations of Mexico City for his ability to travel in the city. This surplus of representations of the city is at once the origin of the lack of personal travel narrative in *México: crónica en espiral* and a 'bridge' to what is arguably the only form of travel chronicle that may be written about contemporary Mexico City. Perea follows the logic of the eighth dimension of the spiral in terms of his displacement from one cultural area to the next, and in the relationships that link present-day reality with its past, its future, its fictional possibilities and its personal resonances. In order to do this he filters every word of his chronicle through other people's representations: historical chronicles, novels and poems; engravings, paintings and photographs. These references might obscure any sense of physical displacement in the text, yet they are also an invitation to a very different type of 'intertextual' and even 'hypertextual' journey. Careful readers who seek to make sense of some of the more elliptical and obscure references find before themselves the unfolding Chinese boxes of a world part Borges, part Fuentes. Instead of analysing this material, Perea appropriates it and extrapolates from it. The journey proposed does not draw readers into the text; instead it forces them to enquire beyond the text in search of a more substantial narrative than that provided by Perea.[26]

Each reference is a challenge to the reader to establish the link. Perea's recurrent references to André Breton ought to signal to the reader that the order of cognition is subliminal, elliptical, quirky. The names of the writers and artists are frequently given in parentheses. At first sight this technique looks heavy-handed, overly academic. Nevertheless, it is an extremely effective shorthand: instead of giving full details, for example, of Óscar de la Borbolla's 'post-apocalyptic' text '¡Llueve sangre!' in his book of fantasy chronicles *Ucronías* (1990), the theory and praxis of which has obviously influenced Perea's style of writing, he notes simply that, in the range of things that Mexico City can represent for its inhabitants, it can been seen as the place 'donde llueve sangre y

---

26 It is in this sense that Perea's text goes beyond traditional intertextuality and into the realms of hypertextuality.

el cielo se colorea como de incendio, como de miles de reflectores (De la Borbolla)' (p. 16). It is the reader who must discover which of De la Borbolla's texts the paraphrase refers to.

In the first paragraph of the same brief chapter Perea makes a similarly discreet reference to Pacheco's short story 'El parque hondo' (1963): the story's title is slipped into the body of the text for the attention of more erudite readers; a phrase in italics is a direct quotation from the opening paragraph of the story (p. 16). The remainder of the paragraph elliptically rewrites Pacheco's text using synaesthesic transpositions of sight and sound, for example, to enhance the impact of the original: it is obvious that Perea is not plagiarising, nor just paraphrasing and analysing Pacheco's text. He is actively participating with this text to produce a new version, sealed with his own sensibilities, yet written to be read side-by-side with the old one. In the reader's flickering eye movements, not just across the page of Perea's chronicle, but between the pages of his text and Pacheco's original story, Perea provokes the reader to experience a hypertextual, spiral journey in the fullest sense of the term.[27]

---

27   In the chapter in question, 'Cuerpo de piedra y asfalto' – a text which is little over a page in length – Perea also incorporates references to the work of Carlos Chimal, Fernando Curiel, Carlos Flores Vargas, and Martín Luis Guzmán. Other substantial readings of the 'chronicles' of Mexico City elsewhere in the text include references to Fuentes's short stories 'Tlactocatzine, del jardín de Flandes' and 'Las dos Elenas' in *Cantar de ciegos* (1964) and *Los días enmascarados* (1966) respectively; to Luis González Obregón's *México viejo, 1521–1821* (1895) and José Luis Martínez's *Nezahualcóyotl: vida y obra* (1972); to Salvador Novo's *Nueva grandeza mexicana* (1946) and Alfonso Reyes's *Visión de Anáhuac* (1915); to Carlos Monsiváis' *Días de guardar* (1970) and to a number of Octavio Paz's poems.

A whole generation of writers ('la generación de los cincuenta') have been influenced by Pacheco's work, particularly in their choice of approach to Mexico City. In 'Caminatas con José Emilio Pacheco', Vicente Quirarte – another member of the generation and a close friend of Perea's – notes that his own vision of Mexico City is irrevocably coloured by his reading of Pacheco, and that what has been most influential in Pacheco's approach has been his treatment of the possibilities of the city rather than its immediate reality. Quirarte also notes the radical effect that the 1985 earthquake had on Pacheco: the implication is that the impact of the earthquake – simultaneously a real event and a metaphor for so many other

Similarly with other media, Perea provides his own suggestive narrative of eighteenth- and nineteenth-century engravings and lithographs, the murals of Diego Rivera, films by Eisenstein and Buñuel, paintings by Remedios Varo and Antonio Rivas, sculptures by Manuel Tolsá, and photography by Casasola 'quizás'. The references to so many works of art can be frustrating for the reader who expects to find these images inserted graphically into the text – relevant images are certainly provided in Celorio's *México: ciudad de papel*. Nevertheless, it is arguable that Perea has treated these images to the same kind of elliptical narration as the texts mentioned above: he does not seek to reproduce and replace them so much as suggest them poetically, and provoke his reader go out in search of them in museums, art galleries, books, or even on the Internet.

Una encrucijada de caminos literarios y vivenciales: A Journey Both Virtual and Real

Many of the dimensions of Perea's spiral come together in two fragments which frame the text. The opening passage describes a route through the old heart of the city in 1914, from a prison in Tlatelolco to another near the Ciudadela where the prisoners undertaking this 'excursión' will be executed (pp. 13–14). The fleeting description of the cloudy night sky and the bloody streets opens a third dimension; comments on the unreal, ghostly nature of the city under curfew suggest a virtual fourth dimension. The spiral of the real journey is made complete in the last chapter of the chronicle where the protagonist is removed from the line of prisoners awaiting their deaths, and returned along the same route to Santiago Tlatelolco prison (pp. 89–90).

---

moments of radical change in Mexico City's history – has provoked an elliptical, fantastic approach to the city (Quirarte, *Enseres para sobrevivir en la ciudad*, Los Cincuenta [Coordinación Nacional de Descentralización; Aguascalientes: Instituto Cultural de Aguascalientes, 1994), pp. 149–53]. These are clearly clues to the literary background of Perea's suggestive reading of the city.

Nevertheless, in the opening passage Perea leaves his protagonist to face the firing squad, brusquely changing to the present, in order to compare and contrast contemporary Mexico City with the one that existed in 1914. Slipped in between these two visions of the city, Perea makes an enigmatic reference to the parallelism between 'excursiones' and 'paseos' in different times and places. He also contrasts the prisoner's experience of the city with that of a certain Víctor Nibelungo (the protagonist of Fuentes's short story 'Las dos Elenas') who made a memorable journey from Coyoacán to Las Lomas exactly fifty years later. The dimensions of imaginative time and space travel are apparent.

However, it requires the addition of a hypertextual dimension for the reader to be able to relate the 'excursiones' of Huertista Mexico to the 'paseos' of Republican Spain. The key to the identity of the 'autor revolucionario' and the relationship between 'paseos' and 'excursiones' lies in Perea's *La rueda del tiempo*.[28] Here, in a discussion of Paz's experiences in Spain during the Civil War, recorded in his *Itinerario* (1993), Perea paraphrases Paz's comments on the term 'paseos' to refer to 'ejecuciones sumarias republicanas'.[29] On the following page of *La rueda del tiempo*, Perea makes an explicit reference to the similarity of these 'paseos' with the 'excursión' described by Guillermo Enríquez Simoní in his *La libertad de la prensa en México: una mentira rosa* (1967), and paraphrased in the opening paragraphs of Perea's *México:*

---

28 *La rueda del tiempo* is a biography of the numerous illustrious Mexican travellers in Spain in the late nineteenth and early twentieth centuries, prior to the Spanish Civil War. The spiralling reciprocity referred to in the title stems from the fact that Perea is exploring the influence of Mexicans on Spanish culture in a period which is immediately prior to that of a major Spanish contribution to Mexican culture as a result of the influx of Spanish exiles in Mexico occasioned by the Spanish Civil War. *La rueda del tiempo* is really the obverse of *México: crónica en espiral*, its companion volume. So many of the proper names that appear in the text on Spain are those that reappear in the travel chronicle concerning Mexico City that this latter text really contributes to completing the circle/spiral of the former in terms of Perea's own literary movement between history and fiction, allowing him to speculate through the historiographic fiction of the travel chronicle on matters which required a more authoritative treatment in his academic work.

29 Perea, *La rueda del tiempo*, p. 467.

crónica en espiral. Yet it is only on the last page of his chronicle that Perea identifies his protagonist as 'el abuelo Guillermo', making it clear that Enríquez Simoní was his own grandfather.[30] Guillermo's spiral journey is thus an intimate part of Perea's own route:

> La ciudad de México es la que recorrió el autor revolucionario, desde Santiago Tlatelolco hasta Belem, para ser fusilado. Es la de Fuentes. Y en realidad no es ninguna ni pertenece a nadie, y la guardamos entre las manos o la seguimos con el dedo sobre un plano. Hoy inicio esta 'Crónica en espiral' sobre la ruta que fue la del pelotón y es la mía. Crónica con final incierto. (p. 15)

The literal and metaphorical dimensions of Perea's spiral are thus intimately enmeshed; at key moments, literature and life fuse together, blurring the division between the writing of personal travels and imaginary travels through reading and writing. Perea really does live in the description of the city. Or perhaps, we should say, of two cities...

Twin Cites: A Mexican Kind of Postcolonialism

Using the defining characteristics of the 'chronotope of the net' to good, potentially postcolonialist, effect, Perea avoids the production of a totalising narrative of the history of Mexico City by offering his reader this 'synthetic' chronicle with its multiple points of view, its abrupt leaps in time, space and the imagination, its intense dialogue between different texts and images, and its ability to accord a sense of protagonism to the city itself. This is a 'speculative' city that, in Perea's account, has the power to reciprocate the gaze of the observer; to challenge it and to change it. Implicitly, then, Perea's Mexico City might present a challenge to imperial eyes.

---

30 The hypertextual feature of jumping from one part of a primary text to another is evident here as the reader is forced to compare and contrast the first and last chapters of the chronicle in order to solve the riddle, as well as to look further afield for clues.

Virtual Journeys: Héctor Perea's 'México: crónica en espiral' 151

Nevertheless, unlike Juan Villoro's travel chronicle with its critique of the legacy of United States imperialist travellers and of contemporary tourists in the Yucatan, Perea's text pays precious little attention to the views expressed by such travellers in their passage through the capital city.[31] Instead, as we have seen, his focus is predominantly on how Mexicans have represented their own city to themselves, and he bypasses any direct association of travel writing as 'un género del Norte' in Pacheco's terms.[32] Perea, like Alfonso Reyes before him, simply posits the chronicle form as the foundation stone of Mexican literature and absorbs unproblematically those texts written by earlier generations of conquistadors and missionaries, *peninsulares* and *criollos*, as part of the canon of Mexican literature concerning the capital city.[33]

However, there is a technically 'postcolonialist' reading to be derived from the narrative – one that is perhaps not recognisably postcolonialist from the point of view of Anglophone Postcolonial Studies, and one that would undoubtedly not merit the term 'postcolonialist' in Mexico, but one that, nevertheless, confronts the main issue that all ex-colonies need to deal with and that Mexico has been dealing with for nearly two hundred years now: that is to say, the relationship with the ex-colonial power. Perea's chronicle is an almost 'loving' account of the intense, 'spiraling', symbiotic relationship between Mexico and Spain that has existed since the time of the Conquest. As Jorge Klor de Alva has noted, Independence in Mexico was not a violent break with colonial rule and a subsequent process of decolonisation. Instead, independent Mexico conceived of its on-going relationship with Spain as more fraternal, or

---

31   Here, I use the term 'imperialist' specifically to refer to those travellers of Northern European or United States origin who have travelled to the city in the years since Mexico gained independence, rather than to earlier generations of travellers of Spanish origin. This distinction is of some importance to my analysis of Perea's 'postcolonialist' stance.
32   For José Emilio Pacheco's critique of travel writing, see the introduction to this study.
33   For Alfonso Reyes's comments on the chronicle as the cornerstone of Mexican literature, see Chapter 1.

sisterly, than antagonistic.[34] It is in this spirit that Mexicans expressed sympathy for Spain at the time that it also succumbed to the imperial designs of France in the 1808,[35] and, just over one hundred years later, it is in this spirit that Mexicans sought haven in Spain during the Mexican Revolution,[36] and subsequently welcomed exiled Spaniards in the wake of the Spanish Civil War – Mexicans have contributed decisively to Spanish cultural life particularly during the last century, and vice versa.[37]

Perea thus charts this specifically Mexican approach to postcolonial relations in *México: crónica en espiral*. Just as Alfonso Reyes's *Visión de Anáhuac: 1519* was a vision of Mexico facilitated by the author's presence in Spain, Perea views Mexico City as both a *chilango*, born and bred in the Valley of Anáhuac, and as an honorary *madrileño*, who makes sporadic return trips to his birth place, and who filters his vision of the Federal District through his knowledge and appreciation of the

---

34   See Jorge Klor de Alva, 'The Postcolonization of the (Latin) American Experience: A Reconsideration of "Colonialism," "Postcolonialism," and "Mestizaje"', in *After Colonialism: Imperial Histories and Postcolonial Displacements*, ed. by Gyan Prakash (Princeton, NJ: Princeton UP, 1995), especially pp. 253–54.

35   See Nancy Vogeley, 'The Discourse of Colonial Loyalty: Mexico, 1808', *in Macropolitics of Nineteenth-Century Literature: Nationalism, Exoticism, Imperialism*, ed. by Jonathan Arac and Harriet Ritvo (Philadelphia: U of Pennsylvania P, 1991), pp. 37–55.

36   This is precisely the subject of Perea's *La rueda del tiempo*.

37   The relationship between Mexico and Spain has suffered some ups and downs since Independence and the image of the 'greedy *gachupín*' has also had some currency. However, Mexico's welcoming of liberal-minded Republican exiles in the late 1930s and 40s has greatly strengthened intellectual and cultural ties between the two countries (Ascensión Hernández de León-Portilla, *España desde México: vida y testimonio de transterrados* [UNAM, 1978]). Miguel León-Portilla also notes that, subsequent to the re-establishment of diplomatic ties between the two countries after the death of Franco, the relationship has been 'excelente', although he does warn about current imbalances in economic relations that see Spain as an neo-imperialist force in Mexico, on a par with the United States and cautions that cultural fraternity might just be a 'postura lírica' rather than a viable way of acting in a globalising world (Miguel León-Portilla, 'España y México: encuentros y desencuentros', *Letras Libres* [November 2006], http://www.letraslibres.com/index.php?art=11577, accessed 30 July 2007).

Spanish capital. Nevertheless, Mexico City is never posited as *inferior* copy – though copy it is in places – nor peripheral *faute-de-mieux*, but simply as a twin city, a city that simply could not be without her sister, and a city that Perea experiences simultaneously with her twin, through imaginative 'hypertextual' links. The volcanoes on the skyline of Mexico City are related – in Perea's imagination – with the Sierra de Guadarrama just outside Madrid; the Museo de San Carlos with El Prado; and Perea's grandfather's 'excursión' at the time of the Mexican Revolution with a Republican 'paseo' during the Spanish Civil War. Perea's travel chronicle of Mexico City even has to be complemented by a reading of his more formal academic study of the influence of Mexicans in early twentieth-century Spain in his *La rueda del tiempo* to complete the spiral of relationships alluded to in the chronicle's title.

Such a subtle and complex relationship as that traced by Perea between Mexico and Spain, Mexico City and Madrid, is clearly facilitated by his use of the 'chronotope of the net' format, particularly in terms of its promotion of dialogue and/or intertextuality, its avoidance of an essentialist us-and-them take on identity, and its ability to reveal the 'interconnectedness' and interdependence of postcolonised and postcolonising peoples in the contemporary world. Arguably, then, even in Perea's rather unlikely travel chronicle, the postmodernist 'chronotope of the net' does achieve postcolonialist objectives, even if this is not entirely the kind of revindicative or oppositional kind of postcolonialism we might have expected.

CHAPTER 6
Archival Travel Writing: Fernando Solana Olivares's *Oaxaca: crónicas sonámbulas*

Archival fictions are often historical, and consist of a complex intertextual web that incorporates the chronicles of the discovery and conquest of America, other fictions, historical documents and characters, songs, poetry, scientific reports, literary figures, and myths, in short, a grab-bag of texts that have cultural significance. The organization of the Archive defies conventional classification because classification is at issue, but it does not abandon this basic function of the Archive to generate an inchoate, heteroglossic mass; a mass of documents and other texts that have not been totally, and sometimes not even partially absorbed, that retain their raw, undisturbed original existence as evidence of the non-assimilation of the Other.[1]

To challenge the impulse to totalize is to contest the entire notion of *continuity* in history and its writing. In Foucault's terms discontinuity, once the 'stigma of temporal dislocation' that it was the historian's professional job to remove from history, has become a new instrument of historical analysis and simultaneously a result of that analysis. Instead of seeking common denominators and homogeneous networks of causality and analogy, historians have been freed, Foucault argues, to note the dispersing interplay of different, heterogeneous discourses that acknowledge the undecidable in both the past and our knowledge of that past. What has surfaced is something different from the unitary, closed, evolutionary narratives of historiography as we have traditionally known it: [...] we now get the histories (in the plural) of the losers as well as the winners, of the regional (and colonial) as well as the centrist, of the unsung many as well as the much sung few, and I might add, of women as well as men.[2] (author's italics)

Oaxaca: crónicas sonámbulas (1994) by Fernando Solana Olivares (né 1954) displays very little obvious evidence of belonging to the genre of the travel chronicle in terms of its 'plot' – indeed, the only evidence of

1   Roberto González Echevarría, *Myth and Archive: A Theory of Latin American Narrative* (Cambridge: Cambridge UP, 1990), p. 176.
2   Linda Hutcheon, *The Politics of Postmodernism* (London: Routledge, 1989), p. 66.

this nature is a brief and somewhat anomalous metatextual digression on the subject of travel writing, diary keeping and the 'writing of place' towards the end. However, this text, I will argue, is an example of the 'chronotope of the net' model of postmodernist travel writing stretched to its extremes. In fact, Solana Olivares's chronicle retains a strong 'archival' consciousness of travel writing and it is the intertextual dialogue that it establishes with such an archive that both retains it within the bounds of the genre as practised in contemporary Mexico, as well as provides it with critical leverage on the genre itself.

In this chapter, I will first examine Solana Olivares's explicit rejection of the travel chronicle form, despite his commission for precisely such a text, before going on to explore the ways in which he presents an archive of intertextual references to travel writing. The chapter will then consider the effects of the particularly allusive presentation of references to this archive of sources, in particular the function of dream in the text as a way of alternately undermining and reinforcing its relationship to the travel chronicle genre. Finally, it weaves together Roberto González Echevarría's definition of Latin American 'archival fictions' from his *Myth and Archive: A Theory of Latin American Narrative* (1990) with Linda Hutcheon's analysis of postmodernist 'historiographic metafiction' in *The Politics of Postmodernism* (1989) in order to reach its conclusions about how such a work might be understood as an example of a postmodernist 'archival' travel chronicle, and how it might achieve postcolonialist objectives, both in terms of its critique of (imperialist) travel writing and its exploration of Mexican postcolonial relations with Spain, thus blending traits that I have previously analysed in the work of Juan Villoro and Héctor Perea.

Elusions: *Decidí no meterme en el género como tal*

Oaxaca: crónicas sonámbulas stems, in part, from a brief journey made by Solana Olivares to the place of his early childhood, made specifically to find material to write a travel chronicle for the CNCA series. During this trip Solana Olivares kept a journal of his experiences and impressions:

> Es una especie de escritura automática, muy impresionista que llevo yo haciendo conforme y durante toda esta semana que estoy en la ciudad. Y estoy en la ciudad vagando, yendo a sitios que conocía, a sitios que no conocía, recordando momentos y escribiendo anotaciones.[3]

Yet for the reader of *Oaxaca: crónicas sonámbulas* there is precious little evidence of this personal 'cuaderno de notas'. Certainly the text is about Oaxaca, but it appears to be an historical novel concerning the lives of a Spaniard, Hermógenes Suárez, proprietor of a clothes shop called El Nuevo Mundo, and his lifetime companions: Catalina Ochoterena Mori, his Oaxacan wife, and 'el licenciado' Zárate, a local lawyer. The narrator plays no part in the action of the novel, and the characters of the novel undertake no journeys in a literal interpretation of the word – the furthest away that Hermógenes and Catalina manage to get from Oaxaca is to Santa María El Tule, about five miles outside of town. As Solana Olivares recognised in interview, given his perceived dearth of personal experience to narrate, he decided quite simply to avoid the travel chronicle genre in any conventional sense.[4]

Instead Solana Olivares chose to fictionalise the lives of members of his own family and their friends, using them as levers to open up facets of Oaxacan history and culture, and as intermediaries between a more general historiography and his personal impressions of his trip to the town.[5] Two members of the Solana family are mentioned in the

---

[3] Personal interview with the author, 22 May 1996.
[4] Solana Olivares's most recent publication, *Parisgótica* (Debate, 2003) also follows this pattern, choosing to fictionalise and intertextually embroider a real journey made by the author.
[5] The germ for this approach is already evident in Solana Olivares's short-story 'Lluvia en Monte Albán', *Casa del Tiempo*, 14 (November 1992), 44,

book by hearsay: Mateo Solana López, Solana Olivares's grandfather and a hard-nosed Spanish millowner, is worked into the dramatic web of the first chapter of the book as a contemporary of Hermógenes, and, secondly, mention is made of Viqui Solana, one of Solana Olivares's great-aunts who committed suicide in the late 1920s following the execution of the military general Manuel García Vigil with whom she had been having an illicit affair. The local legend of Viqui Solana's reappearance as a ghost in El Llano, one of the parks in Oaxaca, shortly after her death is transmuted in the text into the fictional Catalina's vision of her contemporary in the same place over thirty years later.

However, Hermógenes, with his involvement in textiles, his Spanish background and his grudging yet gradual adaptation to Oaxacan life, is clearly a mirror image of three generations of Solana Olivares's family, their fortunes and their attitudes.[6] In the final chapter of the book Solana Olivares offers the reader excerpts from Hermógenes's diary taken from the days shortly before his death, where he sets out to record his impressions of the city for the benefit of his dead wife. Here, his voice blends directly with that of Solana Olivares himself; indeed, these are virtually unadulterated excerpts from the journal Solana Olivares kept during his week in the town.

Hermógenes's journal is also a metatextual vehicle used to justify the actual shape of this 'travel chronicle'. Some of Solana Olivares's qualms about the writing of the text are transposed to a metafictional debate about the relative merits of fact and fiction:

---

      subsequently included in his collection of allusive articles and short stories *El peso de la esperanza* (Breve Fondo Editorial, 1996). Here Solana Olivares narrates an excursion to the Zapotec ruins with his grandfather as the principal protagonist, flanked by his family and his real-life friends Hermógenes and Conzatti.

6   Hermógenes's last days which, from the data given in the course of the narrative, must have taken place in the early 1960s obviously do not coincide perfectly with the data given in Solana Olivares's diary of his own visit in 1994. Nevertheless, the spirit of fusion of voices is perhaps what counts here, not factual accuracy.

      Catalina and Zárate are more fully fictional characters than Hermógenes: Catalina, for instance, stems from Italo Calvino's description of the lives of Colonial nuns in the Oaxacan Convento de Santa Catalina (in 'Under the Jaguar Sun', *Under the Jaguar Sun*, trans. by William Weaver [London: Vintage, 1993], pp. 3–29).

¿Qué haré para escribir este rompecabezas? Ficcionar, inventar, fantasear, y entrar a saco a lo que ya fue escrito. ¿Dónde está registrado el pulso de esta ciudad? ¿Cómo verla? Como algo ajeno, como algo próximo, como algo visto por primera vez, como algo visto una y otra vez. [...]
Se me ocurre que estar aquí no es tanto para acumular datos, impresiones, historias, aunque estos paseos dedicados también sean para eso. Pero quizá el sentido de este cuaderno tiene que ver con mi conciencia profunda, con percepciones más allá de la razón.[7]

Although this discourse seems a little out of place at the end of a narrative which had, until that point, largely eschewed metafictional discourse (although not references to the historiographic activities of some of the central characters), it does contribute to the destabilisation of the historiography narrated thus far by leaving evidence of the 'heteroglossic', 'inchoate' and 'unabsorbed' nature of some of the materials presented, to borrow González Echevarría's terms (see the first epigraph to this chapter), and by revealing, through the conscious qualms over composition expressed by the narrating figure, '[t]he process of making stories out of chronicles, of constructing plots out of sequences' that is central to the composition of 'historiographic metafiction', in Hutcheon's terms.[8]

Allusions: *La red de vínculos oaxaqueños*

Despite the apparent lack of travel narrative structuring *Oaxaca: crónicas sonámbulas*, the text still relies heavily on what might be referred to as an 'archive' of travel writing. In interview Solana Olivares noted that besides visiting Oaxaca to refresh his memories, he also spent a considerable amount of the time available reading books about Oaxaca: histories, tour guides, biographies, cultural studies, and travel narratives. In the event, Solana Olivares incorporates references

---

7   Solana Olivares, *Oaxaca: crónicas sonámbulas*, (CNCA, 1994), p. 152 and pp. 159–60, respectively. All subsequent quotations are from this edition and are indicated parenthetically in the text.
8   Hutcheon, *The Politics of Postmodernism*, p. 66.

or allusions to a dazzling array of travel narratives and their authors, starting with the chronicles of the Colonial era, and ending with the most recent accounts of the region by foreign novelists. The list includes all the obvious references, plus a number of more obscure commentators: Hernán Cortés, Fray Bartolomé de Las Casas, Giovanni Francesco Gemelli Carreri, Francisco Xavier Clavijero, Bernardino de Sahagún, Motolinía, John Chilton, Thomas Gage, Francisco de Ajofrín, Alexander von Humboldt, Désiré Charnay, Charles Étienne Brasseur, Johann Wilhelm von Müller, R. Gordon Wasson, Blas Pablo Reko, Aldous Huxley, André Breton, D.H. Lawrence, Malcolm Lowry, Carlos Castaneda, and Italo Calvino. Solana Olivares also includes references to some foreign (travel) writers, with no first-hand experience in Mexico, let alone Oaxaca (Rudyard Kipling, Sir Richard Burton, Friedrich Nietzsche), and to the travel chronicles of the Mexicans Alejandro Villaseñor, Manuel Toussaint and José Vasconcelos. This mass of travel writing is partly referred to from knowledge of the primary sources, and partly culled from biographies of the writers and histories of the area. There is, thus, a deliberate blurring of the origin of authority and of authorship at work here: references turn into allusions which are further undercut by their presentation in the story itself.

Solana Olivares uses this stock of references to create a collage travel chronicle of Oaxaca, which is held together by the lifestories of the fictional characters of the novel: it is 'una novela mosaica'.[9] In turn, however, the subjects – facts, events, customs, legends, beliefs – introduced by these references are used as the motor for the fictional narrative which advances according to the logic of the literary collage, rather than that of reality, or even verisimilitude. Solana Olivares's account of Oaxaca works through the counterpoint between intertextual references and the fiction of Hermógenes and friends.

In Hermógenes's 'cuaderno' the original mosaic structure of the text, interweaving themes and authors, is made apparent:

> Datos psiquiátricos: la locura en la ciudad. Pitos, falos, sexo en Oaxaca. […] Si una noche de invierno un viajero: ¿estructura? Calvino en Oaxaca. El hongo, la droga y los estados alterados de conciencia. El alcohol en Oaxaca: violencia +

---

9   Personal interview.

mujeres + alcohol. Mezcal, mezcalina, diablos. Oaxaca, reservorio energético y mágico. María Sabina, don Juan, don Genaro, Sancho Panza en Ixtlán. Saul Bellow: 'Oaxaca, no Cuernavaca.' [...] Oaxaca, la Dublín de Joyce. [...] Falta Nietzsche: Andrés Henestrosa vuelve a citarlo. ¿Mircea Eliade fue a Oaxaca? Los amantes de Oaxaca. Los amores de Oaxaca. Las mujeres de Oaxaca. Donaji: ¿neurosis de destino, patrón de comportamiento, fatalidad para todas? Yo y Catalina, Lowry y su mujer, Lawrence y la suya. Huxley y las puertas de la percepción oaxaqueñas: ¿cielo e infierno? (pp. 161–62)

The 'story' element was then laid over this framework. The result is that in each chapter a travel writer (or writers) and a theme is selected. These are subsequently set against a concrete historical background, and woven into the fictional thread of the narrative.

The opening chapter, 'El tedio de Hermógenes', introduces the main protagonist, his nascent relationship with Catalina Ochoterena Mori, and, through his profession, the presence of the textile industry in Oaxaca. It sets the date at 1928, exploring the relationship between upheaval in the textile industry and the post-Revolutionary situation, and introducing a number of historical characters as points of reference and as actors in the outer circles of the fiction: the mill owner Mateo Solana López, the socialist activist Jesús Gonthier, the mill mechanic Manuel González and others. As a contrast to Hermógenes's initially negative impressions of Oaxaca, Solana Olivares uses the more enthusiastic comments of Francisco de Ajofrín, taken from his *Diario del viaje a la Nueva España* (written 1763–67), to introduce some of the more general aspects of the city: its geographical situation and climate, its attractive building materials and city plan, its inhabitants' sleepy, good-natured approach to life and its good chocolate!

Chapter 6, 'El llanto en el Tule', stages Hermógenes's marriage proposal to Catalina at the base of the *ahuehuete* tree in Santa María El Tule. Here, Solana Olivares uses the tree – reputedly the tree with the largest girth in the world and the subject of some considerable attention in most travel guides and chronicles concerning the area – as a catalyst for the fiction through a discussion of the legends and texts concerning the tree (Calvino, Charnay and others). Through the conversation between Hermógenes and Catalina, the belief that the tree is a petrified lake leads the pair to a discussion of water and alchemy. The subject of water leads Catalina onto the subject of crying and the suggestion that Vasconcelos would have come to El Tule to lament his political defeats, and from there the text moves on to Vasconcelos's relationship with Oaxaca. Hermógenes's acceptance of Catalina's unsubstantiated claim concerning Vasconcelos ('¿Contamos con algún testimonio de que Vasconcelos se lamentó desde aquí?' [p. 77]) is an indicator of his growing acceptance of the Oaxacan Catalina and her dependence on allusions, and alternative, simultaneous realities, as opposed to concrete references and causalities. He is starting to show signs of transculturation.

In 'El tedio de Hermógenes' intertextual references are generally explicit: they are quoted verbatim, encased within the correct punctuation and with due credit given in the bibliography at the end of the book. Alternately, they are paraphrased, re-dramatised for economy's sake, without losing sight of their original author, and without being sucked into the fictional narrative – they are used as descriptive aids by the narrator. As the story advances, these references become less clearly defined from the fictional narrative: the quotation marks remain, but the exact identity of the author is obscured. There is, for example, a reference to Octavio Paz's 'Piedra de sol' at the end of the first chapter: '"Inmensa y verdinegra como un arból." Hermógenes entró a la noche oaxaqueña del poeta' (p. 20).[10] Few Mexican readers would have difficulty sourcing this quotation to Paz – he was, after all, 'el poeta' in 1990s Mexico, although he was not in 1928. Already Solana Olivares's fictional liberties with literature and history are evident.

Later, even the quotation marks evaporate. In a passage describing the cathedral: 'fortaleza, espesor de muros, bóvedas rebajadas, escasas cúpulas' (p. 97), all the words and phrases are to be found in Manuel Toussaint's description of 'El templo oaxaqueño'.[11] Whereas earlier in the narrative, the omnipotent narrator comments that Zárate 'hubiera firmado como propias las observaciones arquitectónicas de Toussaint sobre las casas tradicionales del lugar' (p. 64), before quoting them

---

10   From the collection *La estación violenta* (1957), now collected in *Libertad bajo palabra: 1935–57*, ed. by Enrico Mario Santí (Madrid: Cátedra, 1988).

11   Manuel Toussaint, *Oaxaca y Tasco*, ill. by Francisco Díaz de León, Lecturas Mexicanas, 80 (SEP / FCE, 1985), p. 24.

correctly, here the description is woven into Hermógenes's imagined memories of Malcolm Lowry's experiences in Oaxaca, without clear acknowledgement.

The standard structure for facilitating Zárate's and Hermógenes's historical interludes is thus: after nearly seven pages of quotations and reconstructions of the story of the seventeenth-century indigenous Oaxacan Juan Matías's failed trip to Spain to play before the King, there follows, without any transition: 'Pero ¿qué me dice usted del grande Macedonio? – preguntó Zárate, acodado con pereza en el mostrador vespertino de la tienda de Hermógenes' (p. 109). The link between recorded history and the fiction of Hermógenes and Zárate is established, but after the history rather than before, to underline its tenuous nature. This is an efficient way of blending intertextual references with the main narrative. It also undermines the authority of those references and reveals Hermógenes and Zárate as unreliable cultural magpies who 'borrow' liberally from literature and history.

Zárate collects scraps of properly documented Oaxacan history and travel narrative, and shows them off in his conversations with Hermógenes at the end of the day, over the counter of El Nuevo Mundo. Zárate is described as someone who 'tenía fama de intelectual' (p. 43), and as 'el docto repetidor de citas' (p. 85). His intellectual pursuits include the preparation of a history of Oaxaca, which, in a Proustian fashion, the reader might assume to be the text that he or she is currently reading.[12] Nevertheless, Zárate is Oaxacan, and has a 'Oaxacan' understanding of the multiple realities and chronologies that make up history. This local trait somewhat undermines the 'legality' of his history, although Zárate generally remains a mouthpiece for the Western 'chronicle' approach.

Hermógenes attempts to beat Zárate at his own game; however, the former's aptitude and interest in this activity are different from latter's. Initially Hermógenes is bored by the lack of progress (linear time) in Oaxaca (pp. 11–12), where he, like so many nineteenth-century travel writers, stumbles over the non-existent chronology of the area (the Tule tree can only be described as 'Egyptian', to indicate the lack of coincidence

---

12   The key to this is given in the last chapter of the book (pp. 149–50).

with the time of Christianity [p. 73]). His search for concrete historical truths is frustrated. Nevertheless, although his interest in the works of the 'viajeros naturalistas' such as Charnay survives (p. 113), Hermógenes slowly stops worrying about time scales, and redirects his attention to the rituals of daily life, to the all-encompassing Augustinian present of his soul. He starts to indulge in fully-fledged anachronisms, such as his 'reading' and response to Calvino's 'Under the Jaguar Sun'. Finally, we are told, 'después de tantos años en Oaxaca', Hermógenes 'había remplazado su jacobinismo peninsular por una suerte de antropología estupefacta, dispuesta a aceptar cualquier manifestación que rayara los surcos del día' (p. 122). Hermógenes gradually becomes a spokesperson for indigenous models of history (myth and legend), which contrast with Zárate's Western 'chronicle' approach, and, as Linda Hutcheon has argued, work in certain examples of historiographic metafiction to 'foregound the totalizing impulse of western – imperialistic – modes of history-writing' and to undermine them.[13]

Influenced increasingly by Catalina's whimsical, romantic approach to historiography, Hermógenes's contributions to his discussions with Zárate become more tangential and dubious. (Catalina herself is a vehicle for introducing material more properly ascribed to legend rather than history, such as the arrival of the Virgen de la Soledad in town on the back of a mule, or the multiple cases of ill-fated love starting with the Zapotec princess Donaji, and culminating with the apparitions of Viqui Solana. More often than not, she also overtly involves herself in the legends, through implied comparison with her own situation, or through dreams and visions.) In two cases in particular, Hermógenes displays a similar desire to involve himself in historical matters in which he cannot have taken part and to invent connections where there are none.

In the first case, the narrator comments that, 'Años después, cuando la costumbre habría sedimentado los recuerdos [...], Hermógenes afirmó que Malcolm Lowry estuvo en la fiesta de su boda con Catalina' (p. 85). Nevertheless, Hermógenes was married at the latest in 1929 and Lowry

13   Hutcheon, *The Politics of Postmodernism*, p. 65.

did not visit Oaxaca until 1937. Hermógenes goes further, asserting that he helped Lowry get out of jail and accompanied him around town.

In the second case, Hermógenes struggles to relate Macedonio Alcalá's waltz 'Dios nunca muere' to Nietzsche's theory of the death of God and his desire to visit Oaxaca expressed in a letter to his friend Peter Gast.[14] Hermógenes explains the 'phenomenon' as a productive coincidence: 'Puede deberse a la sincronicidad: dos fenómenos que surgen separadamente pero que son complementarios y entre sí elaboran una realidad más amplia' (p. 112). Zárate is not entirely convinced, thus revealing the weakness of Hermógenes's intellectual reasoning, but the fantasy of Zarathustra wandering around Oaxaca still kindles Zárate's imagination. The scene continues with some more forced arguments on Hermógenes's behalf and the story of Zárate's illicit affair with an indigenous child prostitute. As the two characters come to accept each other's weaknesses (Zárate's for women, and Hermógenes's for academic rigour), so they are more frequently likened to Flaubert's infamous pair: 'Los dos, Zárate y Hermógenes, envejecían y jugaban el juego eterno de todas las parejas, aun las simbólicas: Bouvard y Pécuchet' (p. 112).[15] It is also implied that the text that we are reading is a fusion of Zárate's history of Oaxaca with Hermógenes's more

---

14   Nietzsche's desire to visit Oaxaca, however slim a fact, has been mentioned time and again in recent journalistic articles on the subject of Oaxaca that have appeared in the Mexican press, as well as in José Luis Ontiveros's fictional travel chronicle, *El Hotel de las Cuatro Estaciones* (UAM, 1995), especially Chapter 2: 'El secreto de Oaxaca', pp. 31–47.

Carlos Monsiváis also used Alcalá's waltz as the title and epigraph to his travel chronicle of a journey to the Oaxacan coast to record the hippy pilgrimage to see the eclipse of the sun on 7 March 1970 ('Dios nunca muere: Crónica de un eclipse', *Días de guardar*, photographs by Héctor García, 13th repr. [Era, 1991], pp. 91–114).

15   Zárate's response to Hermógenes's claims with regard to Lowry and Nietzsche is described as generously 'crédulo' (p. 110). Hermógenes, on the other hand, continues to enjoy Zárate's company even after he is publicly ostracised for his affair.

Solana Olivares's predilection for pairs of 'lame' characters in the tradition of Flaubert's Bouvard and Pécuchet is also evident in his novel *La rueca y el paraíso* (CNCA / Ediciones del Equilibrista, 1995).

associative version of Oaxaca's 'identity' in his 'cuadernos', dedicated to the memory of Catalina, 'para tejer con ellos una red, porque sabía que sólo así se atrapa una ciudad: por sorpresa' (p. 150).

Of course, Solana Olivares profits from his construction of these 'lame' fictional characters to cover the weak links in his own text. Yet the weaknesses of the fictional characters also help to undermine the authority of the majority of the references. The conversations between Hermógenes and Zárate display the processing of this material as they attempt to 'reconstruir el mundo a golpe de palabras' (p. 98). Through constant retellings, the authority and authorship of even the most inaccurate texts gradually become 'versiones' of common knowledge: 'la red de vínculos oaxaqueños parecían (*sic*) crecer conforme las historias del pueblo eran contadas por el tiempo' (p. 134). The network paradigm of postmodernist Mexican travel writing is very clear here, as is its most important function – the destabilisation of traditional Western conceptions of authority, hierarchy, truth and reliability. In short, 'the chronotope of the net' facilitates the challenging of some of those key tropes that have lent themselves to the strong association between travel writing and imperialism.

Furthermore, although certain writers such as Toussaint, Lowry and Calvino are absorbed into the fiction with a twinge of irony but without criticism, the writings of figures such as Aldous Huxley, D.H. Lawrence, and André Breton are overtly criticised, through the voice of the narrator, for borrowing liberally from local sources, for failing to understand Mexico, and for being commonplace, respectively.[16] Most foreign sources present in this chronicle are thus diminished through allusion and association or through criticism. Furthermore, they are diminished in a way that, following Hutcheon's arguments, makes for a *mestizo*, Mexican, anti-totalising reading of Western modes of history-writing and an implicit critique of the validity of the travel narrative in Mexico.

---

16   *Oaxaca: crónicas sonámbulas*, pp. 30–31, 34–37, 42, & 145, respectively.

Illusions: *Viajes sonámbulos*

If Solana Olivares manages to retain a consciousness of the 'archive' of travel writing through references and allusions, and through his characters' roles as collectors of this kind of material, he also compromises its authority in the process. Another important way in which he contrives to undermine the value of materials taken from travel chronicles and related sources, and promote a Oaxacan/Mexican alternative is through his frequent references to the topic of dreams.

In *Oaxaca: crónicas sonámbulas* the linear time of history is seen to collapse in the face of the main characters' confusion and, above all disinterest, with regard to the accurate identification of historical epochs and in the face of what the narrator of *Oaxaca: crónicas sonámbulas* describes as the on-going state of colonial social relations in the Valley of Oaxaca (p. 36). Furthermore, in the experience of the main characters, particularly Hermógenes, the linear time of the journey from life to death is seen to condense into Saint Augustine's 'eternal present', where everything is held in balance in the imagination and in memories (p. 84). This undermining of linear time, where chronology and causality are substituted by simultaneity, circularity, repetition, and imaginative variations, is also underlined by the prominence of dreams, and dream travels.[17] Dreams, we are told, have particular relevance for our understanding of Oaxaca.

Solana Olivares most probably adapted the somnambulist leitmotif of his chronicle from a conjunction of the writings of Toussaint and Calvino. Toussaint opens his series of vignettes on Oaxaca with the following description of 'El aspecto de la ciudad': 'La vieja Antequera se adormece bajo las caricias del calor incipiente. Se anuncia la

---

17 Saint Augustine's conception of time where past, present and future coexist unproblematically in the mind, is also the leitmotif of *El peso de la esperanza*. The constant preoccupation with Augustine's eternal present in this collection serves to create a dreamlike atmosphere: chronological time sequences and rational causality sink under the weight of philosophical fantasies and distorted memories. Furthermore, a number of the texts make explicit reference to dreams as an integral part of the riddle of time.

primavera en la voluptuosidad de esta mañana, ensoñadora'.[18] Oaxaca is sleepy in itself, and enchanting for the traveller in a hypnotic sense. Thus Calvino, in 'Under the Jaguar Sun', describes his wife and himself as they approach the opulence of the Oaxacan dining table as 'walking like somnambulists, not quite sure we were touching the ground'.[19]

Dreams and the hypnotic magic of Oaxaca are, thus, key themes to be woven into the narrative of the story, on a par with the those of gastronomy and sensuality; themes which have frequently been commented on by visiting writers. Chapters 9 and 10 – 'Los fantasmas del mediodía' and 'El nombre oculto de Monte Albán' – do just this. 'Los fantasmas del mediodía' deals with long-forgotten religious processions and the occasional reappearances of the 'ghosts' of Oaxaca (Viqui Solana). The mention of Viqui Solana and her ill-fated love affair, loops the narrative back round to the recurrent theme of suicidal lovers, and to the sublimation of sexuality in dream images:

> Oaxaca la benemérita favorece a los amantes y a los sueños. No es una ciudad de agua, pero como la piedra con que está construida es camaleónica y cambia de color cuando se moja, la conciencia de quienes duermen entre sus paredes vagabundea con mayor frequencia. (pp. 119–20)

Following on from this, in 'El nombre oculto de Monte Albán', Solana Olivares writes: 'Son frecuentes los sueños oaxaqueños que tienen por oscuro escenario Monte Albán' (p. 131). And thus he links together the inevitable discussion of Oaxaca's greatest pre-Columbian archeological site and all the mysticism that attends it – shamanism, psychedelic drugs, trances and 'trips' –, with the traces of visiting archeologists, anthropologists, hippies and gurus, and with local syncretic beliefs and rites concerning medicine and death, which discussion functions as an omen of Catalina's and then Hermógenes's deaths in the following chapters.

The theme of dreams, as we have seen, is linked to a variety of different topics, but it most frequently prefaces discussions of an anthropological order, particularly in the second of the two chapters.

---

18   Toussaint, *Oaxaca y Tasco*, p. 9.
19   Calvino, *Under the Jaguar Sun*, p. 4.

Thus anthropological knowledge of the region is undermined by being filtered through the wandering minds of two old men and their sonambulist 'paseos'. Indeed, Hermógenes's version of anthropology is simply 'antropología estupefacta'. Yet if dreams undermine the truth value of some of the more anthropological material presented in the text, ironically the theme of 'sueño' – dream, sleep and related concepts/ disturbances such as 'ensueño', 'ilusiones ópticas', 'espejismos', 'insomnio', 'sonambulismo' – also functions as a narrative construct to facilitate the conveyance of some of the less factual aspects of Oaxacan culture. Even in the above-mentioned chapters, where dreams, and the oneiric atmosphere of the text as a whole, work to undermine some of the foreign, anthropological travel writing references, they are also specifically used to introduce material associated with local legends, beliefs and practices, firstly the preserve of Catalina, then Hermógenes, and then even Zárate. The archive, particularly the archive of materials of popular culture and indigenous sources, is thus reinforced. Dreams may also function, then, as a supporting device for the anti-totalising, anti-imperialistic purpose of this chronicle.

Archival Travel Writing

In many ways *Oaxaca: crónicas sonámbulas* fits exactly Roberto González Echevarría's definition of 'archival fiction', outlined in his *Myth and Archive*.[20] González Echevarría argues that narrative in Latin America has always been predicated on certain imported master narratives: the discourse of the law, projected in Latin America through the chronicles of the Conquest and ensuing Colonial era; the discourse of science, projected through the journals of scientific travellers in the nineteenth century; and the discourse of anthropology – a way of generating stories, myths of cultural origins, thus responding to the twentieth century drive for cultural identity –, projected through the

---

20 The following analysis of trends in Latin American literature is glossed from González Echevarría, *Myth and Archive*, especially pp. 1–42 and 142–86.

studies of anthropological investigators in the early twentieth century. Latin American writers of each epoch have achieved a critical absorption of each master narrative, telling the story of their 'otherness' in terms other than their own, hence using, yet simultaneously estranging, the code used to define them. The typical Latin American texts produced under the auspices of such master narratives have devoted much of their attention to masquerading their fictions as legal, scientific and anthropological truths.

Owing to the crisis of legitimacy in the field of anthropology that occurred during the period that followed the end of the Second World War, provoked by the beginning of decolonisation in the British and French empires and the growth of at least a certain feeling of 'postcoloniality' in Latin America (in Jorge Klor de Alva's terms[21]), the anthropological master narrative of Latin American literature also began to founder, and writers started to produce works that critiqued their previous works by juggling all three master narratives at once and hence revealing the insufficiencies of each. These texts advertised themselves now as overt fictions, and through metafiction, they focused attention on their own constructed nature. The icon of this balancing act was the 'Archive', where dead and nearly dead master narratives were stored.

In terms of the most basic, defining features of such archival fiction, the Archive, in González Echevarría's definition, typically requires 'the existence of an inner historian who reads the texts, interprets and writes them', and indeed, this historian or archivist may also synecdochically represent the Archive.[22] The archivist is typically an extremely old, nearly dead, or dead person:

> Death is a metaphor for the impossibility of knowledge, or about the impossibility of there being any discourse about the Other that is not based on a potentially lethal power. [...] Senility is a figure for the gaps in these archival characters.

---

21   Jorge Klor de Alva, 'The Postcolonization of the (Latin) American Experience: A Reconsideration of "Colonialism," "Postcolonialism," and "Mestizaje"', in *After Colonialism: Imperial Histories and Postcolonial Displacements*, ed. by Gyan Prakash (Princeton, NJ: Princeton UP, 1995), pp. 241–75, especially p. 245.

22   González Echevarría, *Myth and Archive*, pp. 22 & 170.

> [...] Senility is [...] a metaphor for the incompleteness of the Archive, but also for the force, the glue by which texts are bound together. There is a whimsical creativity in these characters' recollections that is parallel to how selection takes place in the Archive in the creation of fiction, and which is found in their lapses of memory. [...] Death stands for the gap of gaps, the mastergap of the Archive, both its opening and closing cipher. [...]
> Narrative self-reflexiveness [...] is a figure of death. Self-historicizing brings forth the gap wherein these dead or dying figures spin their web of writing.[23]

And finally, the Archive needs 'the presence of an unfinished manuscript that the inner historian is trying to complete'.[24] On account of the race against time to complete the Archive before death, and the 'whimsical creativity' of the archivist, 'The Archive [...] does not add up'.[25] What the reader reads, are the 'leftovers' of the Archive.

The kind of highly intertextual and self-reflexive narrative that results from the 'leftovers' of the Archive is what González Echevarría terms the 'archival fiction' (see the first epigraph to this chapter). However, although it suggests a novel, 'knowing' approach to the master narratives of old and to earlier Latin American reactions to those master narratives, the 'archival fiction', in its attempt to function as the 'myth of myths', to provide a master key to the cultural origins of Latin America, still generally comes under the sway of anthropological discourse, rather than responds to any newer master narrative or goes beyond master narratives altogether.[26] In essence, then, the limitation of González Echevarría's definition for our purposes here is that what he terms 'archival fiction' fits perfectly the works of the Latin American Boom and these, in his analysis, are generally considered to be more clearly under the sway of high modernism than postmodernism. Nevertheless, González Echevarría notes that 'archival fictions' have not ceased being written in contemporary Latin America, and he cites paradigmatic examples from the late 1980s.[27] In what follows, then, I

---

23 González Echevarría, *Myth and Archive*, pp. 165, 183–84, respectively.
24 González Echevarría, *Myth and Archive*, p. 22.
25 González Echevarría, *Myth and Archive*, p. 180.
26 González Echevarría, *Myth and Archive*, pp. 174–76.
27 González Echevarría, *Myth and Archive*, p. 186.

would like to attempt to sketch out a way in which some 'archival fictions' might be seen to accommodate a more postmodernist worldview.

In the first place, the parallels between González Echevarría's definition of 'archival fictions' and Hutcheon's specifically postmodernist 'historiographic metafiction' are compelling. 'Historiographic metafiction' may be defined as a kind of historical narrative that reveals the seams of its own composition through metatextual asides, anachronisms, loss of causality, etcetera, and that questions the way history is written, the relationship of fact and fiction in such texts.[28] 'Archival fiction' may thus be considered a particular subset or even chronotope of 'historiographic metafiction' – it has certain defining features (the old archivist, the unfinished manuscript, the high degree of intertextuality) but its general objectives are similarly a self-conscious examination of the production of history and knowledge and a response to the more generalised crisis of truth and representation that many see as the cornerstone of postmodernism. Thus works such as García Márquez's *Cien años de soledad* (1967) function as maximum examples of both 'archival fiction' and postmodernist 'historiographic metafiction'.

The point is not that all 'archival fiction' from the Boom onwards should be reclassified as postmodernist, but that there are aspects of González Echevarría's definition of 'archival fiction' that lend themselves to postmodernism, and where they are most prevalent, such narratives might be considered specifically postmodernist examples of 'archival fiction'. Thus, refining González Echevarría's definition, we might add that where 'archival fictions' most clearly eschew issues of classification and where they also show signs of moving beyond the sway of anthropological discourse, and thus cease trying to provide a master key or totalising solution to the cultural origins of Latin America, it is possible to seem them as part of postmodernist cultural production.

Solana Olivares's text clearly fits the general mould of archival fiction. *Oaxaca: crónicas sonámbulas* is historical in its overall structure, and it makes an obvious attempt to balance the three master narratives of Latin American narrative (legal, naturalist and anthropological) in

---

28 Hutcheon, *The Politics of Postmodernism*, pp. 62–92 (see also the epigraph to this chapter).

its mosaic of intertextual references and allusions, undermining these master narratives through their subordinate relationship to the characters in the fictional narrative: the weaknesses of the three main characters weaken the material of the master narratives. Zárate, the lawyer, breaks the law in his relationship with the under-age prostitute. Hermógenes invents coincidences to complement the timelessness of Oaxaca, undermining the naturalist project to fix (natural) history. Catalina, in her dreams, invents and adapts myths to suit herself.

All three characters represent the Archive through their activities in collecting and collating material. As they grow older, the nature of their associations and classifications becomes more fanciful, more creative. In death, only fragments of their knowledge remain: Hermógenes's journal, unfinished and riddled with gaps, is the starting point for the generation of *Oaxaca: crónicas sonámbulas*; a text which is a collation of Zárate's local history and Hermógenes's memories, thus revealing a further archival layer. The metatextual nature of the journal also reinforces the ironic self-awareness which is the crux of archival fiction. And finally, in line with the Archive's ability to accumulate a mass of unabsorbed documents which offer 'evidence of the non-assimilation of the Other' (see the first epigraph to this chapter), Solana Olivares's archival travel chronicle contains a substantial amount of mostly foreign travel writing on the subject of Oaxaca and, in its spurious regurgitation of such material through the mouthpieces of its central characters, it displays its 'non-assimilationist' stance, its critical distance *vis-à-vis* travel writing concerning Mexico and the practice of travel writing in general.

With respect to the more postmodernist aspects of this 'archival fiction', *Oaxaca crónicas sonámbulas* does suggest a move beyond the issue of classification in its central characters' inability to distinguish fact from fiction or, rather, their willingness to leave material unclassified in this respect. And it does suggest a move beyond anthropological discourse in its 'knowing', 'ironic' treatment of the subject, in its consignment of the topics of anthropology and dreams to the same order of truth, and in the acknowledged futility of the characters' attempts to capture the essence of Oaxaca. It may thus be considered an example of postmodernist 'archival fiction'.

But what of the postcolonialist aspects of this postmodernist 'archival fiction'? 'Archival fiction', as mentioned earlier, is strongly related to the emergence of the discourse of postcolonialism in the 1960s and 70s, and the Archive itself offers evidence of 'the non-assimilation of the Other' in its undigested presentation of excepts of Western historical/scientific/anthropological texts. This in essence, is a contestatory, postcolonialist stance towards Western discourses of knowledge. Although Hutcheon's analysis of 'historiographic metafiction' is directed towards its postmodernist rather than potentially postcolonialist aspects, she, too, places particular emphasis on this kind of fiction's need to challenge 'the totalizing impulse of *western – imperialistic* – modes of history-writing' (my italics).[29] Key to both 'historiographic metafiction' and 'archival fiction', then, is the desire to challenge Western, purportedly 'universal', forms of historiography.

It is thus no surprise that an archival text such as *Oaxaca: crónicas sonámbulas* has a strong postcolonialist agenda. In short, it is the text's ability to undermine the attempts made by more traditional, often foreign, travel writers to produce a single, authoritative, essentialising version of what they see and experience during their travels in Mexico, as well as its ability to simultaneously offer a *mestizo*, Mexican alternative in its multiple versions of Oaxaca and its 'realidad más amplia' (p. 112), that comprise its most obvious postcolonialist agenda.

Unlike other contemporary works that we have examined in this study, Solana Olivares's text does, on occasion, suggest a recognisably postcolonialist critique of the Spanish conquest of Mexico and its legacy in its description of social inequality in the region (p. 36). Nevertheless, the real critique in this text is directed at the representatives of Northern European and United States imperialism who have travelled in and written about the region since the beginning of the nineteenth century. Hence the comments about the legacy of Spanish colonialism mentioned above are circumscribed by a critique of D.H. Lawrence's inability to really understand the situation of the indigenous population and its relationship with the 'capa proprietaria y dirigente [...]: española, criolla, mestiza, cacica' (p. 36) since he perceived only a fixed set of

---

29   Hutcheon, *The Politics of Postmodernism*, p. 65.

social relations where the indigenous communities were always posited as 'backward' and as 'savages' rather than a question of historical circumstance. For Solana Olivares, then, colonialism was bad enough, but imperialist ignorance is even worse. This is thus an example of postimperialism in the same vein as that expressed by Juan Villoro rather than an example of postcolonialism proper. Since the criticism is directed at imperialist designs on Mexico and, because such designs are closely associated with their expression in travel writing, Solana Olivares's decision to avoid the genre in his own work also displays a tacit critique of the genre *per se* because of this association.

Complementing this postimperialist stance, and despite the brief evidence of more traditional postcolonialist criticism of the Spanish legacy in Mexico mentioned above, Solana Olivares also shows evidence of the more comprehensive and comprehending attitude to Spanish–Mexican relations that I identified in the work of Héctor Perea as an example of 'Mexican postcolonialism'. Although Solana Olivares's work is perhaps not quite as even-handed as Perea's in its treatment of Spanish–Mexican relations, it nevertheless explores at length the complementarity and inseparability of the components of the Spanish and the indigenous in Oaxacan/Mexican identity, and in particular, it traces the complex process of *mestizaje* that has formed Mexicans' understanding of their own identity through the gradual transculturation of the Spaniard Hermógenes and his Western worldview during his time in Oaxaca.

Oaxaca: crónicas sonámbulas, then, stretches the 'chronotope of the net' format for postmodernist travel writing to its limits and achieves maximum postcolonialist effect in so doing, combining the 'postimperialist' critique I identified as key to Villoro's travel writing in *Palmeras de la brísa rápida* with the 'Mexican postcolonialism' found in Perea's *México: crónica en espiral*. Nevertheless, despite their different approaches, all three writers use postmodernist narrative techniques to productive postcolonialist effect. In particular the critical distance that such texts mark out between themselves (as travel writing) and the (imperialist) genre of travel writing as a whole may be seen as the key to understanding how Mexican writers can reconcile themselves with a genre that has been so closely involved in the history of their colonisation and subsequent imperialist exploitation.

Conclusion
'Mexicans Aren't Great Travellers'

Desde niño sé que el mundo se divide en mexicanos y turistas. Nuestra relación con el extranjero no da para resentimientos de largo alcance; los norteamericanos y los franceses nos han invadido sin que esto impida que hoy sean propietarios del Four Seasons o el Club Med (donde el mexicano es un chaparro que ofrece cocos con ron de bienvenida).

Si los alemanes mandan sus aspirinas al mundo para triunfar ante cualquier dolor de cabeza, nosotros sabemos que nada es universalizable: un sarape es de Saltillo, una guitarra de Paracho, una cecina de Yecapixtla, un libro del sur de la ciudad de México. Las cosas buenas se mueven poco. Si tanto nos necesitan los demás, pos que vengan. Nuestro sistema de correos demuestra a diario que las zonas geográficas alejadas del ombligo son *terra incognita*. El mexicano siente una atracción gravitacional por la milpa o el condominio que lo vio nacer, es decir, que muy rara vez se convierte en explorador ártico. Alzar la vista (acto esencial del viajero con instamátic) no va con el hombre ensimismado. Pero no nos quejemos, que lo nuestro es ser anfitriones.[1]

El cuaderno de viaje es un artículo sospechoso o mal visto en las aduanas de los géneros literarios y aparece de contrabando en el equipaje, en los velices llenos de prosa, como si fuese un alimento fresco o, peor aún, como un ser vivo, una especie infecciosa y escurridiza. Quizá por eso los cuadernos de viaje son tan escasos entre nosotros y, cuando se dan, aparecen revueltos entre la prosa o bien confinados a una categoría inferior, palabra de segunda mano. [...]

Los viajes no son el fuerte del mexicano. Es cierto que nuestros antepasados iniciaron una marcha huyendo del frío y del hambre que nadie sabe muy bien dónde empezó pero que concluyó en el antiguo lago del Anáhuac. Cierto que los aztecas fueron comerciantes aventureros que recorrieron infatigables el territorio mexicano. Cierto que las guerras del XIX y la Revolución – las revoluciones – se verificaron como hazañas peatonales. Pero es también innegable que la nuestra, mestiza, no es una nación impulsada por el espíritu de aventura. Hasta donde sabemos no hay en la Antártida ninguna depresión apellidada Pochotitla ni Morelos o Iturbide – o cualquier otro que fuese el apellido del improbable explorador mexicano.[2]

1 Juan Villoro, 'Todos somos gondoleros', *LJS*, 17 May 1998, 15.
2 Adolfo Castañón, 'Palabras pasajeras (Introducción)', in *Lugares que pasan*, Cuaderno de Viaje (CNCA, 1998), pp. 17–20.

Juan Villoro and Adolfo Castañón, both writing in 1998, continue the tradition of denying the existence of travel and travel writing by Mexicans, whether it concerns travel to the Arctic, the Antarctic, or the provinces of their own country, and despite the fact that they are either known for their published travel books (Villoro), or are including this disclaimer in the opening pages of a book of travel writing (Castañón). As Patrick Holland and Graham Huggan have noted, travel writers frequently announce the death of travel and hence of travel writing in their texts, and indeed such a 'type of lament for "true" travel writing can be used to *promote*, rather than discourage, the circulation of contemporary travel narratives' (authors' italics).[3] However, in the context of Mexican travel writing, such statements are not just bashful or ironic commonplaces – a slash-and-burn technique to clear the ground for new journeys by themselves and others –, but key rhetorical manoeuvres that signal the informed, postcolonialist, nature of some contemporary Mexican writers' practice of the genre. They are a way for these writers to acknowledge the genre's problematic history from a postcolonialist point of view, in order for them to be able to write their own travel books with the weight of such a history thus lightened, if not entirely lifted. Furthermore, even if much of what is published under the rubric of travel writing in contemporary Mexico falls within the parameters of the traditional, realist genre with all its attendant imperialist tendencies intact, radically postmodernist examples of the genre that work according to the principles of the 'chronotope of the net' can and do avoid the pitfalls of such tendencies. Even if such texts threaten to explode the boundaries of the traditional genre, rendering it unrecognisable as such, the importance of their rhetorical challenge to some of the most imperishable and uncomfortable features of the genre from a postcolonialist point of view, justify the importance of their study.

POSTSCRIPT: At the risk of unravelling the argument put forth in this study – that recent developments in postmodernism have helped offer an

---

3   Patrick Holland & Graham Huggan, *Tourists with Typewriters: Critical Reflections on Contemporary Travel Writing* (Ann Arbor: University of Michigan Press, 1998), p. 203.

alternative to the traditional chronotope that defines travel writing and that certain Mexican authors have used this in such a way as to highlight and critique the imperialist associations that the genre has, and that for them, as inevitably postcolonial writers, are singularly uncomfortable – a recent re-reading of Holland and Huggan's *Tourists with Typewriters*, has also reminded me of quite how much contemporary Mexican travel writers have in common with contemporary Anglophone travel writers – even the possibility of postcolonialist-inspired countertravel writing is evident in both contemporary Anglophone and Mexican travel writing.

What might be taken away from this is not that Mexican travel writing is without local particularities which relate to the history of colonial and imperial domination in the region, nor that Mexican travel writing is merely imitative of the models – including the newer countertravel writing models – so powerfully disseminated by the Anglophone publishing industry. Rather, one should conclude that contemporary Mexican travel writing participates in a global cultural economy and where, in some instances, it can be read as contesting Mexico's place in that system, refusing the temptation to generate the traditional knowledge produced by the travel narrative, or to genuflect without irony before previous generations of imperial adventurers, in a great many others the issues with which it wrestles, both in terms of content – the issue of globalisation – and in terms of style – how to incorporate (post)modernist aesthetics into such a traditional genre – are those with which Anglophone writers must also grapple. Now more than ever before, it is impossible to keep travel writers in a particular national box and to ascribe their tendencies and preferences solely to that national origin. The current chronotope foregrounds an increasingly complex dance of transcultural relationality that will continue to play out in challenging and innovative forms in the years to come.

This study cannot claim to be an exhaustive account of Mexican travel writing in Mexico over the last two centuries and it recognises several lacunae. The most glaring of these is the absence of any coverage of travel accounts by Mexican women writers. Though less in number than those penned by men, such accounts do, of course, exist. They have been omitted here because they are significantly different in approach to those written by Mexican men and really merit a study apart to do them justice. Of the material that has been published in recent years, another area that merits further study, and that serendipitously overlaps with the above, is that of the travel writing produced by 'hyphenated' Mexicans – Jewish-Mexicans, Lebanese-Mexicans, Mexican-Americans/ Chicanos and so forth. Such accounts might include Margo Glantz's *Las genealogías* (1981), Rosa Nissán's *Las tierras prometidas: crónica de un viaje a Israel* (1997), and Guillermo Gómez-Peña's *Dangerous Border Crossers: The Artist Talks Back* (2000). It is just such explorations of transcultural relationality, of the frontiers of Mexican society, both within and beyond the nation's borders, and such questionings of the relationship between one's self and the society or societies to which one belongs that are the future of Mexican travel writing.[4]

---

4 Almost inevitably, my future research will concentrate on these areas. A book on Mexican women travellers is planned for publication in 2009.

Bibliography

The place of publication is presumed to be Mexico City unless otherwise stated.

The following abbreviations for Mexican publishers and publications have been used throughout:

CNCA   Consejo Nacional para la Cultura y las Artes
FCE   Fondo de Cultura Económica
LJ(S)   La Jornada (Semanal)
SEP   Secretaría de Educación Pública
UAM   Universidad Autónomo Metropolitana
UNAM   Universidad Nacional Autónoma de México

Primary Texts – Mexican Travel Writing

[This section of the bibliography aims to provide as complete a record as possible of Mexican travel chronicles published in book form, as well as one or two more fictional or essayistic texts that deal extensively with the subject of travel. Inevitably, however, there are omissions, particularly with respect to nineteenth-century publications. The cut-off date for works included here is generally 1998, although some later works have been included where relevant.]

Abreu Gómez, Ermilo. *Andanzas y extravíos: memorias* (Botas, 1965).
Aguilar, Héctor Orestes. *Un disparo en la niebla: recorridos y lecturas desde la otra Europa* (Cal y Arena, 1997).
Agustín, José. *Ciudades desiertas* (Alfaguara, 1995).
——. *Dos horas de sol* (Seix Barral, 1994).
——. *Se está haciendo tarde (final en laguna)* (Mortiz, 1994).
Almada, Pedro J. *99 días en jira con el Presidente Cárdenas* (Botas, 1943).
Almonte, Juan Nepomuceno. *Guía de forasteros, y repertorio de conocimientos útiles*, prol. by Vicente Quirarte (Imprenta de I. Cumplido, 1852; Instituto Mora, 1997).

Altamirano, Ignacio Manuel. *Obras completas*, ed. by Nicole Girón (SEP, 1986–); I: *Discursos y brindis*, ed. by Catalina Sierra Casasús & Jesús Sotelo Inclán, prol. by Jesús Reyes Heroles (1986); V: *Textos costumbristas*, ed, by José Joaquín Blanco (1986); VII: *Crónicas I*, ed. by Carlos Monsiváis (1987); XIII: *Escritos de literatura y arte, II*, ed. by José Luis Martínez (1988).

———. *Paisajes y leyendas: tradiciones y costumbres de México, primera y segunda series*, prol.. by Jacqueline Covo, Sepan Cuantos..., 275, 4th edn (Porrúa, 1989).

Altamirano, Ignacio Manuel & Gonzalo A. Esteva, eds. *El Renacimiento*, 2 vols (Díaz de León & White, 1869), I (2 January–28 August 1869); II (4 September–18 December 1869).

Arróniz, Marcos. *Manual del viajero en México* (Paris: Librería de Rosa y Bouret, 1858; repr. Instituto Mora, 1991).

Avilés, René. *Las estrellas rojas* (Costa-Amic, 1967).

Benítez, Fernando. *China a la vista* (Cuadernos Americanos, 1953).

———. *En la tiera mágica del peyote*, 5th repr. (Era, 1992).

———. *Los hongos alucinantes*, 5th edn (Era, 1983).

———. *Los indios de México*, 7th repr., 5 vols (Era, 1991).

———. *Los indios de México: antología*, ed. by Héctor Manjarrez, prol. by Carlos Fuentes (Era, 1989).

———. *Ki: el drama de un pueblo y de una planta*, Lecturas Mexicanas, 78, 1st repr. (SEP / FCE, 1992).

———. *La Nao de China* (Cal y Arena, 1989).

———. *La ruta de Hernán Cortés*, ill. by Alberto Beltrán, Colección Popular, 56, 3rd edn (FCE, 1974).

———. *La ruta de la libertad*, 3rd edn (Partido Revolucionario Institucional, 1976).

———. *Viaje al centro de México*, Colección Popular, 150, 3rd repr. (FCE, 1987).

Beteta, Ramón. *Camino a Tlaxcalantongo*, 1st repr. (FCE, 1990).

Blanco, Alberto. *Cuenta de los guías* (Era, 1992).

Blanco, José Joaquín. *Cuando todas las chamacas se pusieron medias nylon (y otras crónicas)* (Boldó i Climent / Enjambre, 1988).

Bulnes, Francisco. *Páginas escogidas*, ed. by Martín Quirarte, Biblioteca del Estudiante Universitario, 89, 2nd edn (UNAM, 1995).

Carballo, Emmanuel, ed. *¿Qué país es éste?: los Estados Unidos y los gringos vistos por escritores mexicanos de los siglos XIX y XX*, Sello Bermejo (CNCA, 1996).

Castañón, Adolfo. *Lugares que pasan*, Cuaderno de Viaje (CNCA, 1998).

Castellanos Lira, Arturo. *Nueva crónica de un país bárbaro: diagnóstico crítico de Chihuahua*, prol. by José Antonio Montero, 2nd edn (Costa-Amic, 1974).

Celorio, Gonzalo. *México: ciudad de papel* (Tusquets, 1997).

———. *El viaje sedentario: varia invención*, Colección Andanzas (Tusquets, 1994).

Chavero, Alfredo. *Obras*, 6 vols (Agüeros, 1904), I: *Escritos diversos*, prol. by Dr N. León.

Chimal, Carlos. *Cinco del águila* (Era, 1990).

Clavijero, Francisco Xavier. *Historia de la Antigua o Baja California*, trans. by Nicolás García de San Vicente (Imprenta del Museo Nacional de Arqueología, Historia y Etnografía, 1933).
Correa, Eduardo J. *Viaje a Termápolis* (Botas, 1937).
Covarrubias, Miguel. *Island of Bali* (London: Kegan Paul, 1986).
———. *Mexico South: The Isthmus of Tehuantepec* (London: Cassell, [1946?]).
'Crónica de un día cualquiera: Ciudad de México', issue of *Nexos*, 150 (June 1990).
Cuevas, José Luis. *Historias del viajero* (Puebla: Premiá, 1987).
Curiel, Fernando. *Vida en Londres*, Lecturas Mexicanas, 2nd series, 84 (SEP, 1987).
Dalevuelta, Jacobo. *Cariño a Oaxaca: escrito para viandantes* (Botas, 1938).
Diego Blanco, Hugo. *Ángelus*, Cuaderno de Viaje (CNCA, 1995).
Domenella, Ana Rosa, & Nora Pasternac, eds. *Las voces olvidadas: antología crítica de narradoras mexicanas nacidas en el siglo XIX*, 1st repr. (Colegio de México, 1997).
Dromundo, Baltasar. *Europa lírica* (Costa-Amic, 1969).
Félix, Ofelia de. *Caminos bajo el sol* ([n.p.]: Gobierno del Estado de Sonora, 1959).
Fernández Ledesma, Gabriel. *Viaje Alrededor de mi Cuarto: París, 1938* ('Yolotepec', 1958; repr. Aguascalientes: Instituto Cultural de Aguascalientes / Gobierno del Estado de Aguascalientes, 1992).
Frías Conor, B. *Un yucateco en Zacatecas* (Botas, 1940).
Gante, Pablo C. de. *La Ruta de Occidente: las ciudades de Toluca y Morelia* (Departamento Autónomo de Prensa y Publicidad, 1939).
García, María Victoria. *Vi(r)aje a la memoria* (Puebla, Pue.: Benemérita Universidad de Puebla, 1997).
García Bergua, Ana. *Postales desde el puerto*, Cuaderno de Viaje (CNCA, 1997).
———. *El umbral: Travels and Adventures* (Era, 1993).
García de León, Antonio; Elena Poniatowska; Carlos Monsiváis & others. *EZLN, documentos y comunicados: 1 de enero / 8 de agosto 1994*, photography by Paula Haro, 2nd repr. (Era, 1995).
García Oropeza, Guillermo. *Viaje mexicano: crónica de un vicio*, SEP/80, 58 (SEP / FCE, 1983).
Garibay, Ricardo. *Acapulco* (Grijalbo, 1979).
———. *Chicoasén* (SEP / Gernika, 1986).
Garrido, Felipe. *Viejo continente*, Biblioteca Joven, 23 (FCE / Consejo Nacional de Recursos para la Atención de la Juventud, 1985).
Garrido, Luis. *Días y hombres de España* (Finisterre, 1966).
———. *Evocaciones de Italia* (UNAM, 1958).
———. *La sonrisa de París* (Botas, 1962).
———. *Trasuntos de Egipto* ([n. pub.], 1951).
———. *Venecia, la incomparable*, prol. by Antonio Castro Leal (Editorial Letras, 1966).
———. *Voces de Francia* (Botas, 1957).
Garro, Elena. *Memorias de España, 1937* (Siglo XXI, 1992).
Garza Toba, Manuel. *Hojas sueltas de París*, 2nd edn (Costa-Amic, 1977).
Glantz, Margo. *Las genealogías* (Casillas, 1981).

Gómez-Peña, Guillermo. *Dangerous Border Crossers: The Artist Talks Back* (London: Routledge, 2000).
Gómezperalta Damirón, Manuel. *Viaje en otro compartimiento* (El Caballito, 1993).
Gonzaga Urbina, Luis. *Crónicas*, ed. by Julio Torri, Biblioteca del Estudiante Universitario, 70, 2nd edn (UNAM, 1995).
Gutiérrez Nájera, Manuel. *Cuentos completos, y otras narraciones*, ed. by E.K. Mapes (FCE, 1958).
——. *Cuentos, crónicas y ensayos*, ed. by Alfredo Maillefert, Biblioteca del Estudiante Universitario, 20, 3rd edn (UNAM, 1992).
——. *Viajes extraordinarios*, ed. by Rafael Pérez Gay (Breve Fondo Editorial, 1996).
Guzmán, Martín Luis. *Crónicas de mi destierro* (Empresas Editoriales, 1964).
——. *Obras completas*, 1st repr., 2 vols (FCE, 1992), I, *A orillas del Hudson*, 31–107; *El águila y la serpiente*, 197–498; *La sombra del caudillo*, 501–650.
Hendrichs Pérez, Pedro R. *Por tierras ignotas: viajes y observaciones en la región del río de Las Balsas*, 2 vols ('Cvltvra', 1945–1946).
Hinojosa, Francisco. *Un taxi en L.A.*, Cuaderno de Viaje (CNCA, 1994).
Ibargüengoitia, Jorge. *La casa de usted y otros viajes*, ed. by Guillermo Sheridan (Mortiz, 1991).
——. *¿Olvida usted su equipaje?*, ed. by Jesús Quintero & Aline Davidoff (Mortiz, 1997).
——. *Viajes en la América ignota*, 4th repr. (Mortiz, 1992).
Ibarra, Guillermo, *Alemán en el Sureste* (Ruta, 1950).
Iduarte, Andrés. *Diez estampas mexicanas* (Secretaría de Hacienda y Crédito Público, 1971).
——. *México en la nostalgia* ('Cvltvra', 1965).
Jordán, Fernando. *El otro México: biografía de Baja California* (SEP, 1987).
Juárez, Saúl. *Señales de viaje*, Colección Narrativa, 21 (Planeta Mexicana, 1995).
La Borbolla, Óscar de. *Ucronías* (Mortiz, 1990).
La Cabada, Juan. *La tierra en cuatro tiempos: ida y vuelta*, Colección Popular, 202, 1st repr. (FCE, 1983).
La Colina, José de. *Viajes narrados*, Molinos de Viento, 81 (UAM, 1993).
La Cueva, Eusebio de. *Una primavera en Italia* (Botas, 1924).
Landívar, Rafael. *Por los campos de México*, ed. & trans. by Octaviano Valdés, Biblioteca del Estudiante Universitario, 34 (UNAM, 1942).
Lara Zavala, Hernán. *Viaje al corazón de la península*, Cuaderno de Viaje (CNCA, 1998).
Leal Apaéz, Juan Manuel. *Por los Caminos del Sur: redescubriendo el estado de Guerrero*, prol. by José Sarukhán (UNAM; Acapulco: Universidad Americana de Acapulco, 1995).
Leal Sierra, Manuel, ed. *Medio siglo de excursión: 1920–1970*, 2nd edn (Costa-Amic, 1976).
Leñero, Vicente. *Talacha periodística* (Grijalbo, 1989).
León de Martínez, María Teresa. *Cartas*, ed. by Guadalupe Lozada León (Breve Fondo Editorial, 1996).

León Medellín, Octavio. *Notas de viaje* (Costa-Amic, 1972).
'Literatura de la Ciudad de México: crónicas y cuentos', issue of *Blanco Móvil*, 69 (1996).
López Moreno, Javier. *Diálogo con el sur del mundo* (Costa-Amic, 1975).
Magdaleno, Mauricio. *Agua bajo el puente*, 2nd edn (FCE, 1985).
——. *Tierra y viento* (Stylo, 1948).
Magdaleno, Vicente. *Paisaje y celaje de México* (Stylo, 1952).
Mancisidor, José. 'Ciento veinte días', in *Obras completas* (Xalapa: Gobierno del Estado de Veracruz, 1978-), IV: *Novelas* (1979).
Márquez de Romero Aceves, María del Carmen & Ricardo Romero Aceves. *México en el mundo* (Costa-Amic, 1988).
Martín del Campo, David. *Los mares de México: crónicas de la tercera frontera* (Era, 1987).
Martínez Torres, Gildardo. *Turista contemplativa: Acapulco en hai-kai* (Costa-Amic, 1969).
——. *Viajero sentimental: impresiones de un turista* (Costa-Amic, 1962).
Martínez Torres, José. *Chiapas: crónica de dos tiempos*, Cuaderno de Viaje (CNCA, 1998).
Mastretta, Ángeles. *Puerto libre*, 2nd edn (Cal y Arena, 1993).
Medina, Dante. *Ciudades de por sí*, Más Allá, 20 (Monterrey, NL: Castillo, 1997).
——. *Sólo los viajeros saben que al sur está el verano: un viaje por Francia, Italia, Yugoslavia, Bulgaria y Grecia*, Viajes (Alianza, 1993).
Mejía Madrid, Fabrizio. *Pequeños actos de desobediencia civil* (Cal y Arena, 1996).
Mendoza, María Luisa. *Crónica de Chile* (Diana, 1972).
——. *Raaa, reee, riii, rooo, Rusia (URSS)*, Testimonios del Fondo (FCE, 1974).
Mendoza, María Luisa & Edmundo Domínguez Aragonés. *Allende el Bravo: los días mexicanos* (Diana, 1973).
Moheno, Querido. *Cartas y crónicas: de Washington y La Habana* (Botas, [1920?]).
Molina, Mauricio, ed. *Crónica de Tejas: diario de viaje de la Comisión de Límites* (Gobierno del Estado de Tamaulipas / Gobierno del Estado de Nuevo León / Programa Cultural de las Fronteras / Dirección General de Publicaciones y Medios / Instituto Nacional de Bellas Artes, 1988).
Molina, Silvia. *Campeche, imagen de eternidad*, Cuaderno de Viaje (CNCA, 1996).
Molina Pasquel, Roberto. *Cartas de Etiopía* (Costa-Amic, 1976).
Monsiváis, Carlos. *Días de guardar*, photographs by Héctor García, 13th repr. (Era, 1991).
Monsiváis, Carlos, ed. *A ustedes les consta: antología de la crónica en México* (Era, 1980).
Montañez, Pablo. *Lacandonia y Parque Nacional Montes Azules*, 4th edn, rev. (Costa-Amic, 1985).
——. *Río Grande: la cuenca del Usumacinta (gran reserva de México)* (Costa-Amic, 1970).
Montemayor, Carlos. *Encuentros en Oaxaca* (Aldus, 1995).
Monterde, Francisco. *Páginas escogidas* (Costa-Amic, 1969).

——. *Perfiles de Taxco* ('Cvltvra', 1932).
Montiel, Gustavo. *Memorias de un mexicano detrás de la Cortina de Hierro* (Costa-Amic, 1968).
Morábito, Fabio. *El viaje y la enfermedad* (UAM - Iztapalapa, 1984).
Morales Bermúdez, Jesús. *Por los senderos de lo incierto: antología personal* (Tuxtla Gutiérrez, Chis: Universidad Autónoma de Chiapas, 1994).
Nervo, Amado. *Cuentos y crónicas*, ed. by Manuel Durán, Biblioteca del Estudiante Universitario, 95, 2nd edn (UNAM, 1993).
——. *El éxodo y las flores del camino* (Buenos Aires: Tor, 1952).
——. *Obras completas* 2 vols (Madrid: Aguilar, 1973); I: *Prosas*, ed. by Francisco González Guerrero.
Nissán, Rosa. *Las tierras prometidas: crónica de un viaje a Israel* (Barcelona: Plaza & Janes, 1997).
Novo, Salvador. *Nueva grandeza mexicana: ensayo sobre la Ciudad de México y sus alrededores en 1946*, prol. by Carlos Monsiváis, Cien de México (CNCA, 1992).
——. *Los paseos de la Ciudad de México*, Testimonios del Fondo (FCE, 1974).
——. *Toda la prosa* (Empresas Editoriales, 1964).
——. *Viajes y ensayos, 1*, ed. by Sergio González Rodríguez, Antonio Saborit, Mary K. Long & others (FCE, 1996).
Novo, Salvador, ed. *Seis siglos de la ciudad de México*, Colección Popular, 230 (FCE, 1982).
Obregón, Álvaro. *Ocho mil kilómetros en campaña*, prol. by Francisco L. Urquizo & Francisco J. Grajales, 2nd edn (FCE, 1970).
Ocampo, María Luisa. *Diez días en Yucatán* (Botas, 1941).
Ontiveros, José Luis. *El Hotel de las Cuatro Estaciones*, Molinos de Viento, 88 (UAM, 1995).
Ortiz, Orlando. *Crónica de las Huastecas: en las tierrras del caimán y la sirena*, Cuaderno de Viaje (CNCA, 1995).
Parra Silva, Ignacio. *Memorias de un Colimense alrededor del Mundo*, Club del Libro Colimense, 22 (Costa-Amic, 1978).
Payno, Manuel. *Memorias e impresiones de un viaje a Inglaterra y Escocia*, ed. by Napoleón Rodríguez (*El Siglo XIX*, Imprenta de Ignacio Cumplido, 1853; repr. Fontamara, 1988).
——. *Obras completas* (CNCA, 1996-), I: *Crónicas de viaje: por Veracruz y otros lugares*, ed. by Boris Rosen Jélomer & Blanca Estela Treviño (1996).
——. *Un viaje a Veracruz en el invierno de 1843*, prol. by Esther Hernández Palacios, Colección Rescate (Xalapa: Universidad Veracruzana, 1984).
Paz, Octavio. *Itinerario*, 1st repr. (FCE, 1994).
Paz Paredes, Margarita. *Viaje a la China popular: crónica* (Costa-Amic, 1965).
Pellicer, Carlos. *Cartas desde Italia*, ed. by Clara Bargellini (FCE, 1985).
——. *Cuaderno de viaje*, prol. by Carlos Pellicer López (Ediciones del Equilibrista, 1987).
Perea, Héctor. *México: crónica en espiral*, Cuaderno de Viaje (CNCA, 1996).

Pérez Martínez, Héctor. 'En los caminos de Campeche', in *Obras completas*, ed. by Silvia Molina, 5 vols (Gobierno del Estado de Campeche / Corunda, 1994), V: *Periodismo*, pp. 233–85.
Pérez Rul Falcón, Carlos. *Caminos de Europa: diario de viaje* (Costa-Amic, 1968).
——. *Oriente, mágico y revolucionario* (Costa-Amic, 1979).
Peyrot G., M. *Un viaje a Baja California* (Litorales, 1968).
Pitol, Sergio. *El arte de la fuga* (Era, 1997).
——. *El viaje* (Era, 2000).
Poblett Miranda, Martha, ed. *Cien viajeros en Veracruz: crónicas y relatos*, intro. by José Emilio Pacheco, general project coordination by Ana Laura Delgado, 2nd edn, 11 vols (Veracruz, Ver.: Gobierno del Estado de Veracruz, 1992).
Prieto, Guillermo. *Obras completas*, ed by Boris Rosen Jélomer (CNCA, 1992-), IV: *Crónicas de viaje, 1: Viajes de orden suprema, 1853–1855*, ed. by Francisco López Cámara (1994); XIX: *Actualidades de la semana, 1*, ed. by Carlos Monsiváis (1996).
Puga, María Luisa. *Crónicas de una oriunda del kilómetro X en Michoacán*, Cuaderno de Viaje (CNCA, 1995).
Puga, María Luisa & Mónica Mansour. *Itinerario de palabras* (Folios, 1987).
Quezada, Abel. *Imágenes de Japón* (Mortiz, 1972).
Quirarte, Vicente. *Enseres para sobrevivir en la ciudad*, Los Cincuenta (Coordinación Nacional de Descentralización; Aguascalientes: Instituto Cultural de Aguascalientes, 1994).
Ramírez, Ignacio. *Obras*, prol. by Ignacio Manuel Altamirano, 2 vols (Editora Nacional, 1952).
Ramírez Heredia, Rafael. *Con gusto le canto a Hidalgo* (Diana, 1995).
——. *En un lugar de la mancha... urbana: Iztacalco* (Mortiz, 1993).
——. *Por los caminos del sur: vámonos para Guerrero*, Viajes (Alianza Editorial Mexicana, 1990).
Revueltas, José. *Obras completas*, 26 vols (Era, 1978–1987), XXIV: *Visión del Paricutín, y otras crónicas y reseñas*, prol. by David Huerta, 1st repr. (1986); XXV & XXVI: *Las evocaciones requeridas: memorias, diarios, correspondencia, 1 & 2*, prol. by José Emilio Pacheco (1987).
Rex, Domingo. *Visión de España: paisajes, ciudades, hombres, glosas y recuerdos* (Costa-Amic, 1974).
Reyes, Alfonso. *Berkeleyana (1941)*, Archivo de Alfonso Reyes, Serie A (Reliquías), 2 ([Panamericana], 1953).
——. *Cartones de Madrid*, ed. by Jean Velasco (Madrid: Hiperión, 1988).
——. *Visión de Anáhuac, y otros ensayos*, Lecturas Mexicanas, 14 (SEP / FCE, 1983).
Rico, Dina. *Tierra de promisión* (Costa-Amic, 1964).
Riva Palacio, Vicente. *Antología*, ed. by Clementina Díaz y de Ovando, Biblioteca del Estudiante Universitario, 79, 2nd edn (UNAM, 1993).
Rivas Paniagua, Enrique. *Hidalgo: invitación a un estado de ánimo*, prol. by Luis Rublúo Islas, ill. by Guillermo Palma (author's edition, 1982).

——. *Hidalgo: nueva invitación a un estado de ánimo* (Gobierno del Estado de Hidalgo / Sistema de Educación Pública de Hidalgo / Consejo Estatal para la Cutura y las Artes, 1995).
——. *Trotaméxicos* (author's edition, 1996).
Robles, Vito Alessio. *Mis andanzas con nuestro Ulises* (Botas, 1938).
Rodríguez, Abelardo L. *Notas de mi viaje a Rusia* ('Cvltvra', 1938).
Romero Aceves, Ricardo; & María del Carmen Márquez de Romero Aceves. *China, coloso del Oriente* (Costa-Amic, 1980).
Romero Flores, Jesús. *Un mexicano en la Unión Soviética* (Costa-Amic, 1979).
Ruiz Abreu, Álvaro. *Los ojos del paisaje*, Cuaderno de Viaje (CNCA, 1996).
——. *Tabasco: una cultura del agua*, photographs by Gabriela Iturbide (Villahermosa: Gobierno del Estado de Tabasco, 1985).
Schultz Dantus, Abie Mario. *Viajes de un escritor mexicano de la nobleza realizados de 20 a 30 años después del fin de la segunda guerra mundia*l (Costa-Amic, 1980).
Sheridan, Guillermo. *Cartas de Copilco, y otras postales* (Vuelta, 1994).
Sierra Méndez, Justo. *Obras completas*, 1st repr., 14 vols (UNAM, 1977), VI: *Viajes*, prol. by José Luis Martínez.
Sierra O'Reilly, Justo. *Diario de nuestro viaje a los Estados Unidos: la pretendida anexión de Yucatán*, prol. by Héctor Pérez Martínez, Biblioteca Histórica Mexicana de Obras Inéditas, 12 (Antigua Librería Robredo / Porrúa, 1938).
——. *Páginas escogidas*, ed. by Carlos J. Sierra, Biblioteca del Estudiante Universitario, 82 (UNAM, 1960).
Solana Olivares, Fernando. 'Lluvia en Monte Albán', *Casa del Tiempo*, 14 (November 1992), 44.
——. *Oaxaca: crónicas sonámbulas*, Cuaderno de Viaje (CNCA, 1994).
——. *Parisgótica* (Debate, 2003).
——. *El peso de la esperanza* (Breve Fondo Editorial, 1996).
Soler Frost, Pablo. *Cartas de Tepoztlán* (Era, 1997).
Tablada, José Juan. *La feria de la vida: memorias* (Botas, 1937).
——. *Los días y las noches de París & Crónicas parisienses*, ed. by Esperanza Lara Velázquez, *Obras* 3 (UNAM, 1988).
Taracena, Alfonso. *Viajando con Vasconcelos* (Botas, 1938).
Tavera Alfaro, Xavier, ed. *Viajes en México: crónicas mexicana*s, ill. by Alberto Beltrán, 2nd edn (Secretaria de Obras Públicas, 1972).
Teixidor, Felipe. *Viajeros mexicanos: siglos XIX y XX*, Sepan Cuantos..., 350, 2nd edn (Porrúa, 1982).
Torres, Juan Manuel. *El viaje*, Letras Mexicanas - Third Series, 72 (CNCA, 1993).
Torres, Olga Beatriz. *Memorias de mi viaje / Recollections of My Trip*, preface by Juan Bruce-Novoa, ed. & trans. by Juanita Luna-Lawhn (Albuquerque: U of New Mexico P, 1994).
Torres Bodet, Jaime. *Obras escogidas: poesía, autobiografía, ensayo*, 2nd edn (FCE, 1983).
Toussaint, Manuel. *Guía ilustrada de Tasco*, bilingual edn ('Cvltvra', 1935).

——. *Oaxaca y Tasco*, ill. by Francisco Díaz de León, Lecturas Mexicanas, 80 (SEP / FCE, 1985).
——. *Viajes alucinados: rincones de España*, ill. by the author ('Cvltvra', 1924).
Urquizo, Francisco L. *Memorias de campaña*, Lecturas Mexicanas, 85 (SEP / FCE, 1985).
——. *México-Tlaxcalantongo: mayo de 1920*, 2nd edn ('Cvltvra', 1943).
Vallarino, Roberto. *Las aventuras de Euforión* (Edivisión / Diana, 1988)
——. *Crónicas cotidianas*, Prosa Contemporánea, 7 (Katún, 1984).
Valverde Arciniega, Jaime; & Juan Domingo Argüelles, eds. *El fin de la nostalgia: nueva crónica de la ciudad de México*, prol. by Carlos Monsiváis (Nueva Imagen, 1992).
Vargas, Elvira. *Por las rutas del sureste* (CIMA, [1937?]).
Vasconcelos, José. *Memorias*, 2 vols (FCE, 1993), I (3rd repr.): *Ulises criollo* & *La tormenta*; II (2nd repr.): *El desastre* & El *proconsulado*.
——. *La raza cósmica: misión de la raza iberoamericana, Argentina y Brasil*, Austral 802, 16th edn (Espasa-Calpe Mexicana, 1992).
——. *Temas contemporáneos* (Novaro México, 1955).
Vásquez, Ricardo L. *Por tierras de la América del Sur* (Botas, 1940).
'Viajes: el tiempo del mundo finito'. Edition of *Textual,* 18 (October 1990).
Villoro, Juan. 'La ciudad es el cielo del metro', *Lateral* (March 1995), 17–19.
——. 'La ciudad virtual', *LJ*, 28 April 1996, p. 27.
——. 'Días robados: delitos crónicos', *Letras Libres*, 34 (October 2001), http://www.letraslibres.com/interna.php?sec=5&art=7047, accessed 12 March 2005.
——. 'Nada que declarar: Welcome to Tijuana', *Letras Libres*, 17 (May 2000), http://www.letraslibres.com/interna.php?num=&sec=3&art=6314&pag=0, accessed 12 March 2005.
——. *Los once de la tribu: crónicas* (Aguilar, 1995).
——. *Palmeras de la brisa rápida: un viaje a Yucatán*, Viajes (Alianza Editorial Mexicana, 1989); 2nd edn (Anagrama, 2000).
——. *Safari accidental* (Mortiz, 2005).
——. 'Todos somos gondoleros', *LJS*, 17 May 1998, p. 15.
Volkow, Verónica. *Diario de Sudáfrica* (Siglo XXI, 1988).
Yáñez, Agustín. *Proyección Universal de México: crónica del viaje realizado por el Presidente de México Lic. Adolfo López Mateos a India, Japón, Indonesia y Filipinas, el año 1962* ([n. pub.], 1963).
Zapata, Luis. *Paisaje con amigos: un viaje al occidente de México*, Cuaderno de Viaje (CNCA, 1995).
Zarco, Francisco. *Escritos literarios*, ed. by René Avilés, Sepan Cuantos..., 90, 2nd edn (Porrúa, 1980).
Zavala, Lorenzo de. *Páginas escogidas*, ed. by Fernando Curiel, Biblioteca del Estudiante Universitario, 66 (UNAM, 1972).
Zelis, Rafael de. *Viajes en su destierro*, prol. by Efrén Ortiz Domínguez, Colección Rescate, 29 (Xalapa: Universidad Veracruzana, Instituto Veracruzana de Cultura, 1988).

Secondary Texts – Foreign Travel Writing on Mexico and General Travel Writing

Baudrillard, Jean. *America*, trans. by Chris Turner (London: Verso, 1996).
Burroughs, William S. *Queer* (New York: Viking, 1985).
Calderón de la Barca, Fanny. *La vida en México*, 2 vols, trans. by Enrique Martínez Sobral, prol. by Manuel Romero de Terreros (Librería de la Viuda de Bouret, 1920).
Calvino, Italo. *Under the Jaguar Sun*, trans. by William Weaver (London: Vintage, 1993).
Castaneda, Carlos. *The Teachings of Don Juan: A Yaqui Way of Knowledge* (Harmondsworth: Penguin Arkana, 1990).
Charnay, Desiré. *The Ancient Cities of the New World Being Voyages and Explorations in Mexico and Central America from 1857–1882*, intro. by Allen Thorndike Rice (London: Chapman & Hall, 1887).
Chatwin, Bruce. *In Patagonia* (London: Picador, 1979).
Darío, Rubén. *España contemporánea*, prol. by Antonio Vilanova, Palabra Crítica, 2 (Barcelona: Lumen, 1987).
Fussell, Paul. *The Norton Book of Travel* (New York: Norton, 1987).
Glantz, Margo, ed. & trans. *Viajes en México: crónicas extranjeras (1821–1855)*, ill. by Alberto Beltrán, 2nd edn (Secretaría de Obras Públicas, 1972).
Greene, Graham. *The Lawless Roads* (Harmondsworth: Penguin, 1982).
Humboldt, Alexander von. *Personal Narative of a Journey to the Equinoctial Regions of the New Continent*, ed. & trans. by Jason Wilson, prol. by Malcolm Nicholson, abridged edn (Harmondsworth: Penguin, 1995).
——. *Political Essay on the Kingdom of New Spain*, ed. by Mary Maples Dunn, trans. by John Black, abridged edn (New York: Knopf, 1972).
——. *Views of the Cordilleras and Monuments of the Indigenous Peoples of America*, trans. by Helen Maria Wiliams, 2 vols (London: Longman *et al.*, 1814)
Karinthy, Frigyes. *A Journey Round my Skull*, trans. by Vernon Duckworth Barker (London: Faber and Faber, 1939).
Lawrence, D.H. *Mornings in Mexico* (Harmondsworth: Penguin, 1986).
Lowry, Malcolm. *Under the Volcano*, prol. by Stephen Spender (London: Picador, 1993).
Mayer, Brantz. *México: lo que fue y lo que es* (FCE, 1953), prol. by Juan A. Ortega y Medina.
Mesonero Romanos, Ramón de. *Obras*, 5 vols (Madrid: Biblioteca de Autores Españoles, 1967), I: ed. and prol. by Don Carlos Seco Serrano.
Miller, Tom. *En la frontera: imágenes desconocidas de nuestra frontera norte*, trans. by Federico Patán, Viajes (Alianza, 1991).
Núñez, Estuardo, ed. *Viajeros hispanoamericanos: temas continentales* (Caracas: Biblioteca Ayacucho, 1989).

Sarmiento, Domingo Faustino. *Viajes por Europa, África i América, 1845–1847*, ed. by Javier Fernández (Madrid: FCE, 1993).
Stephens, John Lloyd. *Incidents of Travel in Yucatan*, ill. by Frederick Catherwood, 2 vols (New York: Dover Publications, 1963).
Sterne, Laurence. *A Sentimental Journey, and Other Writings*, ed. by Tom Keymer (London: Dent; Vermont: Tuttle, 1994).
Theroux, Paul. *The Old Patagonian Express: By Train Through the Americas* (Harmondsworth: Penguin, 1980).
Waldeck, Federico de. *Viaje pintoresco y arqueológico a la Provincia de Yucatán, 1834 y 1836*, trans. by Manuel Mestre Ghigliazza (Mérida: Carlos R. Menéndez, 1930).
Waugh, Evelyn. *Robbery Under Law: The Mexican Object Lesson* (London: Chapman & Hall, 1939).

Critical Literature and Other Sources

Alatriste, Sealtiel. Former editor of Alianza Editorial Mexicana. Personal interview, 19 July 1996.
Álvarez, José Rogelio, ed. *Enciclopedia de México*, 14 vols (Encyclopaedia Britannica de México, 1993).
Álvarez Urbajtel, Aurelia. Editor of 'Cuaderno de viaje' series at the CNCA. Personal interview, 20 January 1997.
Anderson, Benedict. *Imagined Communities: Reflections on the Origin and Spread of Nationalism*, 2nd edn, revised & extended (London: Verso, 1991).
Appiah, Kwame Anthony. 'Is the Post- in Postmodernism the Post- in Postcolonial?', *Critical Inquiry*, 17:2 (1991), 336–57.
Bakhtin, Mikhail. 'Forms of Time and of the Chronotope in the Novel: Notes toward a Historical Poetics', in *The Dialogic Imagination: Four Essays by M.M. Bakhtin*, ed. by Michael Holquist, trans. by Caryl Emerson & Michael Holquist (Austin: U of Texas P, 1981), pp. 84–258.
Barth, John. 'La literatura postmoderna', *Quimera*, 46–47 (1985), 12–21.
Bellinghausen, Hermann. 'Testigos del caso: la crónica en México', *Nexos*, 162 (June 1991), 15–17.
Bhabha, Homi K., ed. *Nation and Narration* (London: Routledge, 1990).
Blanco, José Joaquín. *Crónica literaria: un siglo de escritores mexicanos* (Cal y Arena, 1996).
——. *Se llamaba Vasconcelos: una evocación crítica* (FCE, 1977).
Blanton, Sarah C. 'Departures: Travel Writing in a Post-Bakhtinian World' (unpublished doctoral thesis, University of South Florida, 1992).

Bono López, María. 'Frances Erskine Inglis Calderón de la Barca y el mundo indígena mexicano', http://www.bibliojuridica.org/libros/1/252/8.pdf, accessed 5 September 2005.
Brading, David Anthony. *Los orígenes del nacionalismo mexicano*, trans. by Soledad Loaeza Grave, 2nd edn, augmented, 6th repr. (Era, 1997).
Bradu, Fabienne. N. de Saint Phalle, *Hoteles literarios, viaje alrededor de la tierra*, review, *Vuelta*, 208 (March 1994), 42–44.
Brushwood, John S. *La barbarie elegante: ensayos y experiencias en torno a algunas novelas hispanoamericanas del siglo XIX*, trans. by Lucía Garvito (FCE, 1988).
Caesar, Terry. 'The Book in the Travel: Paul Theroux's *The Old Patagonian Express*', *Arizona Quarterly Review*, 46:2 (Summer 1990), 101–10.
Campbell, Federico. *Periodismo escrito* (Ariel, 1994).
Cantón, Wilberto. *Justo Sierra: héroe blanco de México* (SEP, 1967).
Carballo, Emmanuel, ed. *Historia de las letras mexicanas en el siglo XIX* (Guadalajara: Universidad de Guadalajara / Xalli, 1991).
Cárdenas, Noé. 'Otros tiempos y lugares', H. Perea, *México: crónica en espiral*, review, *Nexos*, 233 (May 1997), 99–102.
——. '"Toma el Llavero, Abuelita"', J. Villoro, *Palmeras de la brisa rápida*, review, *Textual*, 2 (June 1989), 52–53.
Castañón, Adolfo. *Arbitrario de literatura mexicana: paseos I*, 2nd edn (Vuelta, 1995).
——. 'Brevísima relación de los que ensayaron y sobrevivieron en México a fin de siglo', *Vuelta*, 234 (May 1996), 33–41.
——. 'Magnitudes del Jíbaro: literatura hispanoamericana contemporánea', *Vuelta*, 241 (December 1996), 82–85.
Castillo, Susan. *Performing America: Colonial Encounters in New World Writing, 1500–1786* (London: Routledge, 2006).
Cedillo, Jesús R. 'Viajeros en el norte de México', in *Ensayistas de Tierra Adentro*, ed. by José María Espinasa (Fondo Editorial Tierra Adentro (CNCA), 1994), pp. 201–05.
Chambers, Iain. *Border Dialogues: Journeys in Postmodernity* (London: Routledge, 1990).
Clark, Steve, ed. *Travel Writing and Empire: Postcolonial Theory in Transit* (London: Zed Books, 1999).
Cooper Alarcón, Daniel. *The Aztec Palimpsest: Mexico in the Modern Imagination* (Tucson: University of Arizona Press, 1997).
——. 'The Ruins of Manifest Destiny: John L. Stephens's *Incidents of Travel in Central America, Chiapas, and Yucatan*', in *A través del espejo: viajes, viajeros y la construcción de la alteridad en América Latina*, ed. by Lourdes de Ita Rubio and Gerardo Sánchez Díaz, (Morelia: Instituto de Investigaciones Históricas, Universidad Michoacana de San Nicolás Hidalgo, 2005), pp. 333–42.
Corona, Ignacio. 'Contesting the Lettered City: Cultural Mediation and Communicative Strategies in the Contemporary Chronicle in Mexico', in *Latin American*

Literature and Mass Media, ed. by Edmundo Paz-Soldán, & Debra A. Castillo (New York: Garland, 2001), pp. 193–206.

Corona, Ignacio & Beth E. Jörgensen, eds., *The Contemporary Mexican Chronicle: Theoretical Perspectives on the Liminal Genre* (Albany: State U of New York P, 2002).

Costeloe, Michael P. 'Prescott's *History of the Conquest* and Calderón de la Barca's *Life in Mexico*: Mexican Reaction, 1843–44', *The Americas*, 47:3 (1991), 337–48.

Domínguez Michael, Christopher. 'Lecciones de la tormenta', *Gaceta del Fondo de Cultura Económica*, 285 (September 1994), 50–54.

——. Personal interview, 15 April 1996.

——. Personal letter, 12 February 1996.

——. *Tiros en el concierto: literatura mexicana del siglo V* (Era, 1997).

Domínguez Michael, Christopher, ed. *Antología de la narrativa mexicana del siglo XX*, 2nd edn, 2 vols (FCE, 1996).

——. 'Diccionario de Octavio Paz', *Vuelta*, 259 (June 1998), 56–69.

Durán, Manuel. *Genio y figura de Amado Nervo* (Buenos Aires: Editorial Universitaria de Buenos Aires, 1968).

Enríquez Simoní, Guillermo. *La libertad de prensa en México: una mentira rosa* (Costa-Amic, 1967).

Fabrizio (Mexico), J. Villoro, *Palmeras de la brisa rápida*, review, 30 April 2000, http://www.amazon.com/exec/obidos/tg/detail/-/9686001948/qid=1108128196/sr=8–2/ref=sr_8_xs_ap_i2_xgl14/104–1683169–0902342?v=glance&s=books&n=507846, accessed 12 March 2005.

Feifer, Maxine. *Going Places: The Ways of the Tourist from Imperial Rome to the Present Day* (London: MacMillan, 1985).

Fernández Ruiz, Consuelo; Leticia Gámez Ludgar; & María de los Ángeles Sobrino Figueroa. *El paisaje mexicano en la pintura del siglo XIX y principios del XX*, exhibition catalogue: June–October 1991, Mexico City (Fomento Cultural Banamex, 1991).

Fuentes, Carlos. 'Las dos Elenas', in *Cantar de ciegos*, in *Obras completas*, prol. by Octavio Paz, 2 vols (Aguilar, 1980), II, 85–97.

——. 'Tlactocatzine, del Jardín de Flandes', in *Los días enmascarados*, in *Obras completas*, II, 41–49.

García Canclini, Néstor; Alejandro Castellanos; & Ana Rosas Mantecón. *La ciudad de los viajeros: travesías e imaginarios urbanos, México, 1940–2000* (UAM-Iztapalapa / Grijalbo, 1996).

García-Tort, Carlos. 'Escriba (una crónica de viajes) ahora, viaje (con un premio) después', *LJS*, 23 May 1999, p. 11.

Gilbert, Helen & Anna Johnston, *In Transit: Travel, Text, Empire* (New York: Lang, 2002).

Glaser, Elton. 'The Self-Reflexive Traveler: Paul Theroux on the Art of Travel and Travel Writing', *The Centennial Review*, 33:3 (Summer 1989), 193–206.

Gómez Méndez, Josefina; Nicolás Ortega Cantero; Dolores Brandis & others. *Viajeros y paisajes* (Madrid: Alianza Editorial, 1988).

González, Aníbal. *La crónica modernista hispanoamericana* (Madrid: Porrúa Turanzas, 1983).
——. *Journalism and the Development of Spanish American Narrative* (Cambridge: Cambridge UP, 1993).
González Echevarría, Roberto. *Myth and Archive: A Theory of Latin American Narrative* (Cambridge: Cambridge UP, 1990).
——. *La ruta de Severo Sarduy* (Hanover, NH: Ediciones del Norte, 1987).
González Obregón, Luis. *Cronistas e historiadores* (Botas, 1936).
——. *México viejo, 1521–1821: noticias históricas, tradiciones, leyendas y costumbres*, revised edn (Paris: Librería de la Viuda de C. Bouret, 1900).
Gran diccionario de la lengua española. 2nd edn (Madrid: Sociedad General Española de Librería, 1988).
Greenblatt, Stephen. *Marvelous Possessions: The Wonder of the New World* (Chicago: U of Chicago P, 1991).
Granillo Vázquez, Lilia, ed. *Identidades y nacionalismos: una perspectiva interdisciplinaria* (UAM / Gernika, 1993).
Gutiérrez Nájera, Manuel. *Obras: crítica literaria, I*, ed. by E.K. Mapes (UNAM, 1959).
Hahner, June E., ed., *Women through Women's Eyes: Latin American Women in Nineteenth-Century Travel Accounts* (Wilmington, DE: Scholarly Resources, 1998).
Hernández de León-Portilla, Ascensión. *España desde México: vida y testimonio de transterrados* (UNAM, 1978).
Hobsbawm, Eric, & Terence Ranger, eds. *The Invention of Tradition* (Cambridge: Cambridge UP, 1983).
Holland, Patrick, & Graham Huggan. *Tourists with Typewriters: Critical Reflections on Contemporary Travel Writing* (Ann Arbor: U of Michigan P, 1998).
Hutcheon, Linda. *The Politics of Postmodernism* (London: Routledge, 1989).
El Informador, J. Villoro, *Palmeras de la brisa rápida*, review, 23 May 2000, http://www.informador.com.mx/lastest/2000/mayo/23May2000/23ar03b.htm, accessed 12 March 2005.
Iturriaga de la Fuente, José. *Anecdotario de viajeros extranjeros en México, siglos XVI-XX*, repr., 4 vols (FCE, 1993–94).
Johnson, David E. '"Writing in the Dark": The Political Fictions of American Travel Writing', *American Literary History*, 7:1 (1995), 1–27.
Klor de Alva, Jorge. 'The Postcolonization of the (Latin) American Experience: A Reconsideration of "Colonialism," "Postcolonialism," and "Mestizaje"', in *After Colonialism: Imperial Histories and Postcolonial Displacements*, ed. by Gyan Prakash (Princeton, NJ: Princeton UP, 1995), pp. 241–75.
Kraniauskas, John. 'Border Issues', *Travesía: The Border Issue*, 3: 1/2 (1994), 5–13.
Krauze, Enrique. 'Humboldt y México: un amor correspondido', *Vuelta*, 212 (July 1994), 21–24.
Larsen, Michael. 'The Bakhtinian Chronotope: Origins, Modifications and Additions' (unpublished doctoral dissertation, U. of Kent at Canterbury, 1997).

Leask, Nigel. *Curiosity and the Aesthetics of Travel Writing, 1770–1840: 'From an Antique Land'* (Oxford: Oxford UP).
——. 'The Ghost of Chapultepec: Fanny Calderón de la Barca, William Prescott and 19th Century Mexican Travel Accounts', in *Voyages and Visions: Towards a Cultural History of Travel*, ed. by Jás Elsner and Joan-Pau Rubiés (London: Reaktion Books, 1999), pp. 184–209.
Leitner, Ulrike. 'Humboldt's Works on Mexico', in *Alexander von Humboldt im Netz*, 1:1 (2000), http://www.uni-potsdam.de/u/romanistik/humboldt/hin/leitner3.htm, accessed 22 June 2006.
León-Portilla, Miguel. 'España y México: encuentros y desencuentros', *Letras Libres* (November 2006), http://www.letraslibres.com/index.php?art=11577, accessed 30 July 2007.
Litvak, Lily. *El ajedrez de estrellas: crónicas de viajeros españoles del siglo XIX por países exóticos, 1800–1913* (Barcelona: Laia, 1987).
Long, Mary Kendall. 'Salvador Novo: 1920–1940, Between the Avant-Garde and the Nation' (unpublished doctoral dissertation, Princeton University, 1995).
López Cámara, Francisco. *Los viajes de Guillermo Prieto: estudio introductorio* (Cuernavaca: Centro Regional de Investigaciones Multidisciplinarias, UNAM, 1994).
Lloréns García, Ramón F. *Los libros de viajes de Miguel de Unamuno* (Alicante: Caja de Ahorros Provincial de Alicante, 1991).
Magris, Claudio. 'El mundo según Internet', interview, trans. by Héctor Abad Faciolince, *Nexos*, 237 (September 1997), 25–27.
Maples Arce, Manuel. *El paisaje en la literatura mexicana* (Porrúa, 1944).
Marentes, Luis Antonio. 'Narrativizing the Storm: José Vasconcelos and the Writing of the Mexican Revolution' (unpublished doctoral dissertation, University of Texas at Austin, 1994).
María y Campos, Alfonso de. Director of publications at the CNCA. Personal interview, 21 May 1996.
Martínez, José Luis. *La expresión nacional*, Cien de México (CNCA, 1993).
——. *Netzahualcóyotl: vida y obra* (FCE, 1972).
Mazzoleni, Donatella. 'The City and the Imaginary', trans. by John Koumantarakis, in *Space and Place: Theories of Identity and Location*, ed. by Erica Carter, James Donald & Judith Squires (London: Lawrence & Wishart, 1993), pp. 296–300.
McLean, Malcolm D. *Vida y obra de Guillermo Prieto* (El Colegio de México, 1960).
Mejía Madrid, Fabrizio. 'Diet Coke, ba hux?', J. Villoro, *Palmeras de la brisa rápida*, review, *Nexos*, 146 (February 1990), 73–74.
Mendieta, María de los Ángeles. *El paisaje en la novela de América*, prol. by Alberto Delgado Pastor, Tercera Época, 203 (SEP, 1949).
Mignolo, Walter D. 'Human Understanding and (Latin) American Interests: The Politics and Sensibilities of Geohistorical Locations', in *A Companion to Postcolonial Studies*, ed. by Henry Schwarz & Sangeeta Ray (Oxford: Blackwell, 2000), pp. 180–202.
Miranda, José. *Humboldt y México* (UNAM, 1962).

'Modernidad y posmodernidad en América Latina (I)'. Special issue of *Nuevo Texto Crítico*, 3:6 (1990).
'Modernidad y posmodernidad en América Latina (II)'. Special issue of *Nuevo Texto Crítico*, 4:7 (1991).
Monsiváis, Carlos. 'Apocalipsis y utopías', *LJS*, 4 April 1999, pp. 2–5.
——. 'Muerte y resurrección del nacionalismo mexicano', *Nexos*, 109 (January 1987), 13–22.
——. 'Notas sobre la cultura mexicana en el siglo XX', in *Historia general de México*, ed. by Daniel Cosío Villegas, 2nd edn, 4 vols (Colegio de México, 1977), IV: 305–476.
——. Personal interview, 30 January 1997.
——. 'Los viajeros y la invención de México', *Aztlán*, 15:2 (1985), 201–29.
Monterde, Francisco. *Aspectos literarios de la cultura mexicana*, ed. by Evodio Escalante (UNAM / Universidad de Colima, 1987).
Núñez, Estuardo. *La imagen del mundo en la literatura peruana* (FCE, 1971).
Ortega y Medina, Juan A. *Humboldt desde México* (UNAM, 1960).
Pacheco, José Emilio. 'Bitácoras', *Hoja por Hoja*, 13 December 1997, pp. 12–13.
——. *El viento distante, y otros relatos*, 2nd edn, revised & extended (Era, 1969).
Pacheco, José Emilio, ed. *Antología del modernismo: 1884–1921*, 2 vols, Biblioteca del Estudiante Universitario, 90, 2 vols (UNAM, 1970).
Paz, Octavio. *Libertad bajo palabra: 1935–57*, ed. by Enrico Mario Santí (Madrid: Cátedra, 1988).
——. '¿Posmodernidad?', *Vuelta*, 127 (June 1987), 1.
Perea, Héctor. *Océano de colores* (Aldus, 1996).
——. Personal interview, 27 January 1997.
——. *La rueda del tiempo: mexicanos en España* (Cal y Arena, 1996).
Perea, Héctor, ed. *España en la obra de Alfonso Reyes* (FCE, 1990).
——. *Nuestras naves: imágen de México en España*, Colección Cultural Universitaria, 57 (UAM, 1993).
'The Postmodernist Debate in Latin America'. Special issue of *Boundary 2*, 20:3 (1993).
Pratt, Mary Louise. *Imperial Eyes: Travel Writing and Transculturation* (London: Routledge, 1992).
Publi.com, J. Villoro, *Palmeras de la brisa rápida*, review, [no date], http://www.publi.com/news/2000/ 0409/a15.htm, accessed 12 March 2005.
Quayson, Ato. 'Postmodernism and Postcolonialism', in *A Companion to Postcolonial Studies*, ed. by Henry Schwarz & Sangeeta Ray (Oxford: Blackwell, 2000), pp. 87–111.
Rea Spill, Jefferson. *Bridging the Gap: Articles on Mexican Literature* (Libros de México, 1971).
Reyes, Alfonso. *Obras completas*, 26 vols (FCE, 1955–92), VIII: *Tránsito de Amado Nervo* (1958), XII: *Letras de la Nueva España* (1960).
Riva Palacio, Raymundo. *Más allá de los límites: ensayos para un nuevo periodismo* (Gobierno del Estado de Colima / Fundación Manuel Buendía, 1995).

Román, Alberto. J. Villoro, *Palmeras de la brisa rápida*, review, *Nexos*, 141 (September 1989), 64–65.
Ruiz Abreu, Álvaro. 'Novela de la crisis y crisis de la novela', *Nexos*, 241 (January 1998), 183–92.
Russell, Alison. *Crossing Boundaries: Postmodern Travel Literature* (New York: Palgrave, 2000).
Santamaría, Francisco de, ed. *Diccionario de Mejicanismos*, 5th edn (Porrúa, 1992).
Schulman, Iván A. & Manuel Pedro González. *Martí, Darío y el modernismo*, prol. by Cintio Vitier (Madrid: Gredos, 1969).
Segre, Erica. 'An Italicised Ethnicity: Memory and Renascence in the Literary Writings of Ignacio Manuel Altamirano', *Forum for Modern Language Studies*, 36:3 (2000), 266–78.
Shaw, Donald L. *The Post-Boom in Spanish American Fiction* (Albany: State U of New York P, 1998).
Solana Olivares, Fernando. *La rueca y el paraíso* (CNCA / Ediciones del Equilibrista, 1995).
Solís, René. Former director of Alianza Editorial Mexicana. Personal interview, 24 May 1996.
——. Personal letter, 8 November 1995.
Spurr, David. *The Rhetoric of Empire: Colonial Discourse in Journalism, Travel Writing, and Imperial Administration* (Durham, NC: Duke UP, 1993).
Steele, Cynthia. *Politics, Gender and the Mexican Novel, 1968–1988: Beyond the Pyramid* (Austin: U of Texas P, 1992).
Stevens-Middleton, Rayfred Lionel. *La obra de Alexander von Humboldt en México: fundamento de la geografía moderna* (Instituto Panamericano de Geografía e Historia / Sociedad Mexicana de Geografía y Estadística, 1956).
Tercero, Magali. '¿Existe el postmodernismo?'. *Casa del Tiempo*, 81 (January 1989), pp. i-xx.
Torres Sánchez, Rafael. 'Ignacio Manuel Altamirano: la cotidianidad en perspectiva', *LJS*, 2 May 1993, pp. 16–20.
Turner Wellman, Esther. *Amado Nervo: Mexico's Religious Poet* (New York: Instituto de las Españas en los Estados Unidos, 1936).
Ucelay da Cal, Margarita. *Los españoles pintados por sí mismos, 1843–1844: estudio de un género costumbrista* (El Colegio de México, 1951).
Urry, John. *The Tourist Gaze: Leisure and Travel in Contemporary Societies*, 6th repr. (London: SAGE Publications, 1996).
Vasconcelos Aguilar, Mario. *José Vasconcelos: maestro de América* (Jus, 1978).
Villoro, Juan. Personal interview, 19 February 1996.
——. *Tiempo transcurrido: crónicas imaginarias* (FCE, 1993).
Vogeley, Nancy. 'The Discourse of Colonial Loyalty: Mexico, 1808', in *Macropolitics of Nineteenth-Century Literature: Nationalism, Exoticism, Imperialism*, ed. by Jonathan Arac and Harriet Ritvo (Philadelphia: U of Pennsylvania P, 1991), pp. 37–55.

Ward, Philip, ed. *The Oxford Companion to Spanish Literature* (Oxford: Clarendon Press, 1978).
Williams, Raymond Leslie. *The Postmodern Novel in Latin America: Politics, Culture, and the Crisis of Truth* (London: MacMillan, 1995).
Wright-Rios, Edward N. 'Indian Saints and Nation-States: Ignacio Manuel Altamirano's Landscapes and Legends', *Mexican Studies/Estudios Mexicanos*, 20:1 (2004), 47–68.
Zamudio, Luz Elena, ed. *Espacio, viajes y viajeros* (Aldus and UAM – Unidad Iztapalapa, 2004).
Zermeño, Sergio. 'La tentación posmoderna', *Nexos*, 124 (April 1988), 5–8.

Index

Abreu Gómez, Ermilo 80
Academia Nacional de Ciencias y Literatura 57
Addison, Joseph 41
aesthetics in travel writing
  Altamirano 63
  Gutiérrez Nájera 64, 66
  Humboldt 16–17, 22
  Sierra 69, 71, 72
Ajofrín, Francisco de 160, 161
Alatriste, Sealtiel 9, 26, 106
Alcalá, Macedonio 165
Alianza Editorial Mexicana 25–6, 27, 105
Altamirano, Ignacio Manuel 12, 21–4, 27
  impact 24, 25
  imperialist discourse 83–4
  lack of Mexican travel writing 23–4, 92
  national identity 23, 37
  and Sierra 69
  tradition of Mexican travel writing 57–8, 59–63, 66
  and Vasconcelos 76, 77
Álvarez Urbajtel, Aurelia 26
American New Journalism 35
Anderson, Benedict 50
anthropological narrative 168–70, 173
Appiah, Kwame Anthony 90, 127
architecture
  Humboldt 17
  Perea's *Mexico: crónica en espiral* 137, 140
  Villoro's *Palmeras de la brisa rápida* 119
archival travel writing, Solana Olivares's *Oaxaca: crónicas sonámbulas* 155–6, 159, 167, 169–75

Arróniz, Joaquín 60
Arróniz, Marcos 51
Augustine, Saint 167
availability of foreign travel writing in Mexico 13–14
Azorín (José Augusto Trinidad Martínez Ruiz) 69, 77

Baedecker guidebooks 71
Bakhtin, Mikhail 46–7, 48, 97, 98
Balzac, Honoré de 41
Barcelona 144
Baroja, Pío 69
Barth, John 94
Barthes, Roland 96
Baudrillard, Jean 88, 96, 105, 112, 120
Bayo, Ciro 69
Beat Generation, North America 18
belatedness, trope of 126
Bellinghausen, Hermann 20–1, 35
Benítez, Fernando 8, 91, 127, 133
Bhabha, Homi K. 92
Blanco, José Joaquín 63, 133
Blanton, Sarah C. 98–9, 102
Blasco Ibáñez, Vicente 77
Bolívar, Simón 52
Borges, Jorge Luis 146
Bradu, Fabienne 125
Brasseur, Charles Étienne 160
Breton, André 146, 160, 166
bridges, Perea's *Mexico: crónica en espiral* 144
British novelists, expatriate 18
Brushwood, John S. 39
Buffon, Comte de 16
Bulnes, Francisco 65
Buñuel, Luis 148
Burroughs, William 19
Burton, Sir Richard 160
Bustamante, Carlos María de 62

Caesar, Terry 112
Calderón de la Barca, Marquise
    Frances 12, 13, 18–19, 53, 85
Calvino, Italo 96, 158, 160, 161, 164, 166, 167
Campbell, Federico 35
'capitalist vanguard' 17–18, 20, 74
    disappointment, trope of 127–8
    Stephens 127
    Vasconcelos 83
Carballo, Emmanuel 23, 24, 42, 62
Cárdenas, Noé 125, 134
carnivalised travel writing 99
Casasola, Agustín Víctor 148
Castaneda, Carlos 108, 160
Castañón, Adolfo 27, 64, 177, 178
Castelar y Ripoll, Emilio 71
Castillo, Susan 82
Castro Leal, Antonio 78–9
Catherwood, Frederick 17, 114, 115, 116, 128
Catholicism 92
Cedillo, Jesús R. 125
Celorio, Gonzalo 131, 133, 135, 148
Cervantes, Miguel de 41
Cervantes de Salazar, Francisco 132
Chadourne, Marc 77
Chambers, Iain 100, 102, 103
Charnay, Désiré 160, 161, 164
Chateaubriand, François René de 40, 56, 69, 77
Chatwin, Bruce 98, 102, 106–7
Chilton, John 160
Chimal, Carlos 147
chroniques 33, 34
chronological order in travel writing
    crónica de viaje 35, 37, 49
    postmodernist travel writing 99
    Solana Olivares's *Oaxaca: crónicas en espiral* 167
    Villoro's *Palmeras de la brisa rápida* 111, 112
chronotopes 27–8, 31, 46
    of the net 27, 48, 97–100, 178
    Perea's *Mexico: crónica en espiral* 135, 151, 153
    postcolonialism 102–3

Solana Olivares's *Oaxaca: crónicas sonámbulas* 156, 166, 175
Villoro's *Palmeras de la brisa rápida* 112–13
    of the road 27, 46–8, 81, 84
Científicos 58, 69
civilisations, pre-Columbian 17
Clavijero, Francisco Xavier 17, 160
climate, descriptions of 17
colonialism *see* imperialism/colonialism
Colonialistas 79–80
competitions, travel writing 27
Comte, Auguste 58
conferences, Mexican travel writing 27
Congreso Social y Económico Hispanoamericano (1901) 68
Connor, Steve 101
Conquest of America 32, 33, 35
Consejo de la Crónica de la Ciudad de México 132
Consejo Nacional para la Cultura y las Artes (CNCA) 14, 26, 125, 157
Conservatives 51
consumerism 87
Constant de Rebecque, Henri Benjamin 40
contemporary travel writing, substance of 91–4
Cooper Alarcón, Daniel 74, 120, 127
Coppée, François 66
Córdoba 143
Corona, Ignacio 134
El Correo de México 62
Cortés, Hernán 160
costumbrismo 38–9, 40–3, 58
    Prieto 55
    revival of *crónicas* 33
    travel chronicles in 19th-century Mexico 44–5, 49
    Vasconcelos 77
countertravel writing 103, 179
creolisation 23–3, 82–4
criollo 22
La Crisis 88
crónica de viaje
    abandonment of tradition 80–1
    Altamirano 62–3

Colonialistas 80
Gutiérrez Nájera 64
as literary genre 32–7, 85
Payno 52
postmodernism 94–5, 96
Prieto 52
revival of 85–6
substance of contemporary Mexican travel writing 91–2
Vasconcelos 75–9, 80
see also Perea, Héctor, *Mexico: crónica en espiral*; Solana Olivares, Fernando, *Oaxaca: crónicas sonámbulas*; Villoro, Juan, *Palmeras de la brisa rápida*
crónicas de Indias 32, 36
Cuéllar, José Tomás de 62
Curiel, Fernando 133, 147

Darío, Rubén 68
Day of the Dead 50
Debord, Guy 88
Del Castillo, Bernal Díaz 60
Díaz, Porfirio 43
Diego Blanco, Hugo 27
disappointment, trope of 127–8
Domingo Argüelles, Juan 134
Domínguez Michael, Christopher 34–5, 81
Donaji, Zapotec princess 164
Dostoyevsky, Fyodor Mikhailovich 46
dreams, Solana Olivares's *Oaxaca: crónicas sonámbulas* 167–9
drugs trade 88
Dumas, Alexandre (père) 40, 53

earthquake (1985, Mexico City) 143, 147–8
Eco, Umberto 96
Ediciones B 27
Editorial Botas 75
Eisenstein, Sergei Mikhailovich 148
'encyclopaedists' 17
Enríquez Simoní, Guillermo 150–1
Estébanez Calderón, Serafín 43
Esteva, Gonzalo 59
Europe
    Altamirano 61–2

Gutiérrez Nájera 66
Mexican travel writers in 56–7, 68–9
Nervo 72–4
Sierra 71–2
exoticism, discourse of 47–8
    Altamirano 83
    Nervo 73–4
expatriate British novelists 18

fauna, descriptions of 17
federalism 51
Feifer, Maxine 122
feminised national identity 93
Fernández, Emilio 85
Flaubert, Gustave 40, 165
    Bouvard et Pécuchet 165
flora, descriptions of 17
Fondo de Cultura Económica (FCE) 13–14
foreign travel writers 11–12, 26, 34
    archival fiction 173, 174
    dearth of Mexican travel writing 21, 22, 24
    imperialist politics 82
    legacy 13–20
    and Nervo 73–4
    and Perea's *México: crónica en espiral* 134, 136, 146–8
    Solano Olivares's *Oaxaca: crónicas sonámbulas* 160, 166, 169, 173
    Villoro's *Palmeras de la brisa rápida* 110, 114–17, 126, 127–8
Foucault, Michel 155
France
    chroniques 33, 34, 62
    culture 33, 34, 40, 42
    Gutiérrez Nájera 66, 67
    Nervo 73
    imperialism 42, 152
    Mexican travellers 57, 68
    Mexico compared with
        Altamirano 61, 62
        Payno 53
    postcolonialism 91
    Revolution 16
    Sierra 71
    Surrealism 18

Fuentes, Carlos 145, 146, 147, 149
Fussell, Paul 122–3

Gage, Thomas 160
García Bergua, Ana 27
García Canclini, Néstor 132, 141, 142
García Cubas, Antonio 24, 77
García Márquez, Gabriel 172
García Vigil, Manuel 158
Gasset, José Ortega y 69
Gautier, Théophile 40
Gemelli Carreri, Giovanni Francesco 160
Generation of 98: 59, 69
Giner de los Ríos, Francisco 58, 59
Glantz, Margo 180
Glaser, Elton 112
globalisation 88, 92, 179
  postmodernist travel writing 96
  substance of contemporary Mexican travel writing 92, 93–4
  Villoro's *Palmeras de la brisa rápida* 120, 126, 128
Goethe, Johann Wolfgang von 40, 71
Gómez Carillo, Enrique 68
Gómez-Peña, Guillermo 180
Gonthier, Jesús 161
González, Aníbal 62, 63, 72
González, Manuel 161
González Echevarría, Roberto 81, 87, 95, 98
  archival fictions 98, 155, 156, 159, 169, 170–2
González Obregón, Luis 147
Graff, Gerald 94
Grand Tour 57
Greenblatt, Stephen 32
Greene, Graham 19
Groussac, Paul 68
Gutiérrez Nájera, Manuel 59–60, 63–7, 72, 85
Guzmán, Martín Luis 127, 144, 147

Hinojosa, Francisco 27, 94
historiographic metafiction 155, 159, 164, 172, 174
Hobsbawm, Eric 50
Holiday Inn chain 119

Holland, Patrick 179
  'death' of travel writing 178
  middle-class nature of contemporary travel writing 95
  postmodernism 96, 97, 99, 102, 110
Holy Land, Mexican travellers to the 57
Huggan, Graham 179
  'death' of travel writing 178
  middle-class nature of contemporary travel writing 95
  postmodernism 96, 97, 99, 102, 110
Hugo, Victor 40, 53
Humboldt, Baron Alexander von 12, 15–18, 22
  Altamirano 60
  Payno 53
  Prieto 54, 55
  Romantic aesthetic 39, 40
  Solana Olivares's *Oaxaca: crónicas sonámbulas* 160
  Stephens 17, 127
  Vasconcelos 77, 78
Hurricane Gilbert (1988) 109
Hutcheon, Linda 95–6, 101, 117, 124, 166
  historiographic metafiction 155, 159, 164, 172, 174
Huxley, Aldous 160, 166
hypertextuality, Perea's *Mexico: crónica en espiral* 135, 146–8, 149, 150, 153
'hyphenated' Mexicans 180

Ibargüengoitia, Jorge 7–8, 91, 133
impact of foreign travel writing in Mexico 14–15
  Calderón de la Barca 18–19
  Humboldt 15–18
imperialism/colonialism
  chronotopes 28
  of the road 48
  Colonialistas 79–80
  creolisation and transculturation 82–4
  crónica de viaje 32
  dearth of Mexican travel writing 25
  foreign travel writers 16, 18, 20, 23

Index

Humboldt 18
genre of travel writing 12, 27–8, 80, 81
globalisation as 88
racism 22
United States of America 82, 93–4, 119, 127
Vasconcelos 78
Villoro's *Palmeras de la brisa rápida* 119
see also postcolonialism; postimperialism
indigenous communities
  Altamirano 22, 83
  postcolonialism 90
  Solana Olivares's *Oaxaca: crónicas sonámbulas* 174–5
  Vasconcelos 73, 83
  Villoro's *Palmeras de la brisa rápida* 118, 119
innovation in travel writing genre 179
  Altamirano 60
  Gutiérrez Nájera 60, 64
  modernism and postmodernism 27, 28, 179
  Perea 137
  Sierra 70
Institución Libre de Enseñanza 58
insurrection against Spanish crown 15
integrated model of travel writing 16–17
intelligentsia
  Mexican 13, 14
    Calderón de la Barca 18–19
    Humboldt 15
  Spanish 42
Internet 142
intertextuality 49–50
  archival fiction 171, 172, 173
  Celorio 135
  chronotope of the net 98
  crónica de viaje 37
  Nervo 72
  Perea's *Mexico: crónica en espiral* 135, 146
  postmodernism 98, 100
  Solana Olivares's *Oaxaca: crónicas sonámbulas* 160–6, 173

Villoro's *Palmeras de la brisa rápida* 106, 113–17, 123
irony, postmodern 93, 96, 124
  chronotope of the net 100
  and postcolonialism 101
  Villoro's *Palmeras de la brisa rápida* 124, 126, 128
Irving, Washington 43
Italy, Mexican travellers to 57, 68
Iturbe, Luis 118, 119
Iturriaga de la Fuente, José 14

Jouy, Joseph Étienne de 41, 43

Kapuściński, Ryszard 98
Karinthy, Frigyes 107
Kipling, Rudyard 160
Klor de Alva, Jorge 23, 24, 80
  postcolonialism 89–90, 151, 170

La Borbolla, Óscar de 133, 146–7
Lamartine, Alphonse Marie Louis de Prat de 40, 53, 55
landscapes
  appreciation of, *see paisajismo*
  Humboldt 17
Larra, Mariano José de 43, 44
Las Casas, Fray Bartolomé de 160
Lawrence, D.H. 7, 19–20, 77
  Solana Olivares's *Oaxaca: crónicas sonámbulas* 160, 166, 174–5
Leask, Nigel
  and Humboldt 15, 17
  integrated model of travel writing 17
  'Mexican travel accounts' 11
leisure
  Altamirano 61, 62, 66
  Gutiérrez Nájera 66–7
  Villoro 117–18, 119–24
León-Portilla, Miguel 152
Lerdo de Tejada, Sebastián 61
Liberal writers
  and *Científicos* 58
  costumbrismo 43
  federal approach to government 51
  travel 51
Lisbon 143

Litvak, Lily   49
Lizardi, Fernández de   42
Long, Mary K.   79
López Cámara, Francisco   23
Los Herreros, Manuel Bretón de   43
Lowry, Malcolm   160, 163, 164–5, 166
Luis Mora, José María   62
luxury tourism   66–7
Lyotard, Jean-François   88

Madrid   136, 143, 153
Madrid Hurtado, President Miguel de la   88
Magris, Claudio   141
Maistre, Xavier de   133
Malanco, Luis   21
Mansour, Mónica   127
Marentes, Luis Antonio   78
marginalised voices, privileging of   87
María Heredia, José   69
María y Campos, Alfonso de   26
Martí, José   68
Martínez, José Luis   41, 70, 147
Matías, Juan   163
Maupassant, Guy de   40
Mayans   118, 119, 128
Mayer, Brantz   13–14
Mazzoleni, Donatella   100
Medina, Dante   26
Mejía Madrid, Fabrizio   125, 133
Mercier, Louis-Sébastien   41
Mesonero Romanos, Ramón de   43, 44
mestizaje, discourse of   78, 83
mestizos   22
metafiction   170
  historiographic   155, 159, 164, 172, 174
  Solana Olivares's *Oaxaca: crónicas sonámbulas*   155, 158–9, 164
metaphor, Villoro's *Palmeras de la brisa rápida*   109
metatextuality
  postmodernism   96
  Solana Olivares's *Oaxaca: crónicas sonámbulas*   155, 158–9, 164
  Villoro's *Palmeras de la brisa rápida*   105–13, 114, 123, 136
Mexican Revolution (1910-20)   90

Mexico City   131–5
  earthquake (1985)   143, 147–8
  Perea's *Mexico: crónica en espiral*   135, 136–40
    alternative dimensions of Perea's journey   141–8
    postcolonialism   151–3
    virtual and real journeys   148–51
  postmodernism   88–9
Michelet, Jules   40
Mignolo, Walter D.   51, 89
migration, Villoro's *Palmeras de la brisa rápida*   118
Miller, Tom   26
modernism   81, 179
  archival fiction   171
  and postmodernism, relationship between   94–5, 96
  and Realism   95, 108
  Villoro's *Palmeras de la brisa rápida*   108, 109, 110
modernismo   67–9
  Gutiérrez Nájera   60, 64
  leisured travel   67
  Nervo   72, 74
  Sierra   69, 70, 71
  Spain   59, 69
Molina, Silvia   27, 70
Monsiváis, Carlos   24
  'Dios nunca muere'   165
  costumbrismo   44–5
  crónicas   34, 36, 79, 85, 91–2
  Mexico City   131, 133, 134, 143
  modernismo   72
  in Perea's *Mexico: crónica en espiral*   147
  postcolonialism   91
  postmodernism   88–9
  postnationalism   88, 92–3, 120
  tradition   50
Montalvo, Juan   52
Monterde, Francisco   62, 79
Motolinía   160
Müller, Johann Wilhelm von   160
Musset, Louis Charles Alfred de   40, 65

Naipaul, V.S.   98
narcotics trade   88

Index

narrative voice and style 49, 81
  crónica de viaje 37
  Gutiérrez Nájera 64
  Perea's *Mexico: crónica en espiral* 137–41
  postmodernism 93, 95
  Romanticism 39
national identity
  Mexico 49
    Altamirano's agenda 23, 37
    chronotope of the road 47
    costumbrismo and *paisajismo* 38, 43
    crónica de viaje 37, 80
    Prieto 56
    substance of contemporary Mexican travel writing 92–3
    tradition of Mexican travel writing 50, 51, 57, 81
    Vasconcelos 78, 83
    Villoro's *Palmeras de la brisa rápida* 120
  Spain 42, 58
nationalism in Mexican travel writing 7, 92
nation-building
  Altamirano 22, 23, 83
  Payno 52–3
  Prieto 55
Naturalism 38–9
Nerval, Gérard de 40
Nervo, Amado 67, 68, 72–5, 82
New Journalism, American 35
Nietzsche, Friedrich 160, 165
Nissán, Rosa 180
Noble Savage 41
Novo, Salvador 7–8, 79, 85
  Mexico City 132–3
  in Perea's *Mexico: crónica en espiral* 147
  and Villoro 127
Núñez, Estuardo 33, 52

Ocampo, Gabriel 118, 119
Ocampo, Melchor 52
offensive foreign travel books 14–15, 18–20
Ontiveros, José Luis 165

Ortega y Medina, Juan A. 16
Ortiz, Luis G. 62
Ortiz, Orlando 27

Pacheco, José Emilio 12, 24–5, 126
  influence 147–8
  Mexico City 133, 142, 147
  Perea's *Mexico: crónica en espiral* 147, 151
paisajismo 38, 39–40, 49, 58
  Vasconcelos 77
Pardo Bazán, Emilia 69
Payno, Manuel 43
  Altamirano's style compared to 60, 61
  Mexican national literature 60
  tradition of Mexican travel writing 52–4, 55, 56, 58, 64
  Vasconcelos's style compared to 76, 77
Paz, Octavio
  Mexico City 133
  and Perea 145, 147, 150
  Solana Olivares's *Oaxaca: crónicas somámbulas* 162
  and Vasconcelos 77–8
  and Villoro 127
  Vuelta 86
'paz porfiriana' 60
Perea, Héctor 156
  México: crónica en espiral 27, 28, 29, 135
  alternative dimensions of Perea's journey 141–8
  postcolonialism 28, 29, 135, 150–3, 175
  time travel 142–3
  traditional travel narrative, vestiges of 136–40
  virtual and real journeys 141–3, 148–50
  Océano de colores 145
  on Reyes's *Visión de Anáhuac* 134–5
  La rueda del tiempo 149, 152, 153
Pérez Martínez, Héctor 70
Pitol, Sergio 137

plane journeys, pointlessness of
     narrating   105, 111
political issues
   Colonialistas   80
   crónicas   63
   Humboldt's influence   16, 17
   Nervo   72
   North American versus European
      travel   56
   postcolonialism   101, 102
   Sierra   69, 71, 72
   Vasconcelos   78, 80
Porfiriato   65, 67
positivism
   Altamirano   69
   Científicos   58
   Sierra   69
Post-Boom era   87, 95
postcolonialism   21, 24–5, 29, 86, 178,
     179
   anthropological narrative   170
   archival fiction   174–5
   chronotopes   28
      of the net   99, 100
   Perea's *Mexico: crónica en
      espiral*   28, 29, 135, 150–3
   Post-Boom works   95
   and postmodernism   88, 89–91,
      101–3
   seeds of   23, 80
   Solana Olivares's *Oaxaca: crónicas
      sonámbulas*   156, 174–5
   substance of contemporary Mexican
      travel writing   92, 93
   Villoro's *Palmeras de la brisa
      rápida*   106, 125–9
postimperialism   86, 90
   critique of travel writing genre   34,
      80
   Nervo   74
   Perea   150–3
   Solana Olivares   156, 174–5
   Villoro   28, 175
postmodernism   8, 29, 81, 86–9, 178–9
   aesthetic innovations   27–8, 179
   archival fiction   28–9, 171, 172, 173
   chronotope of the net   135, 156
   and modernism   94–98

Perea's *Mexico: crónica en
      espiral*   139
   possibility of postmodernist travel
      writing   94–100
   and postcolonialism   88, 89–91,
      101–3
   Solana Olivares's *Oaxaca: crónicas
      sonámbulas*   28–9, 156, 166, 173,
      175
   substance of contemporary Mexican
      travel writing   92, 93
   Villoro's *Palmeras de la brisa
      rápida*   28, 106, 107, 110, 113,
      116, 117–25, 128–9
postnationalism   88, 92–3, 96
   Villoro's *Palmeras de la brisa
      rápida*   120, 141
post-tourism, Villoro's *Palmeras de la
   brisa rápida*   122–4, 128
Pratt, Mary Louise   17–18, 32, 108, 140
pre-Columbian civilisations   17
Prieto, Guillermo   43, 45
   and Altamirano   24, 60, 61
   internal exile   54, 55
   Mexican national literature   60
   Payno's writing   53
   Sierra's writing   70
   tradition of Mexican travel
      writing   52, 54–6, 58, 64
   Vasconcelos's writing   76
Puga, María Luisa   27

Quayson, Ato   101–2
Quirarte, Vicente   147

racism and racial prejudice   19, 22
Ramírez, Ignacio   24, 58, 76
Ramírez Heredia, Rafael   26, 133
Ranger, Terence   50
Raynal, Abbé   16
Realism   38–9
   contemporary travel writing   28
   costumbrismo   38, 41
   crónica de viaje   37
   and modernism   95, 108
   Payno   53
   and postmodernism   95, 97
   and Romanticism   38–9, 41, 53

tradition of Mexican travel
    writing 53
Villoro's *Palmeras de la brisa
    rápida* 108
Rea Spill, Jefferson 42, 43
Reko, Blas Pablo 160
religion 60, 92
El Renacimento 24, 59, 62
Renan, Ernest 71
reprints of foreign travel writing 14
Revueltas, José 127
Reyes, Alfonso 145, 152
    crónica de viaje 33, 151
    and Perea 134–5, 147
    Visión de Anáhuac 134, 147, 152
Riva Palacio, Raymundo 35
Rivas, Antonio 148
Rivera, Diego 85, 148
Roa Bárcena, José María 65
Robertson, William 16
Rojas González, Francisco 85
Román, Alberto 125
Romanticism 38–9, 40–1
    Altamirano 61
    costumbrismo 38, 41
    French and Spanish cultures 42
    paisajismo 38, 39, 40
    Payno 53
    postmodernism 95
    Prieto 55
    Sierra 71
Rosaldo, Renato 126
Rousseau, Jean-Jacques 17, 39, 40
Ruiz Abreu, Álvaro 27, 125
Russell, Alison 97, 99, 102, 139

Sahagún, Bernardino de 160
Sand, Georges
Sangari, Kumkum 101
Santa Anna, General Antonio López
    de 54, 61
Santos Chocano, José 68
Sarmiento, Domingo Faustino 51–2
Scherpe, Klaus R. 132
Secretaría de Educación Pública (SEP)
    14
Segre, Erica 63, 84
Senancour, Étienne Pivert de 40

Shaw, Donald L. 81, 87, 95
Sierra, Justo 67, 68, 69–72
Sierra O'Reilly, Justo 56, 69, 70, 116
El Siglo XIX 62
simile, Villoro's *Palmeras de la brisa
    rápida* 109
Solana, Viqui 158, 164, 168
Solana López, Mateo 158, 161
Solana Olivares, Fernando
    Oaxaca: crónicas sonámbulas 26–7,
        28–9, 155–6
    intertextuality 159–66
    archival travel writing 172–5
    traditional travel writing,
        avoidance of 157–9
    dreams 167–9
    Parisgótica 157
    La rueca y el paraíso 165
Solís, René 26, 106
Spain
    Altamirano 61
    Conquest of America 32, 33, 35
    costumbrismo 41, 42, 43, 44
    crónicas 32, 34
    culture 34, 42, 59
    France's imperialist designs 42, 152
    imperialist discourse 82
    Institución Libre de Enseñanza 58
    Madrid 136, 143, 153
    Mexican travellers 57, 68
    modernismo 59, 69
    Perea 149, 151–2
    postcolonialism 90, 91, 151–2
    Sierra 71
Spanish–Mexican postcolonial
    relations 28, 80, 175
The Spectator 41
Staël, Mme de 40
Steele, Sir Richard 41
Stendhal (Henri-Marie Beyle) 40
Stephens, John Lloyd 74
    Humboldt's influence 17, 127
    Villoro's *Palmeras de la brisa
        rápida* 114–16, 118, 127–8
Sterne, Laurence 53, 66
substance of contemporary travel
    writing 91–4
Surrealists 18

Taine, Hippolyte Adolphe 41–2, 71
The Tatler 41
Tavera Álfaro, Xavier 11, 12
Teixidor, Felipe 23, 58, 92
Tercero, Magali 87
Theroux, Paul 102, 105, 111, 112
Thompson, Sir Eric S. 115
Tiffin, Helen 101
time travel, Perea's *Mexico: crónica en espiral* 142–3
Tlatelolco massacre (1968) 34, 85
Tocqueville, Alexis de 40, 56
Tolsá, Manuel 148
Torre Repetto, Carlos 118
Torres Sánchez, Rafael 63
tourism
   Gutiérrez Nájera 66–7
   luxury 66–7
   Nervo 74
   Sierra 71–2
   substance of contemporary Mexican travel writing 93
   Villoro's *Palmeras de la brisa rápida* 106, 107, 110, 117, 118, 119–24
   postcolonialism 126, 128
Toussaint, Manuel 69, 160, 162–3, 166, 167–8
tradition of Mexican travel writing 49–50
   creation 51–7
   demise 75–81
   imperialist discourse, creolisation and transculturation 82–4
   literary travels and early tourism 57–67
   postmodernism 94–100
   stifling tradition 67–75
traditions, rescuing of 87
transculturation 82–4, 179, 180
   Solana Olivares's *Oaxaca: crónicas sonámbulas* 162
   Villoro's *Palmeras de la brisa rápida* 116
translations of foreign travel writers 13–14, 20
Turner, John Kenneth 118
Tyndall, John 70

Unamuno, Miguel de 69
understatement, Villoro's *Palmeras de la brisa rápida* 109
United Kingdom, imperialist discourse 82
United States of America
   border with Mexico 118
   globalisation 93–4
   imperialism 82, 93–4, 119, 127
   and Mexican national identity 93
   Mexican travel writers 56
   Sierra 70, 71, 72
   tourists 119–21, 128
   Villoro's *Palmeras de la brisa rápida* 119–21, 128
Universal Exhibition 68
Urry, John 122

Vallarino, Roberto 133
Valle-Arizpe, Artemio de 80
Valle-Inclán, Ramón María del 77
Valverde Arciniega, Jaime 134
Varo, Remedios 148
Vasconcelos, José 52, 75–80
   imperialist discourse 83, 84
   and Solana Olivares 160, 162
   and Villoro 127
Verlaine, Paul 40
Verne, Jules 77
Vidaurre, Manuel Lorenzo de 52
Vigneaux, Ernest de 60
Vigny, Alfred Victor, comte de 40, 65
Villaseñor, Alejandro 160
Villoro, Juan 105, 140, 156, 177, 178
   Mexico City 132
   Palmeras de la brisa rápida 26, 28, 29, 105–6
      intertextuality 106, 113–17, 123
      metatextuality 106–13, 114, 123, 136
      postcolonialist reading 125–9
      postmodernity, post-tourism and postmodern irony 106, 107, 110, 113, 116, 117–25, 128–9
      postnationalism 120, 141
      postimperialism 28, 175
      postmodernism 93, 94, 106, 107, 110, 113, 116, 117–25, 128–9

Virgin of Guadalupe, cult of the 88
Virilio, Paul 132
virtual journeys, Perea's *Mexico: crónica en espiral* 141–3, 148–50
Vuelta 86

Waldeck, Jean Frederic de 13
Wasson, R. Gordon 160
Waugh, Evelyn 19, 20
Weltanschauung 87

Williams, Raymond Leslie 87, 88, 95
Wilson, Jason 16
women writers 179
Wright-Rios, Edward N. 61

Yáñez, Agustín 81

Zapata, Luis 27
Zavala, Lorenzo de 56, 62, 69
Zermeño, Sergio 87, 88

Hispanic Studies: Culture and Ideas

Edited by
Claudio Canaparo

This series aims to publish studies in the arts, humanities and social sciences, the main focus of which is the Hispanic World. The series invites proposals with interdisciplinary approaches to Hispanic culture in fields such as history of concepts and ideas, sociology of culture, the evolution of visual arts, the critique of literature, and uses of historiography. It is not confined to a particular historical period.

Monographs as well as collected papers are welcome. Languages of publication are English, Spanish and Spanish-American.

Those interested in contributing to the series are invited to write with either the synopsis of a subject already in typescript or with a detailed project outline to either Dr Claudio Canaparo, Centre for Latin American Studies, School of Arts, Languages and Literatures, University of Exeter, Exeter EX4 4QH, UK, c.canaparo@exeter.ac.uk, or to Hannah Godfrey, Peter Lang Publishing, Evenlode Court, Main Road, Long Hanborough, Witney, Oxfordshire OX29 8SZ, UK, h.godfrey@peterlang.com.

Vol. 1 Antonio Sánchez
Postmodern Spain. A Cultural Analysis of 1980s–1990s Spanish Culture. 220 pages. 2007.
ISBN 978-3-03910-914-2

Vol. 2 Geneviève Fabry and Claudio Canaparo (eds)
El enigma de lo real. Las fronteras del realismo en la narrativa del siglo XX. 275 pages. 2007.
ISBN 978-3-03910-893-0

Vol. 3 William Rowlandson
Reading Lezama's *Paradiso*. 290 pages. 2007.
ISBN 978-3-03910-751-3

Vol. 4   Claudio Canaparo, Fernanda Peñaloza and Jason Wilson (eds)
         Patagonia. Myths and Realities. *Forthcoming*.
         ISBN 978-3-03910-917-3

Vol. 5   Xon de Ros
         Primitivismo y Modernismo. El legado de María Blanchard.
         238 pages. 2007.
         ISBN 978-3-03910-937-1

Vol. 6   Sergio Plata
         Visions of Applied Mathematics. Strategy and Knowledge.
         284 pages. 2007.
         ISBN 978-3-03910-923-4

Vol. 7   Annick Louis
         Borges ante el fascismo. 374 pages. 2007.
         ISBN 978-3-03911-005-6

Vol. 8   Helen Oakley
         From Revolution to Migration. A Study of Contemporary Cuban and
         Cuban American Crime Fiction. *Forthcoming*.
         ISBN 978-3-03911-021-6

Vol. 9   Thea Pitman
         Mexican Travel Writing. 209 pages. 2008.
         ISBN 978-3-03911-020-9

Vol. 10 Francisco J. Borge
         A New World for a New Nation. The Promotion of America in Early
         Modern England. 240 pages. 2007.
         ISBN 978-3-03911-070-4

Vol. 11 Helena Buffery, Stuart Davis and Kirsty Hooper (eds)
         Reading Iberia. Theory/History/Identity. 229 pages. 2007.
         ISBN 978-3-03911-109-1

Vol. 12   Sheldon Penn
         Writing and the Esoteric. Identity, Commitment and Aesthetics in
         Mexican Literature since the Revolution. *Forthcoming.*
         ISBN 978-3-03911-101-5

Vol. 13 Angela Romero-Astvaldsson
         La obra narrativa de David Viñas. La nueva inflexión de *Prontuario*
         y *Claudia Conversa*. 300 pages. 2007.
         ISBN 978-3-03911-100-8

Vol. 14 Aaron Kahn
         The Ambivalence of Imperial Discourse. Cervantes's *La Numancia*
         within the 'Lost Generation' of Spanish Drama (1570–90).
         243 pages. 2008.
         ISBN 978-3-03911-098-8

Vol. 15 Turid Hagene
         Negotiating Love in Post-Revolutionary Nicaragua. The role of love
         in the reproduction of gender asymmetry. 341 pages. 2008.
         ISBN 978-3-03911-011-7

Vol. 16 Yolanda Rodríguez Pérez
         The Dutch Revolt through Spanish Eyes. Self and Other in historical
         and literary texts of Golden Age Spain (c. 1548–1673). 346 pages. 2008.
         ISBN 978-3-03911-136-7

Vol. 17 Stanley Black (ed.)
         Juan Goytisolo: Territories of Life and Writing. 202 pages. 2007.
         ISBN 978-3-03911-324-8

Vol. 18 María T. Sánchez
         The Problems of Literary Translation. A Study of the Theory and
         Practice of Translation from English into Spanish. *Forthcoming.*
         ISBN 978-3-03911-326-2

Vol. 19 Matías Bruera
         Meditations on Flavour. *Forthcoming.*
         ISBN 978-3-03911-345-3

Vol. 20   Ana Cruz García
           Re(de-)generando identidades. Locura, feminidad y liberalización en la
           obra de Elena Garro, Susana Págano, Ana Castillo y María Amparo
           Escandón. *Forthcoming*.
           ISBN 978-3-03911-524-2

Vol. 21   Idoya Puig
           Tradition and Modernity. Cervantes's Presence in Spanish
           Contemporary Literature. *Forthcoming*.
           ISBN 978-3-03911-526-6

Vol. 22   Charlotte Lange
           Modos de parodia. Guillermo Cabrera Infante, Reinaldo Arenas,
           Jorge Ibargüengoitia y José Agustín. 252 pages. 2008.
           ISBN 978-3-03911-554-9

Vol. 23   Claudio Canaparo
           Geo-Epistemology. Latin America and the Location of Knowledge.
           Forthcoming.
           ISBN 978-3-03911-573-0

Vol. 24   Jesús López-Peláez Casellas
           Honourable Murderers. El concepto del honor en *Othello*,
           de Shakespeare, y en los 'dramas de honor' de Calderón. *Forthcoming*.
           ISBN 978-3-03911-825-0

Vol. 25   Marian Womack and Jennifer Wood (eds)
           Beyond the Back Room. New Perspectives on Carmen Martin Gaite.
           Forthcoming.
           ISBN 978-3-03911-827-4

Vol. 26   Manuela Palacios and Laura Lojo (eds)
           Writing Bonds. Irish and Galician Contemporary Women Poets.
           Forthcoming.
           ISBN 978-3-03911-834-2

Vol. 27   Myriam Osorio
           Agencia femenina, agencia narrativa. Una lectura feminista de la obra
           en prosa de Albalucía Angel. *Forthcoming*.
           ISBN 978-3-03911-893-3